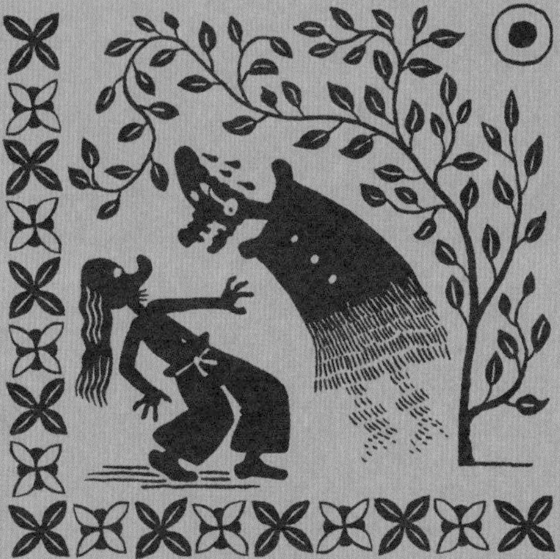
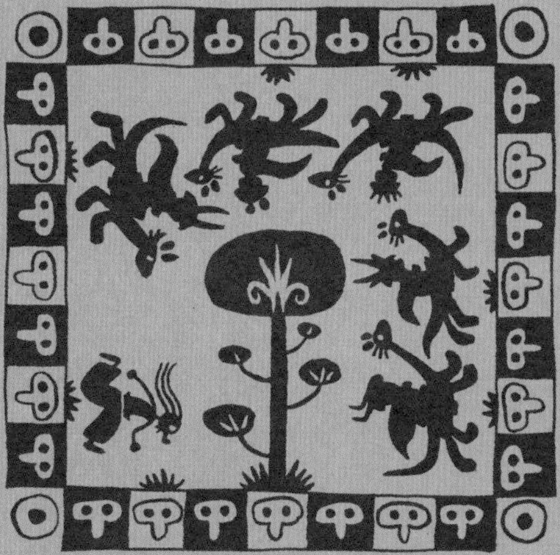
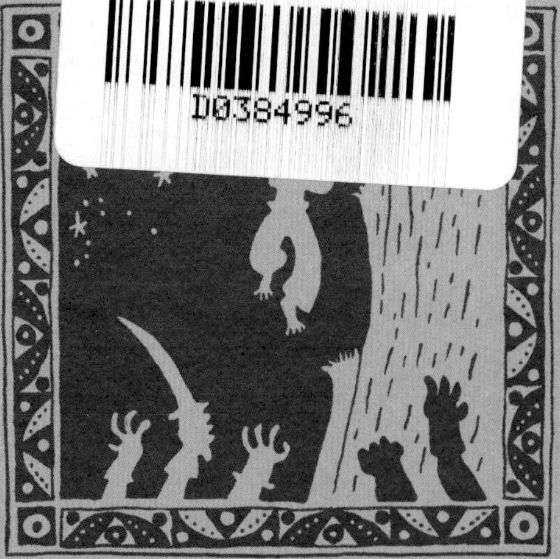

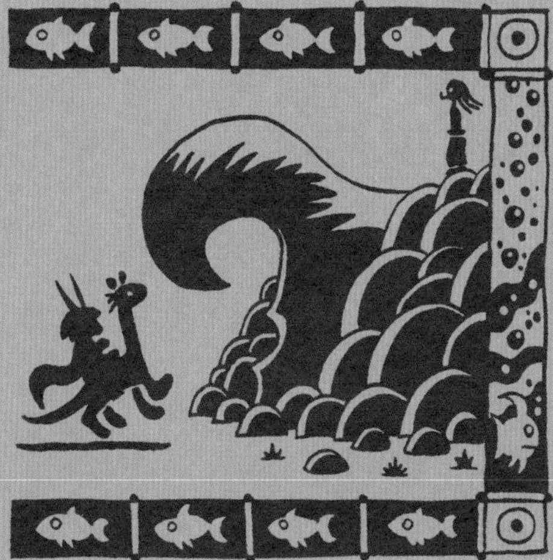
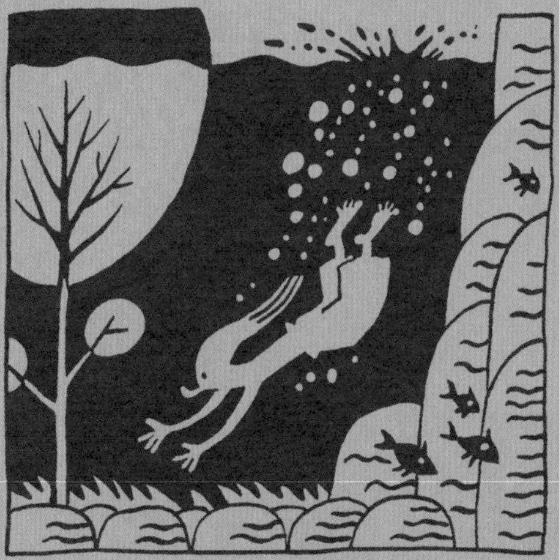
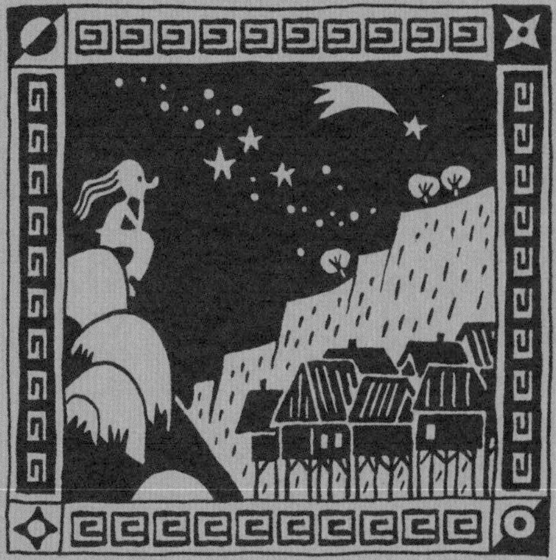

Ralph Azham

Ralph Azham

1

Why Would You Lie to Someone You Love?

Story and Art: Lewis Trondheim
Colors: Brigitte Findakly
Translation: Kim Thompson

FANTAGRAPHICS BOOKS

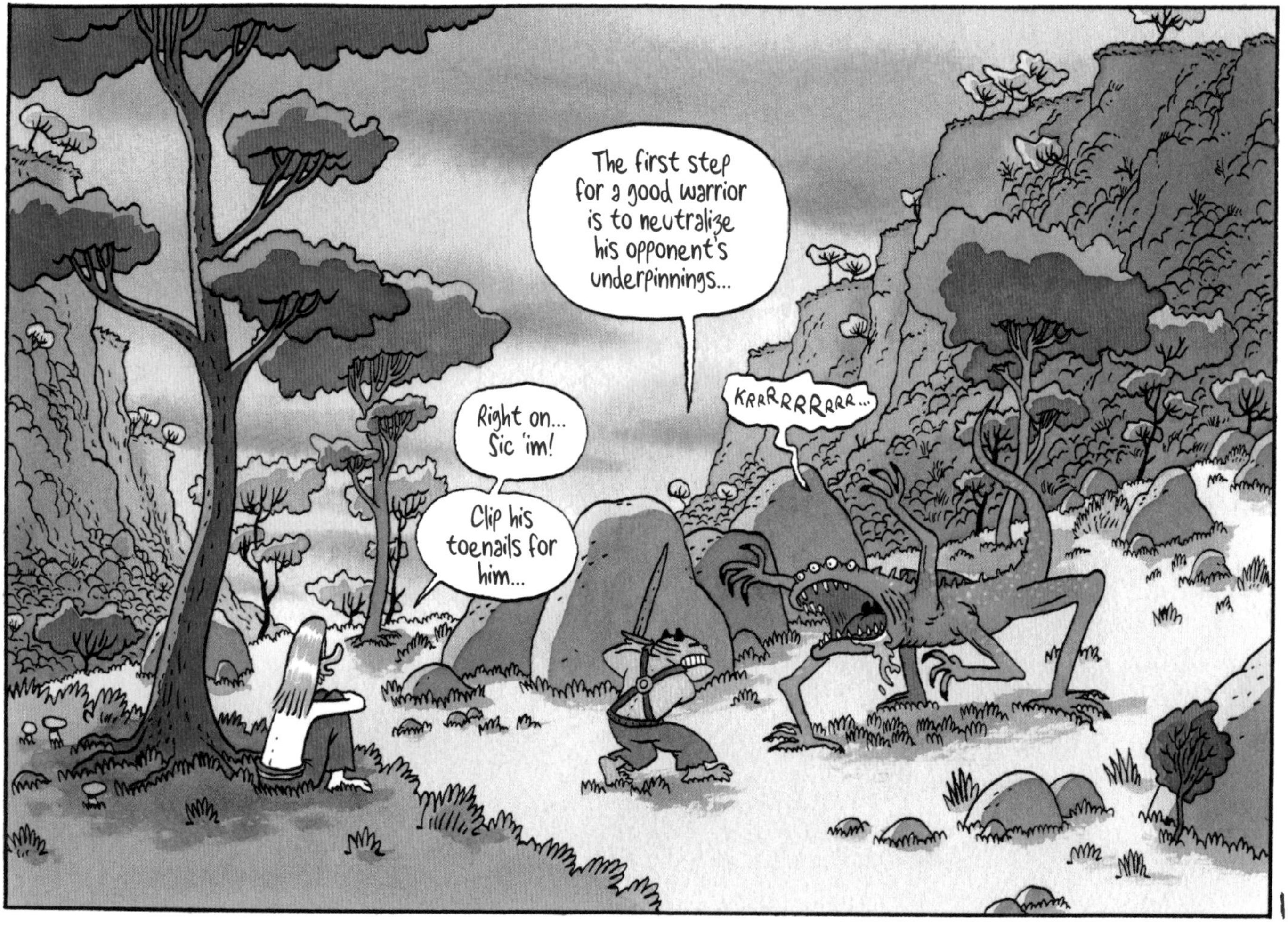
The first step for a good warrior is to neutralize his opponent's underpinnings...
Right on... Sic 'im!
Clip his toenails for him...
KRRRRRRRRRR...

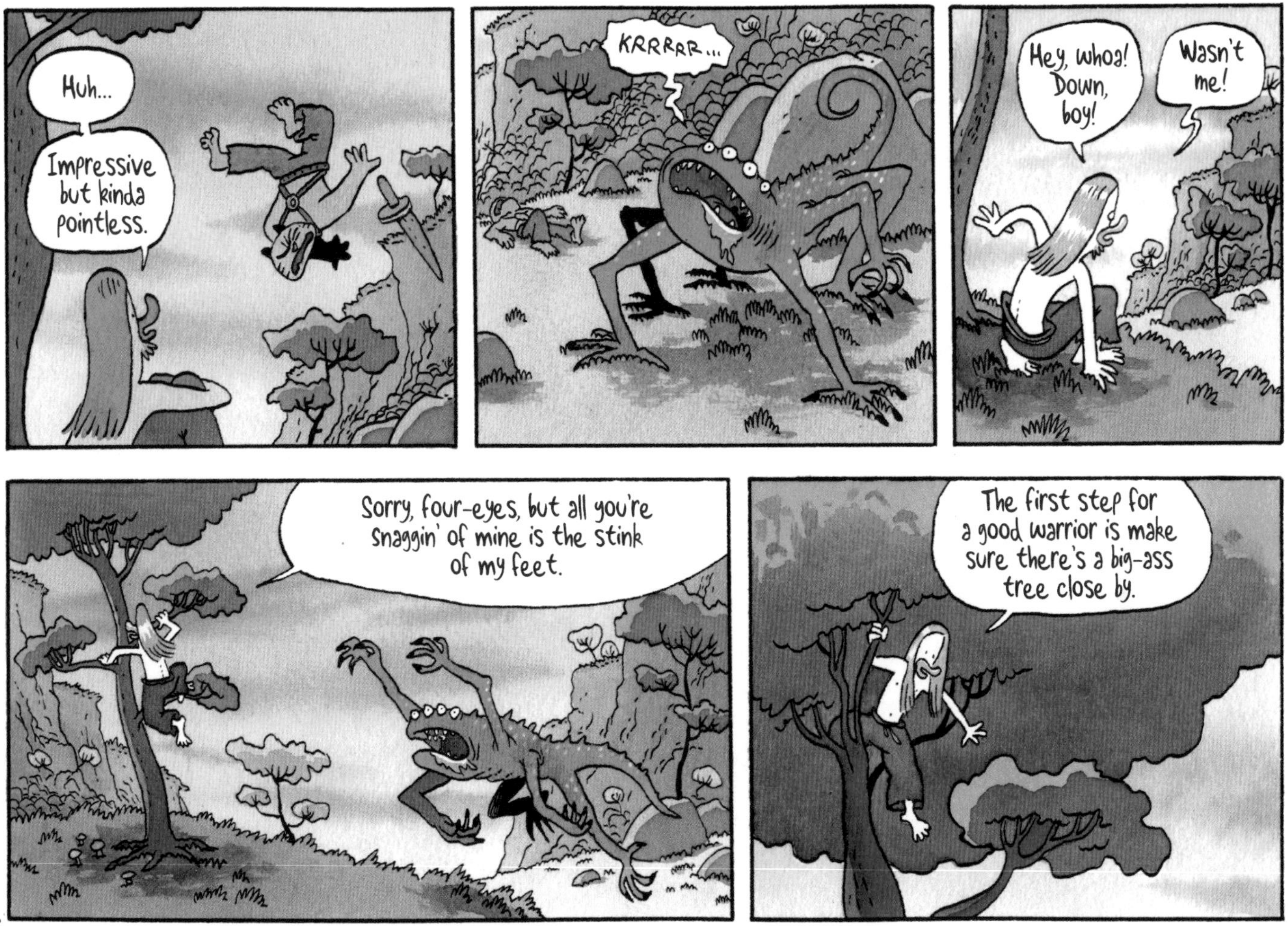
Huh...
Impressive but kinda pointless.
KRRRRR...
Hey, whoa! Down, boy!
Wasn't me!
Sorry, four-eyes, but all you're snaggin' of mine is the stink of my feet.
The first step for a good warrior is make sure there's a big-ass tree close by.

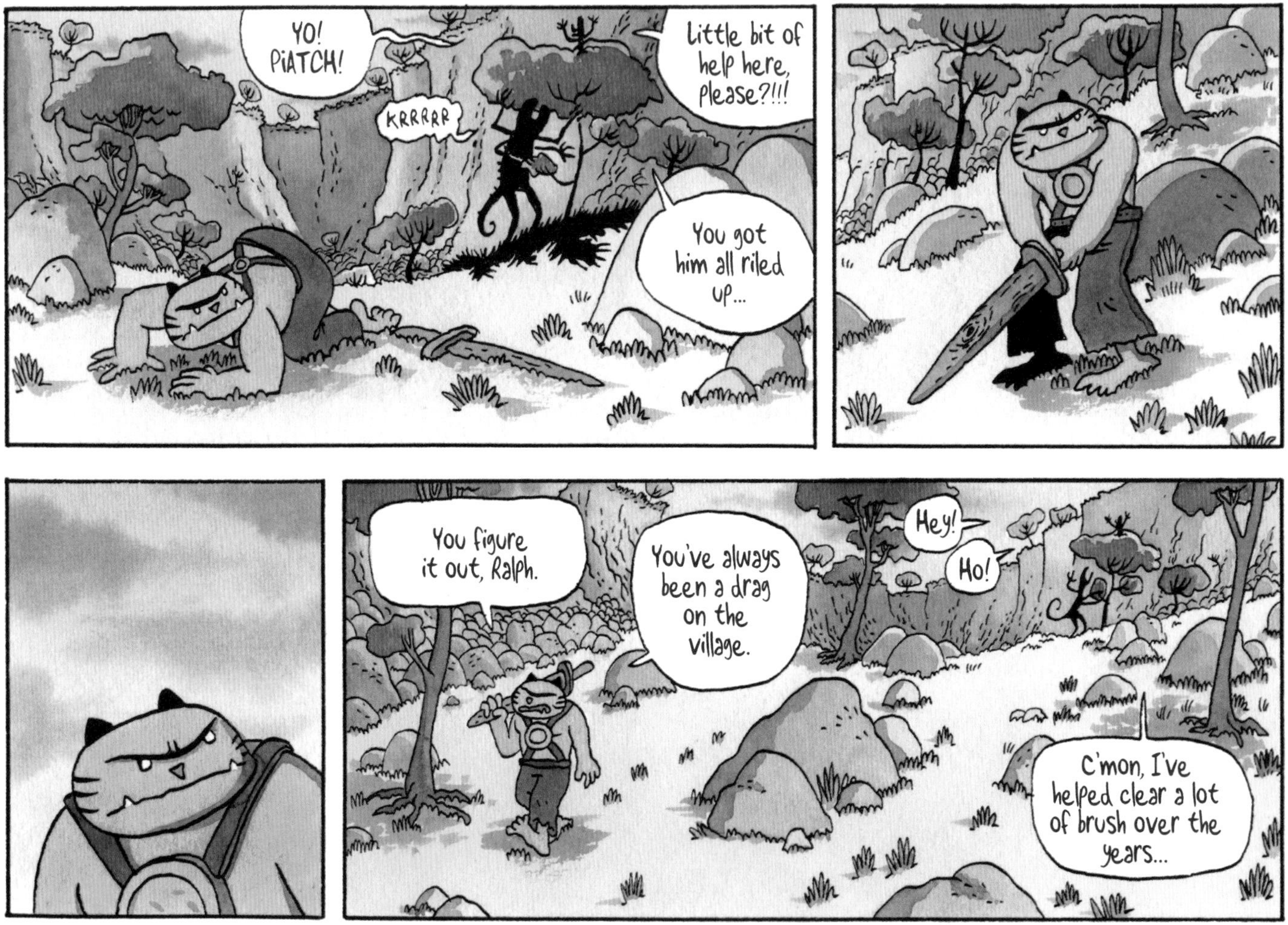

YO! PiATCH!
KRRRRR
Little bit of help here, please?!!!
You got him all riled up...
You figure it out, Ralph.
You've always been a drag on the village.
Hey!
Ho!
C'mon, I've helped clear a lot of brush over the years...

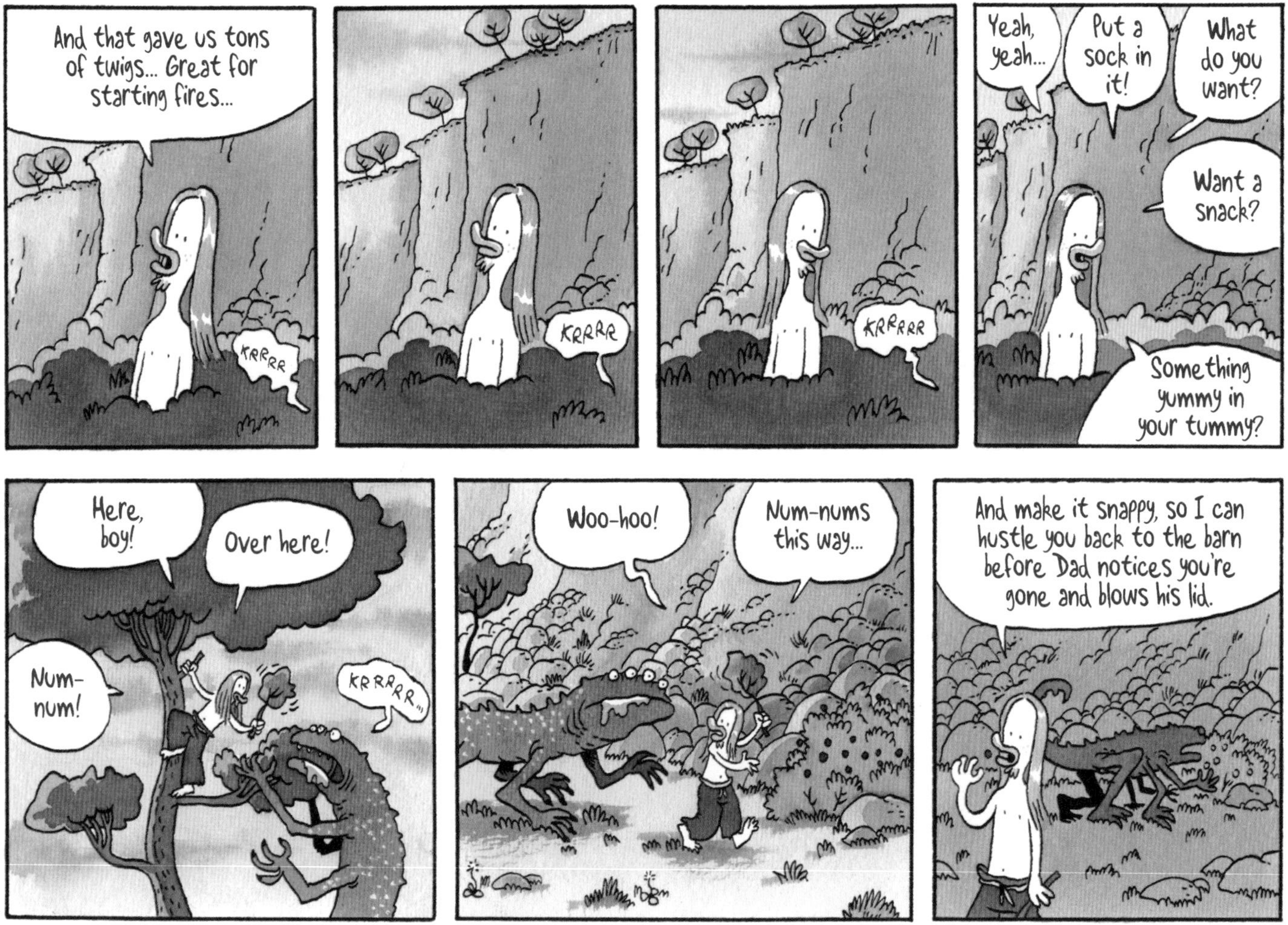

And that gave us tons of twigs... Great for starting fires...
KRRRR
KRRRR
KRRRRR
Yeah, yeah...
Put a sock in it!
What do you want?
Want a snack?
Something yummy in your tummy?
Here, boy!
Over here!
Num-num!
KRRRRR...
Woo-hoo!
Num-nums this way...
And make it snappy, so I can hustle you back to the barn before Dad notices you're gone and blows his lid.

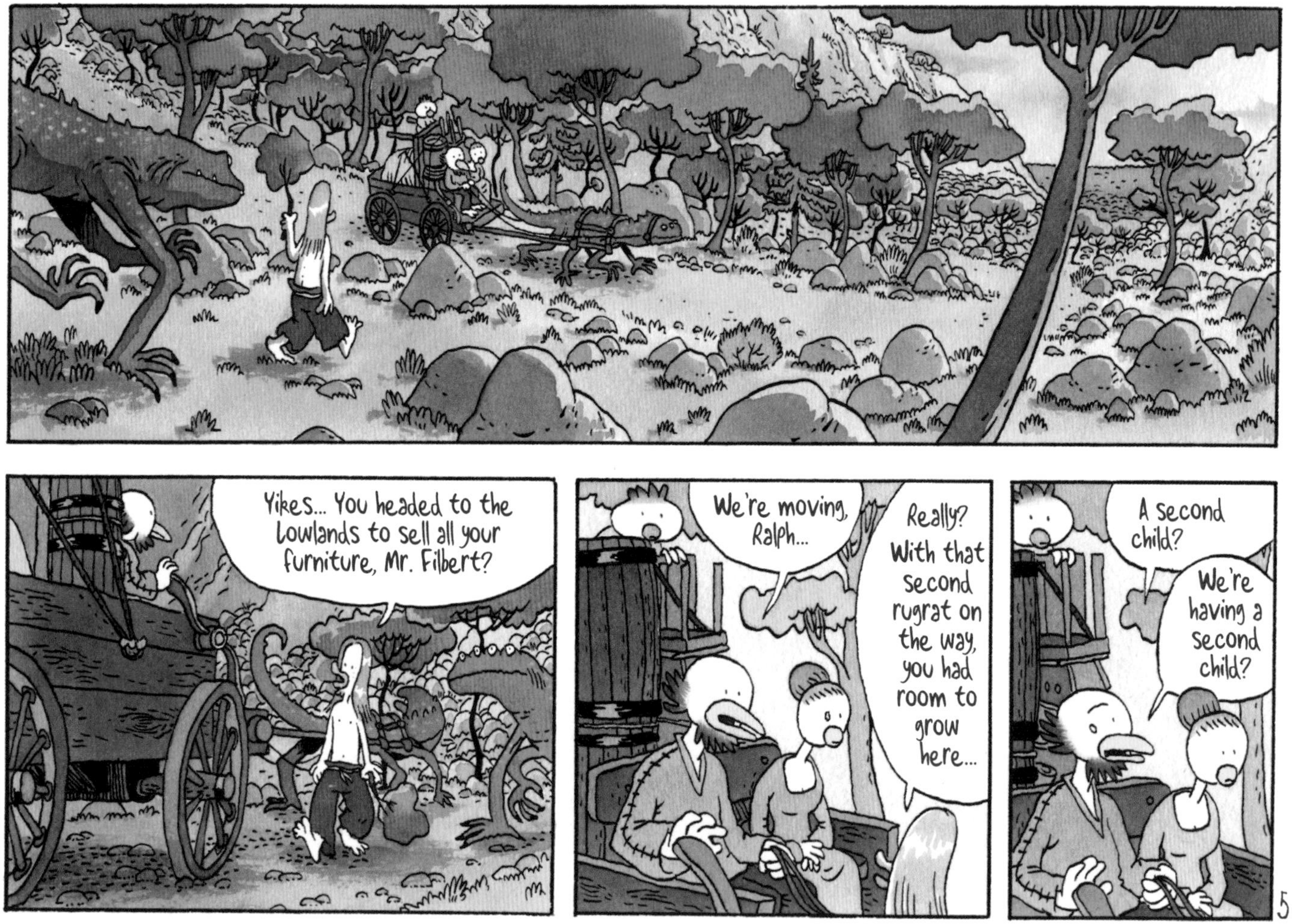
Yikes... You headed to the Lowlands to sell all your furniture, Mr. Filbert?
We're moving, Ralph...
Really? With that second rugrat on the way, you had room to grow here...
A second child?
We're having a second child?

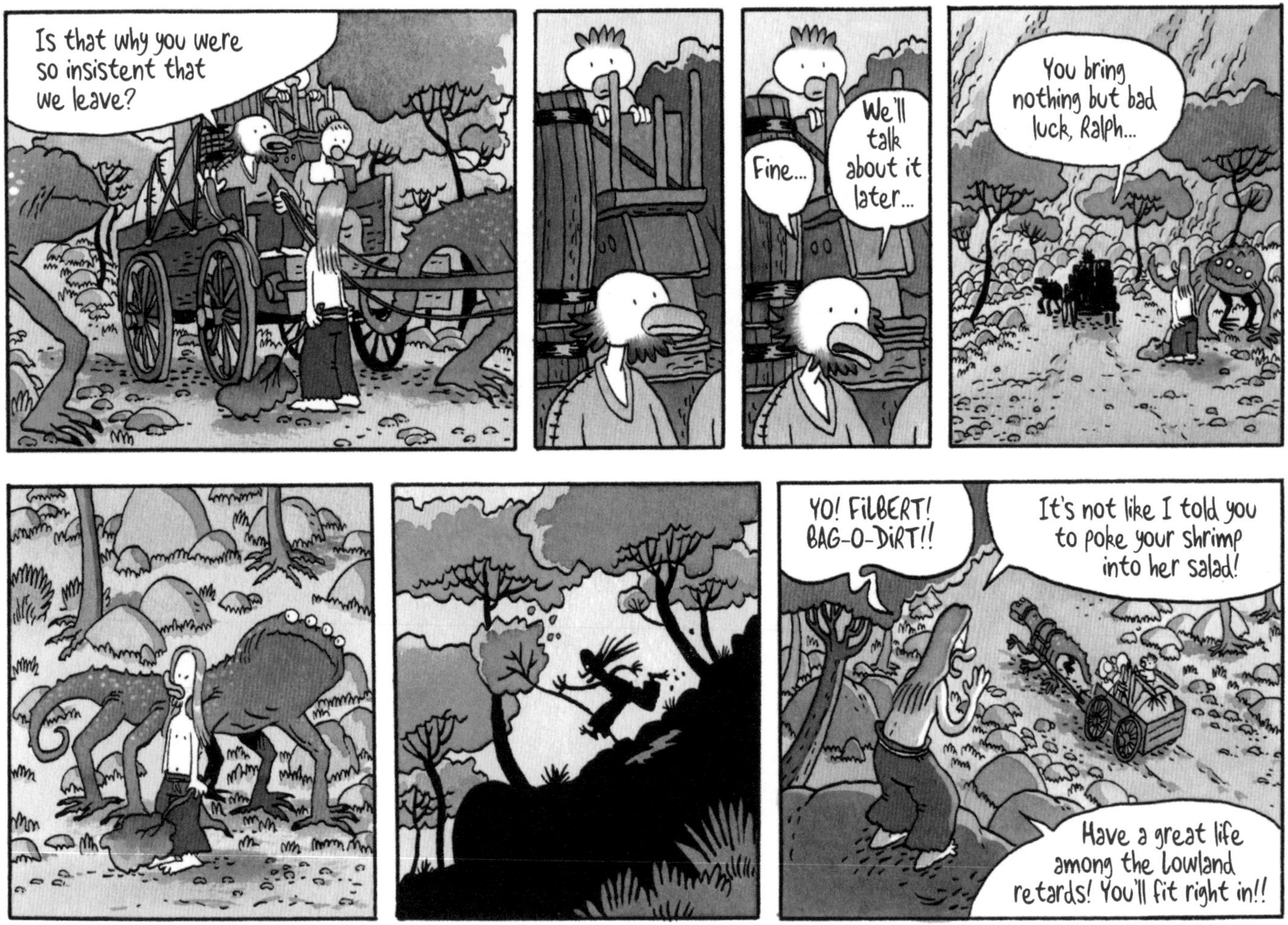

Is that why you were so insistent that we leave?
Fine...
We'll talk about it later...
You bring nothing but bad luck, Ralph...
YO! FILBERT! BAG-O-DIRT!!
It's not like I told you to poke your shrimp into her salad!
Have a great life among the Lowland retards! You'll fit right in!!

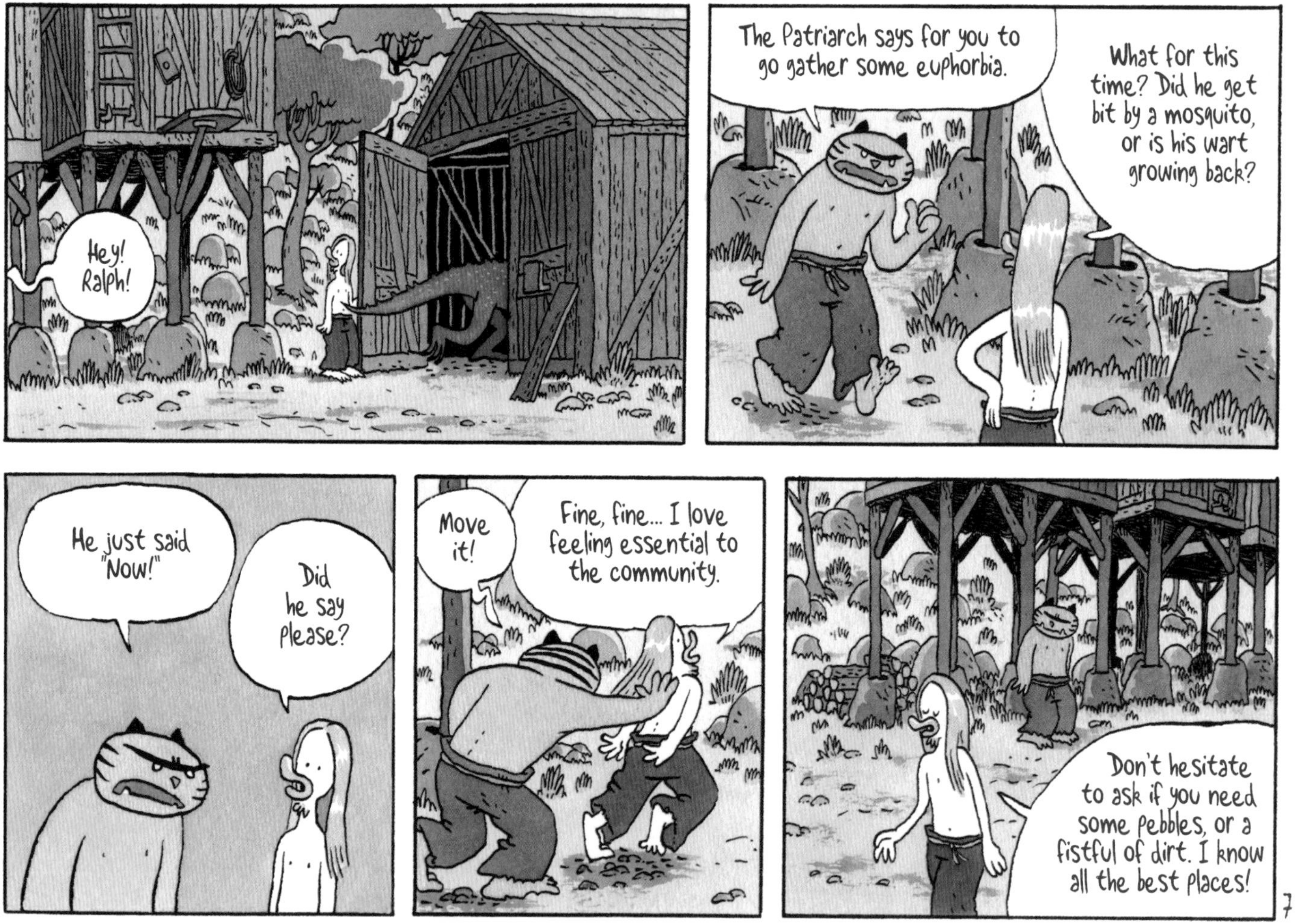
Hey! Ralph!
The Patriarch says for you to go gather some euphorbia.
What for this time? Did he get bit by a mosquito, or is his wart growing back?
He just said "Now!"
Did he say please?
Move it!
Fine, fine... I love feeling essential to the community.
Don't hesitate to ask if you need some pebbles, or a fistful of dirt. I know all the best places!

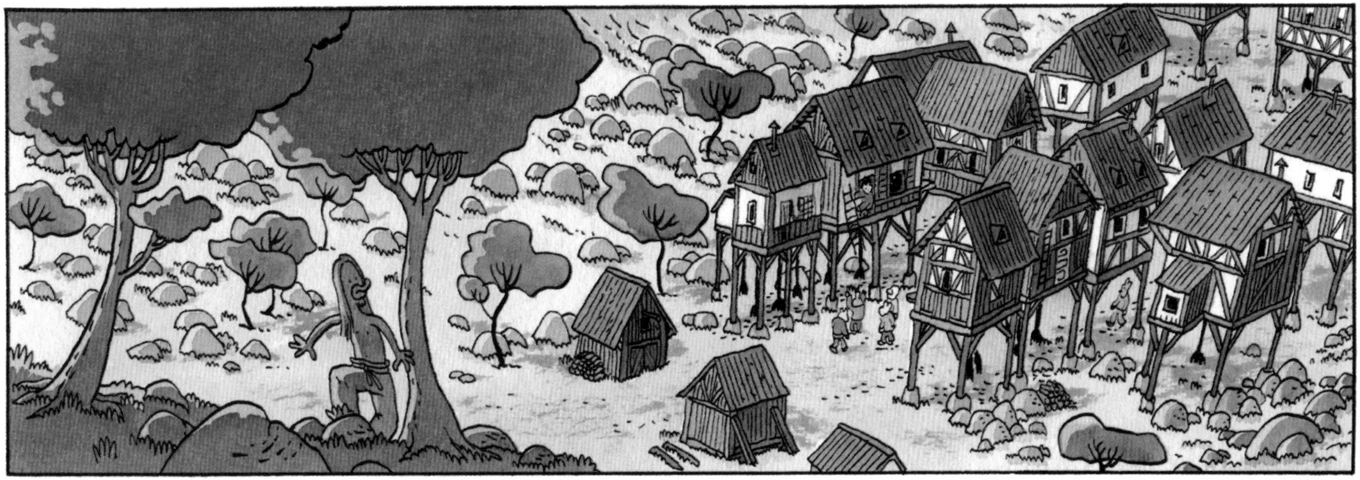

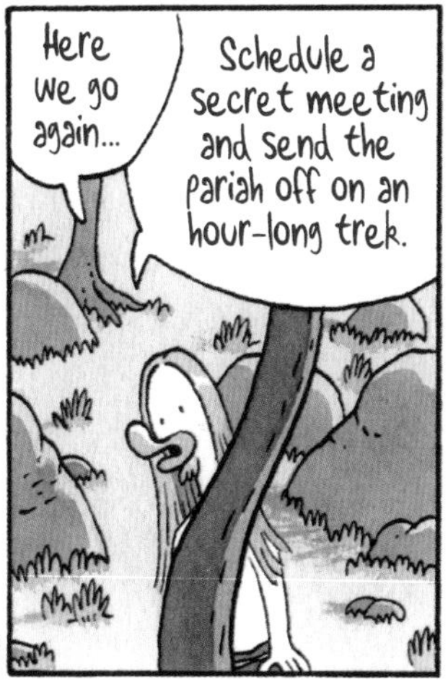
Here we go again...
Schedule a secret meeting and send the pariah off on an hour-long trek.

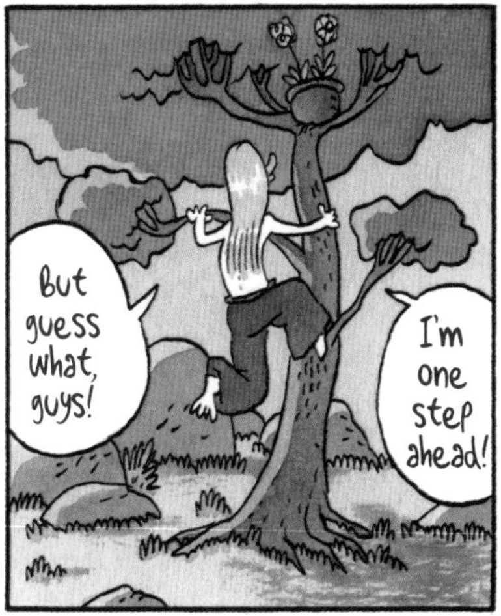
But guess what, guys!
I'm one step ahead!

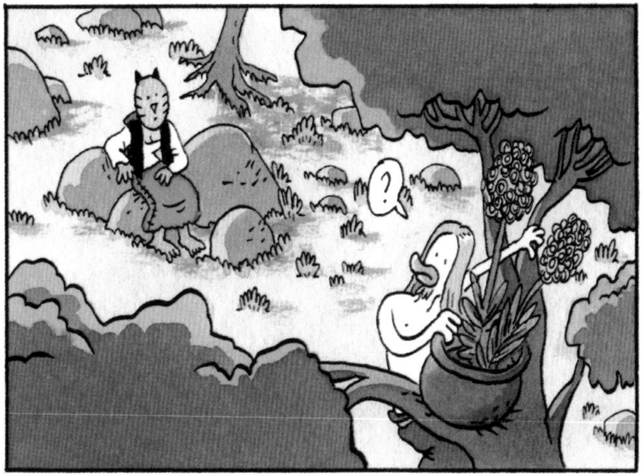
?

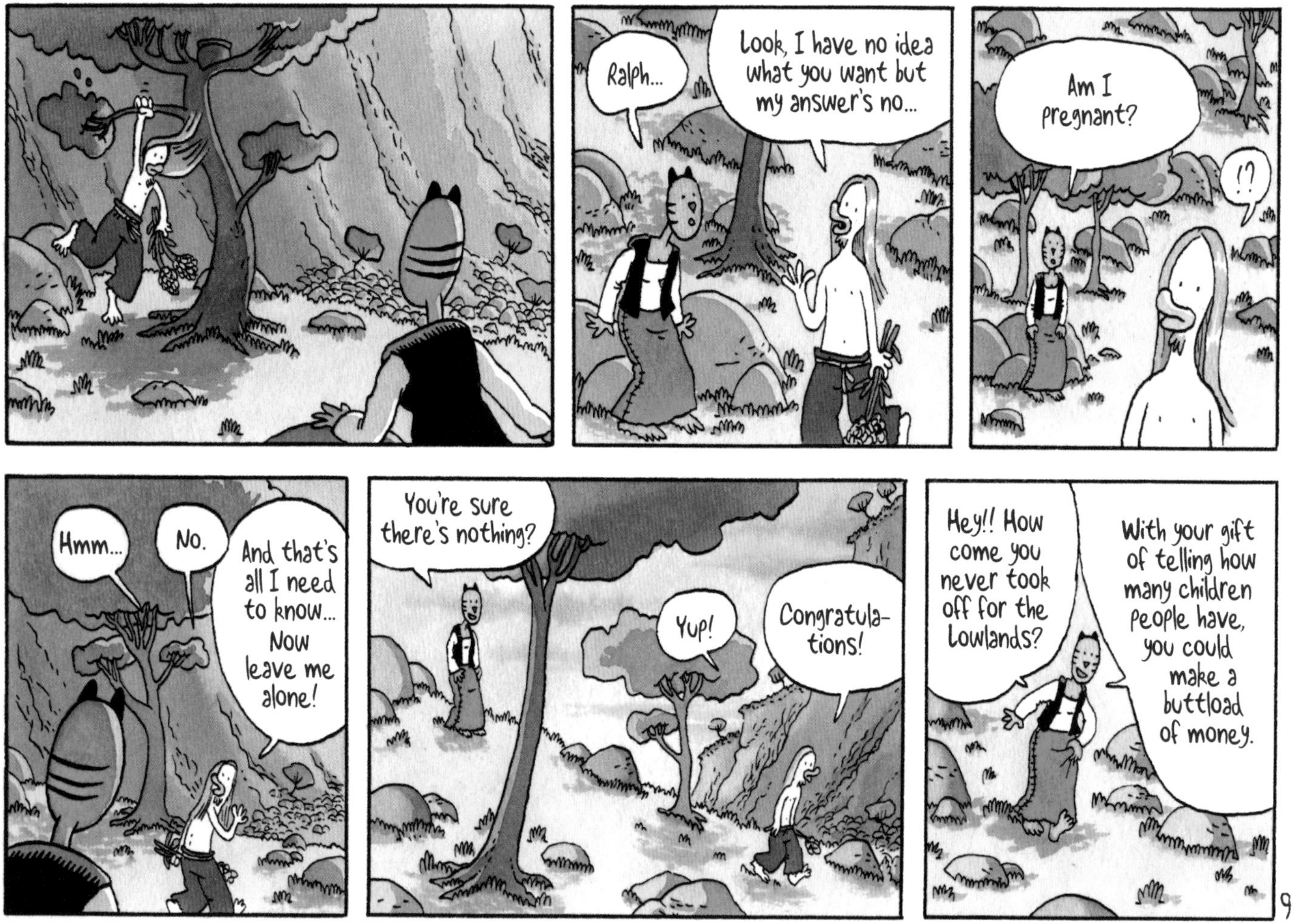
Ralph...
Look, I have no idea what you want but my answer's no...
Am I pregnant?
!?
Hmm...
No.
And that's all I need to know... Now leave me alone!
You're sure there's nothing?
Yup!
Congratulations!
Hey!! How come you never took off for the Lowlands?
With your gift of telling how many children people have, you could make a buttload of money.

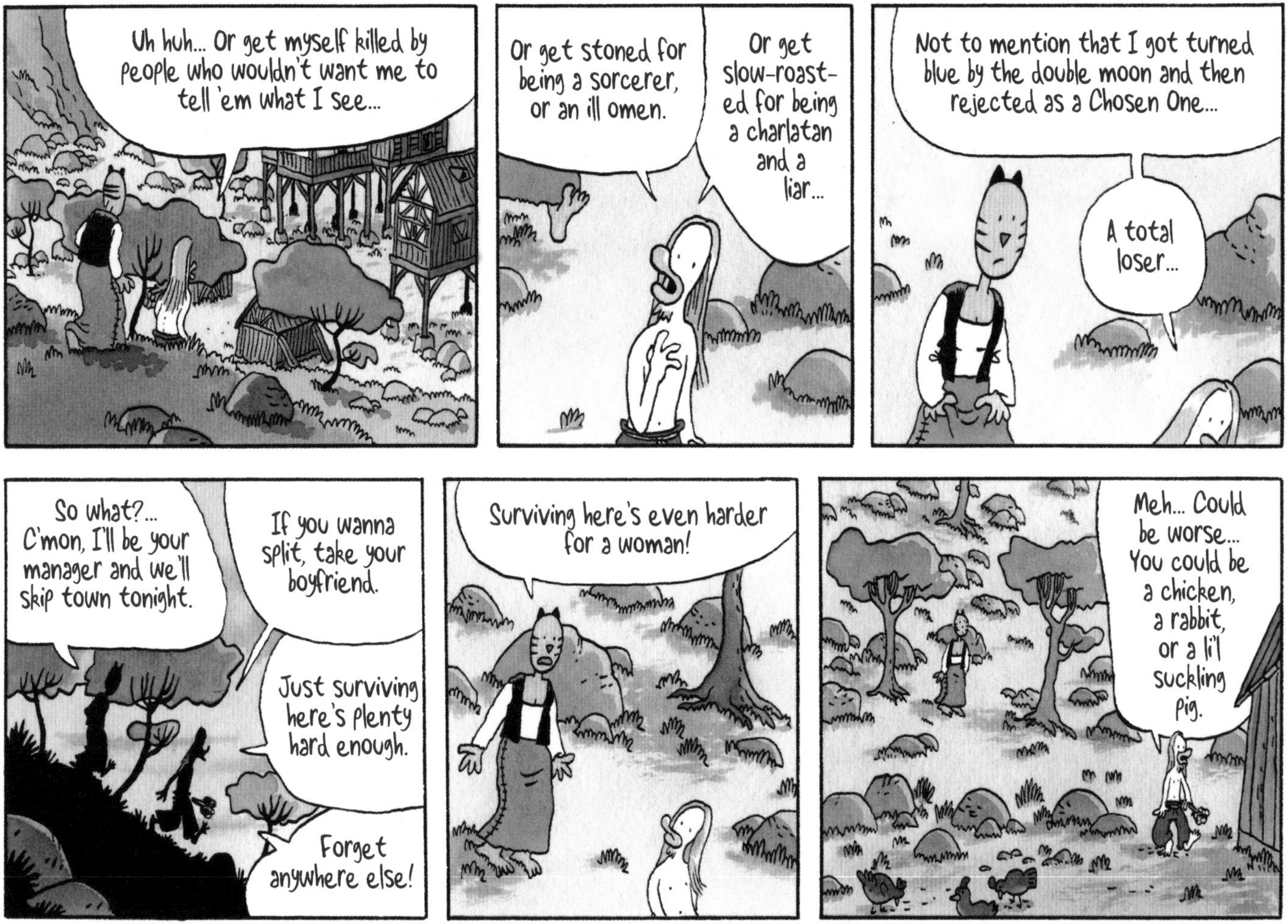
Uh huh... Or get myself killed by people who wouldn't want me to tell 'em what I see...
Or get stoned for being a sorcerer, or an ill omen.
Or get slow-roast-ed for being a charlatan and a liar...
Not to mention that I got turned blue by the double moon and then rejected as a Chosen One...
A total loser...
So what?... C'mon, I'll be your manager and we'll skip town tonight.
If you wanna split, take your boyfriend.
Just surviving here's plenty hard enough.
Forget anywhere else!
Surviving here's even harder for a woman!
Meh... Could be worse... You could be a chicken, a rabbit, or a li'l suckling pig.

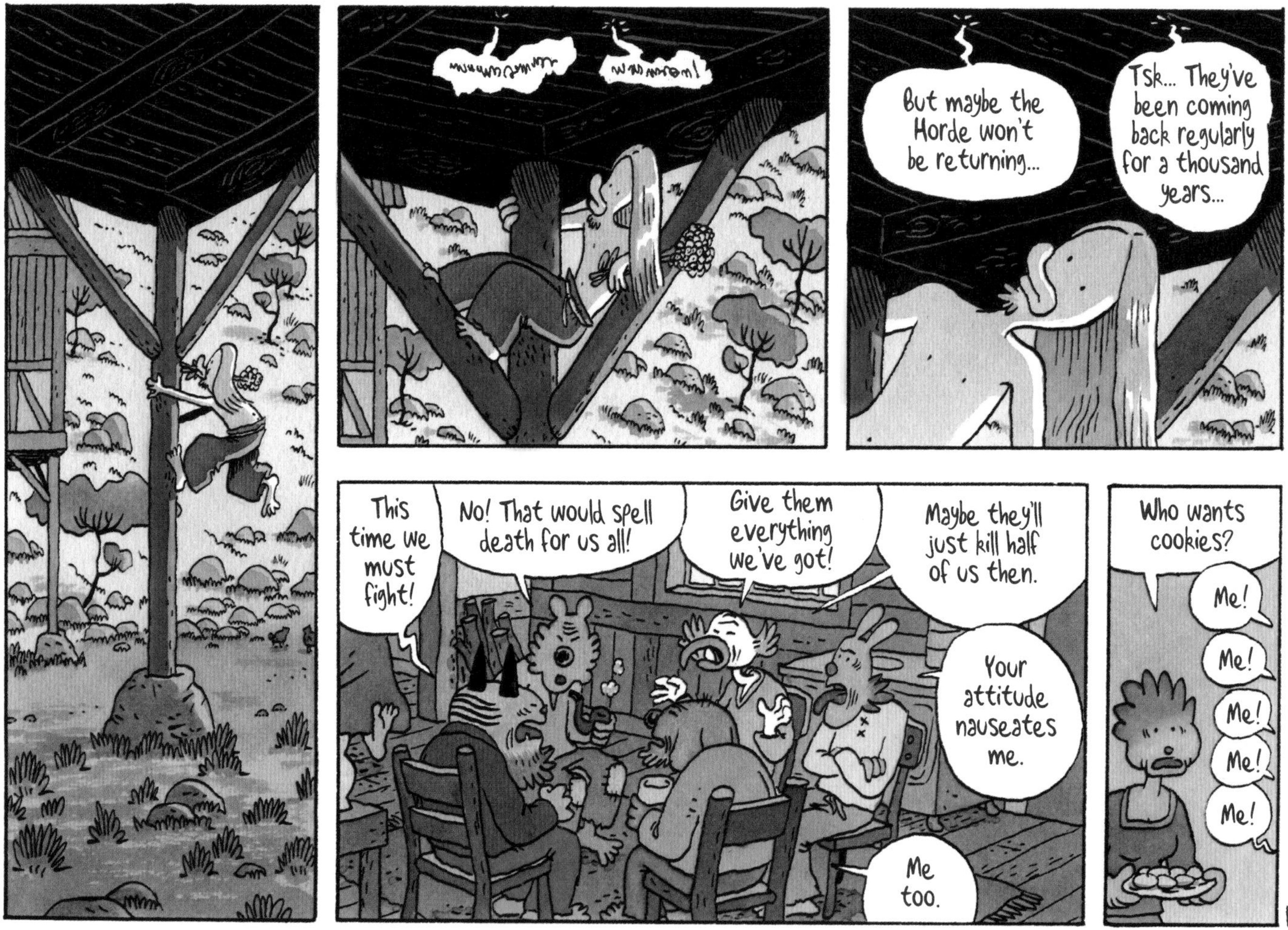
But maybe the Horde won't be returning...
Tsk... They've been coming back regularly for a thousand years...
This time we must fight!
No! That would spell death for us all!
Give them everything we've got!
Maybe they'll just kill half of us then.
Your attitude nauseates me.
Me too.
Who wants cookies?
Me!
Me!
Me!
Me!
Me!

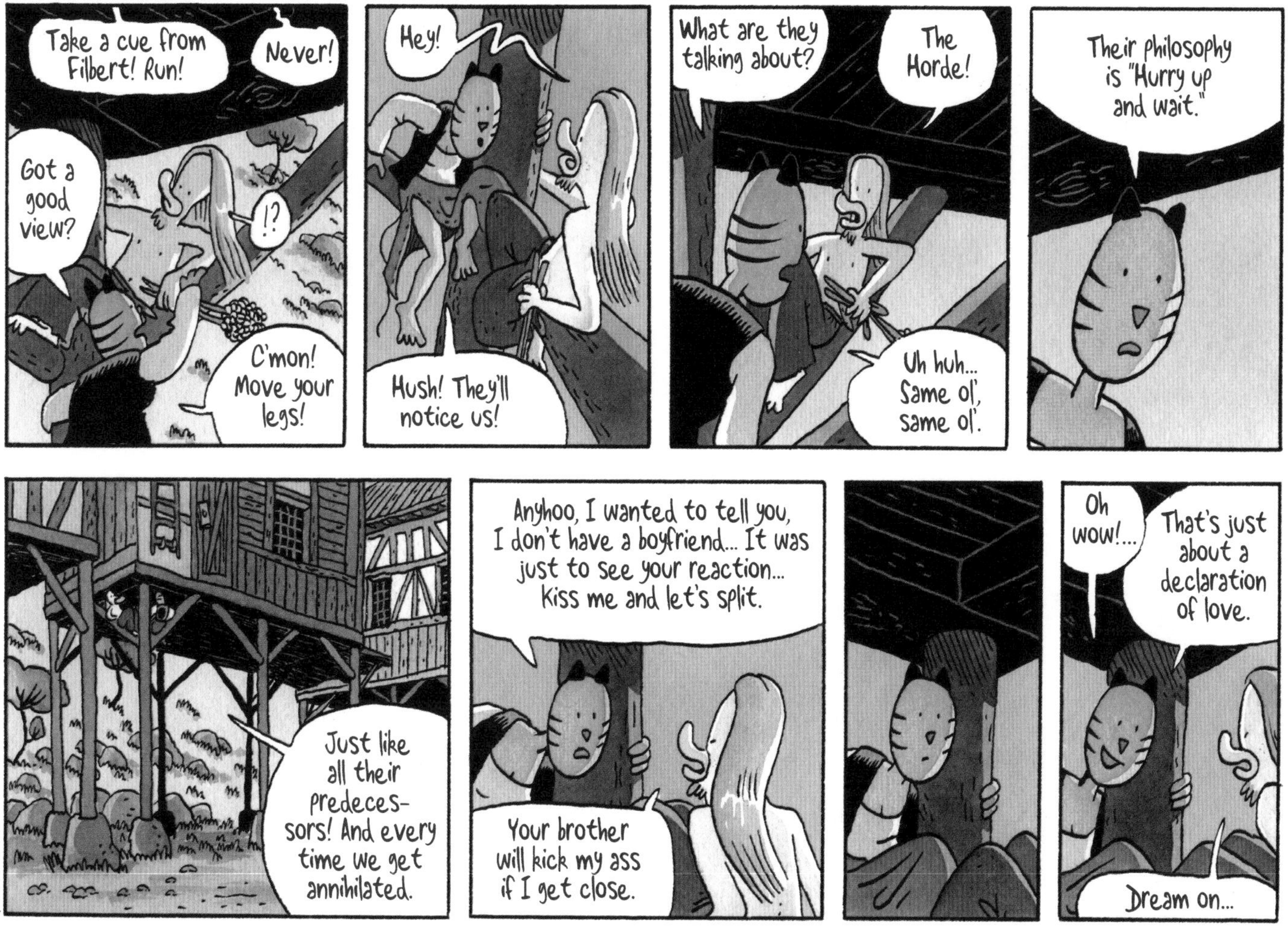
Take a cue from Filbert! Run!
Never!
Got a good view?
!?
C'mon! Move your legs!
Hey!
Hush! They'll notice us!
What are they talking about?
The Horde!
Uh huh... Same ol', same ol'.
Their philosophy is "Hurry up and wait."
Just like all their predeces-sors! And every time we get annihilated.
Anyhoo, I wanted to tell you, I don't have a boyfriend... It was just to see your reaction... Kiss me and let's split.
Your brother will kick my ass if I get close.
Oh wow!...
That's just about a declaration of love.
Dream on...

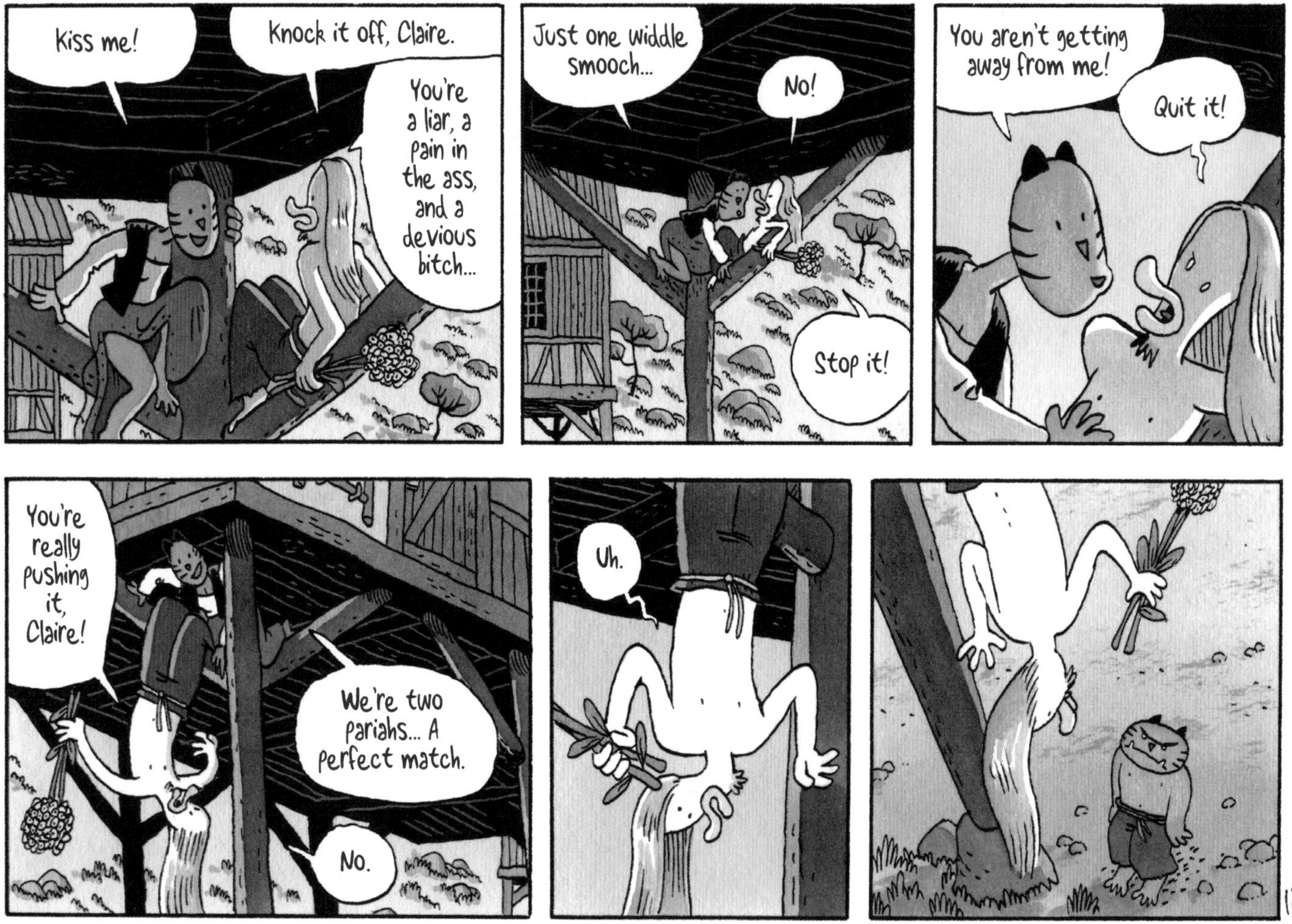
Kiss me!
Knock it off, Claire.
You're a liar, a pain in the ass, and a devious bitch...
Just one widdle smooch...
No!
Stop it!
You aren't getting away from me!
Quit it!
You're really pushing it, Claire!
We're two pariahs... A perfect match.
No.
Uh.

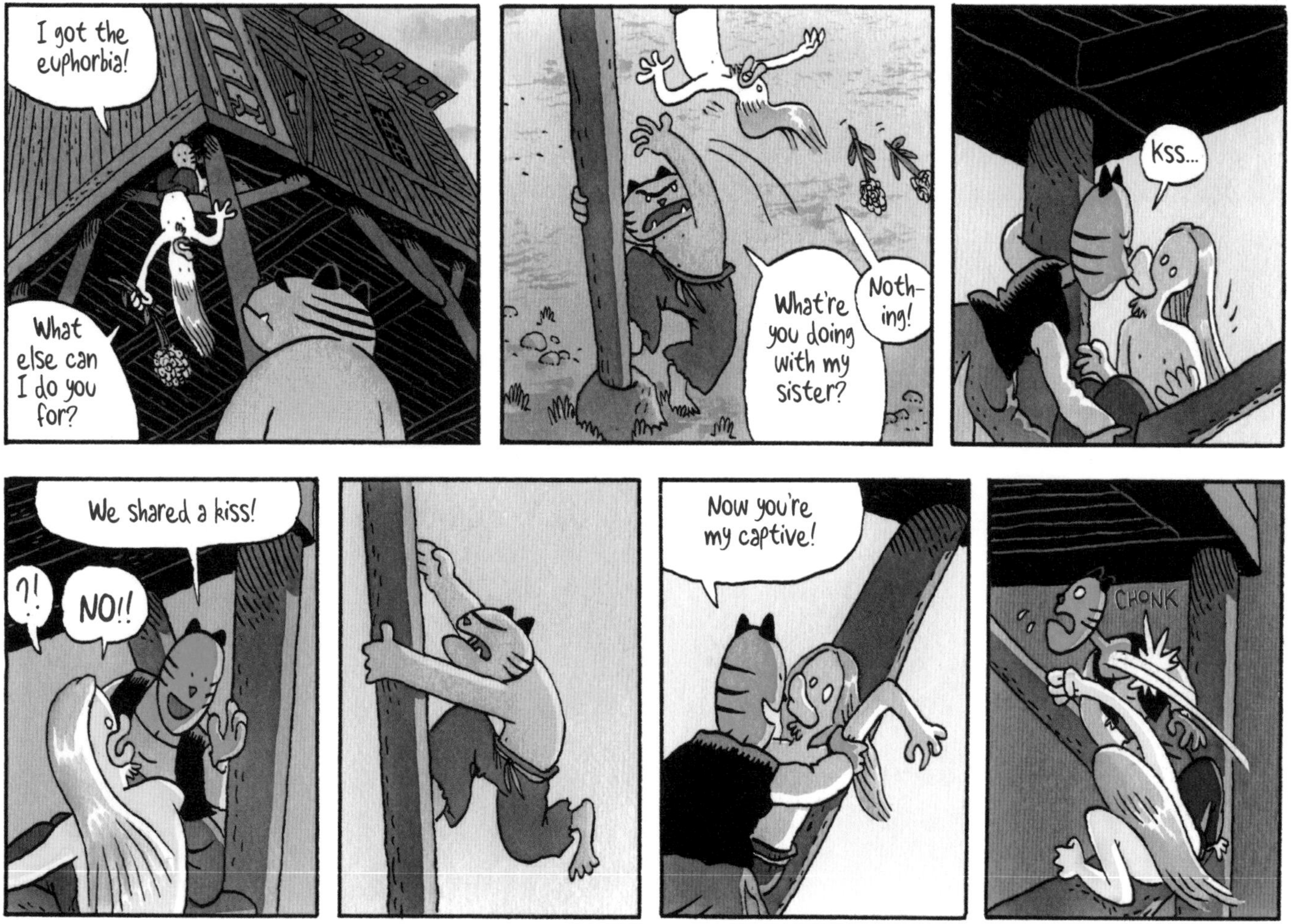
I got the euphorbia!
What else can I do you for?
What're you doing with my sister?
Noth-ing!
KSS...
We shared a kiss!
?!
NO!!
Now you're my captive!
CHONK

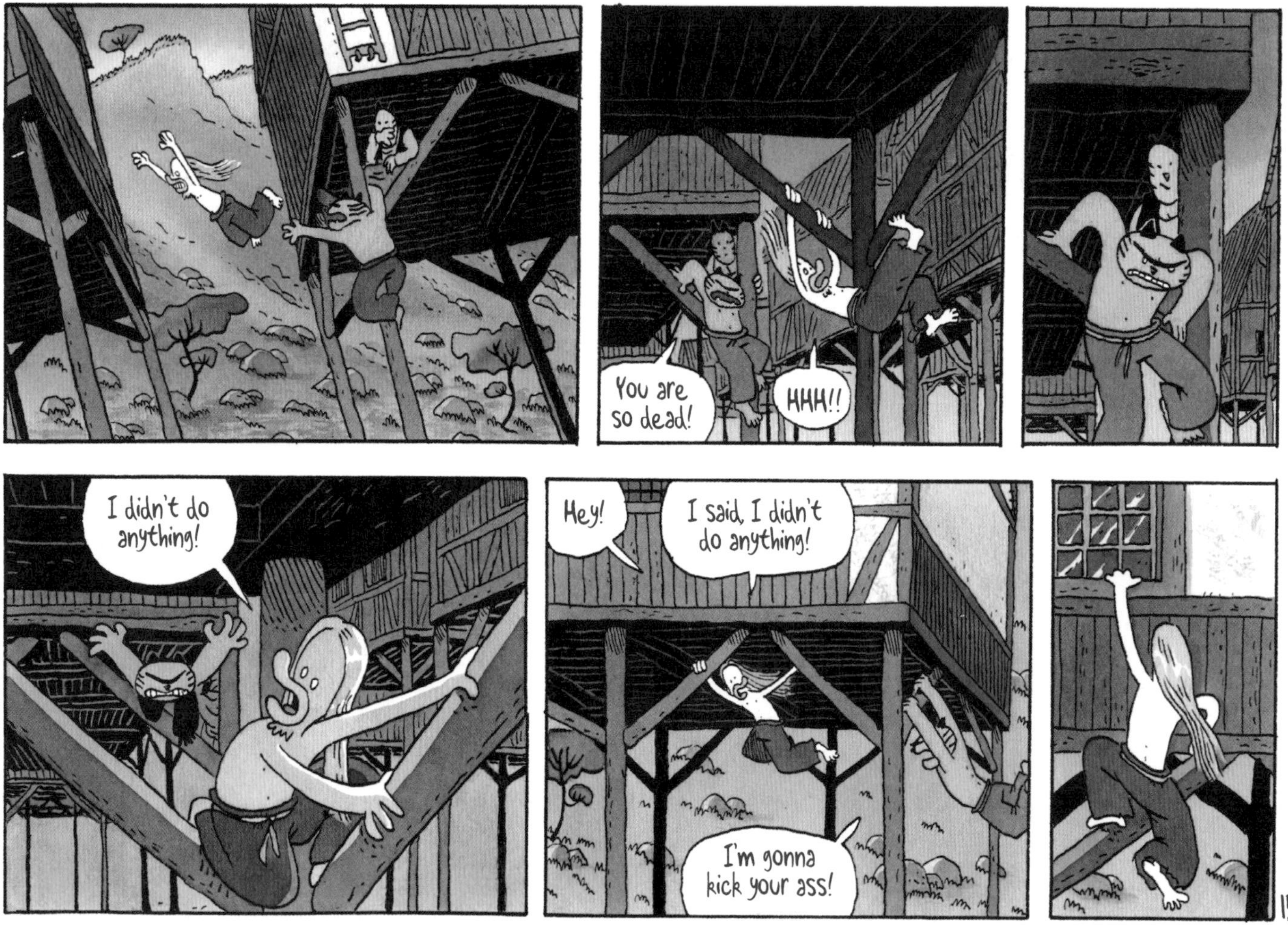
You are so dead!
HHH!!
I didn't do anything!
Hey!
I said, I didn't do anything!
I'm gonna kick your ass!

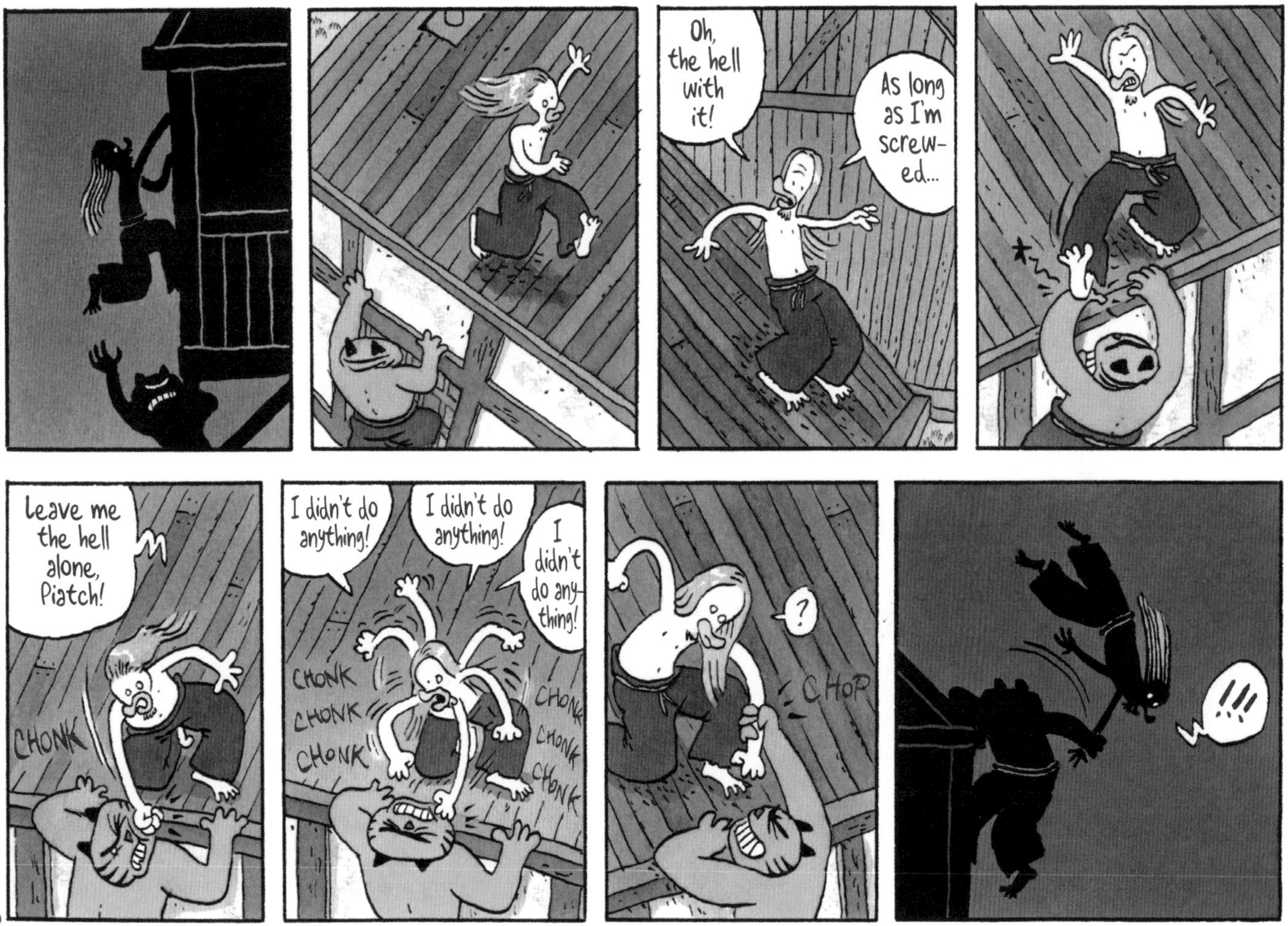

Oh, the hell with it!
As long as I'm screw-ed...
Leave me the hell alone, Piatch!
CHONK
I didn't do anything!
I didn't do anything!
I didn't do any-thing!
CHONK
CHONK
CHONK
CHONK
CHONK
CHONK
?
CHOP
!!!

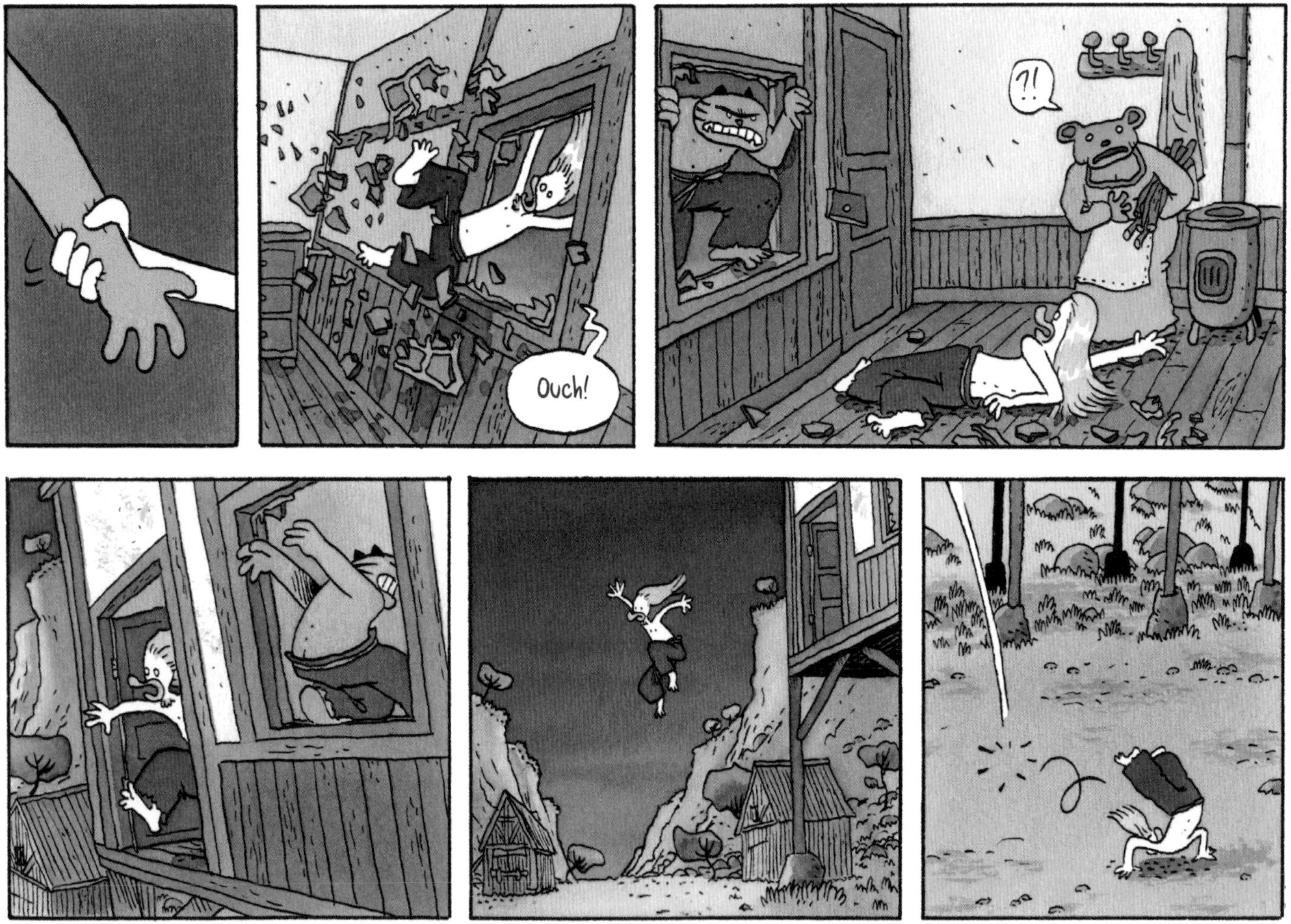
Ouch!
?!

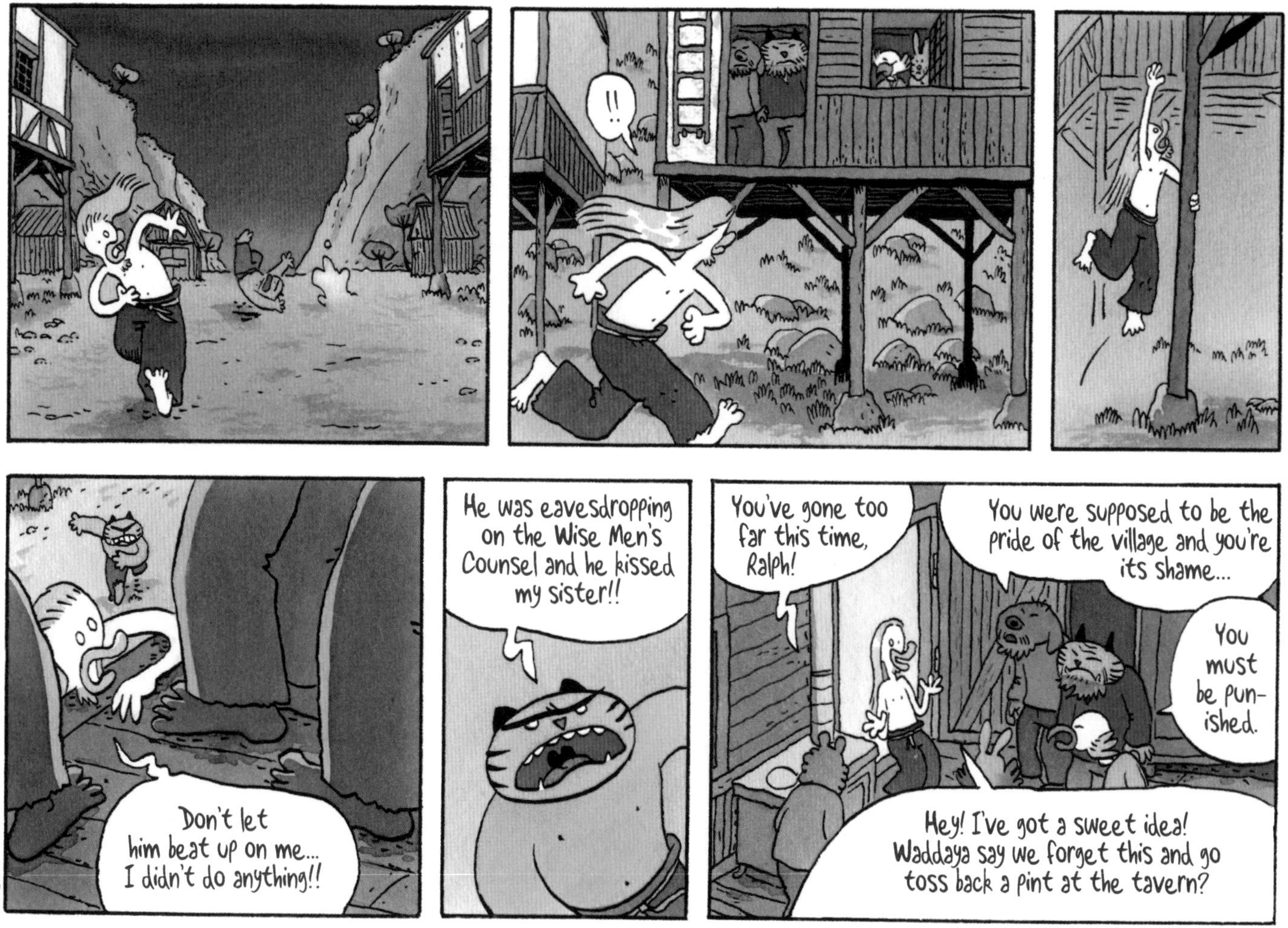

!!
Don't let him beat up on me... I didn't do anything!!
He was eavesdropping on the Wise Men's Counsel and he kissed my sister!!
You've gone too far this time, Ralph!
You were supposed to be the pride of the village and you're its shame...
You must be pun-ished.
Hey! I've got a sweet idea! Waddaya say we forget this and go toss back a pint at the tavern?

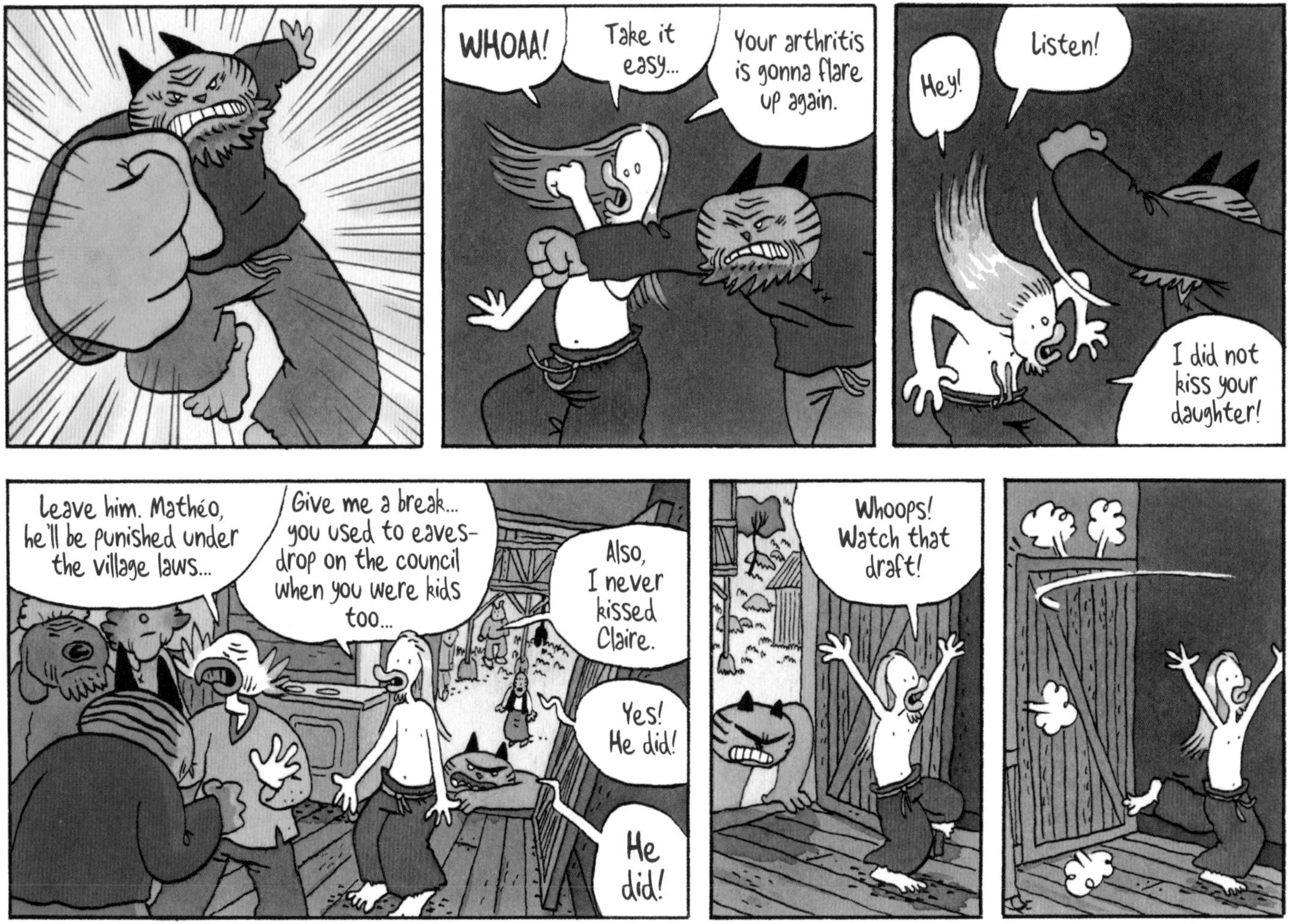
WHOAA!
Take it easy...
Your arthritis is gonna flare up again.
Hey!
Listen!
I did not kiss your daughter!
Leave him. Mathéo, he'll be punished under the village laws...
Give me a break... you used to eaves-drop on the council when you were kids too...
Also, I never kissed Claire.
Yes! He did!
He did!
Whoops! Watch that draft!

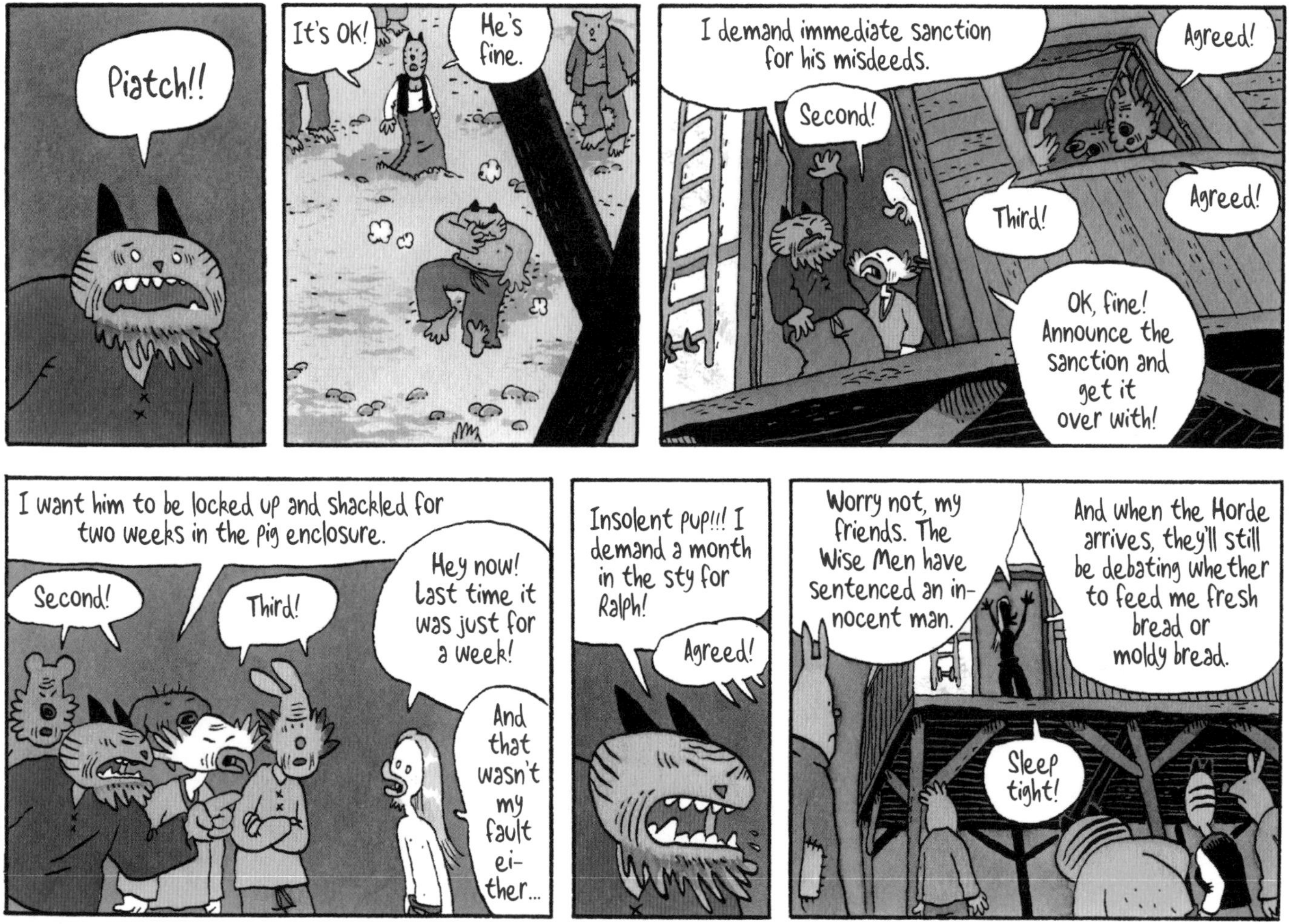

Piatch!!
It's OK!
He's fine.
I demand immediate sanction for his misdeeds.
Agreed!
Second!
Third!
Agreed!
OK, fine! Announce the sanction and get it over with!
I want him to be locked up and shackled for two weeks in the pig enclosure.
Second!
Third!
Hey now! Last time it was just for a week!
And that wasn't my fault ei-ther...
Insolent pup!!! I demand a month in the sty for Ralph!
Agreed!
Worry not, my friends. The Wise Men have sentenced an in-nocent man.
And when the Horde arrives, they'll still be debating whether to feed me fresh bread or moldy bread.
Sleep tight!

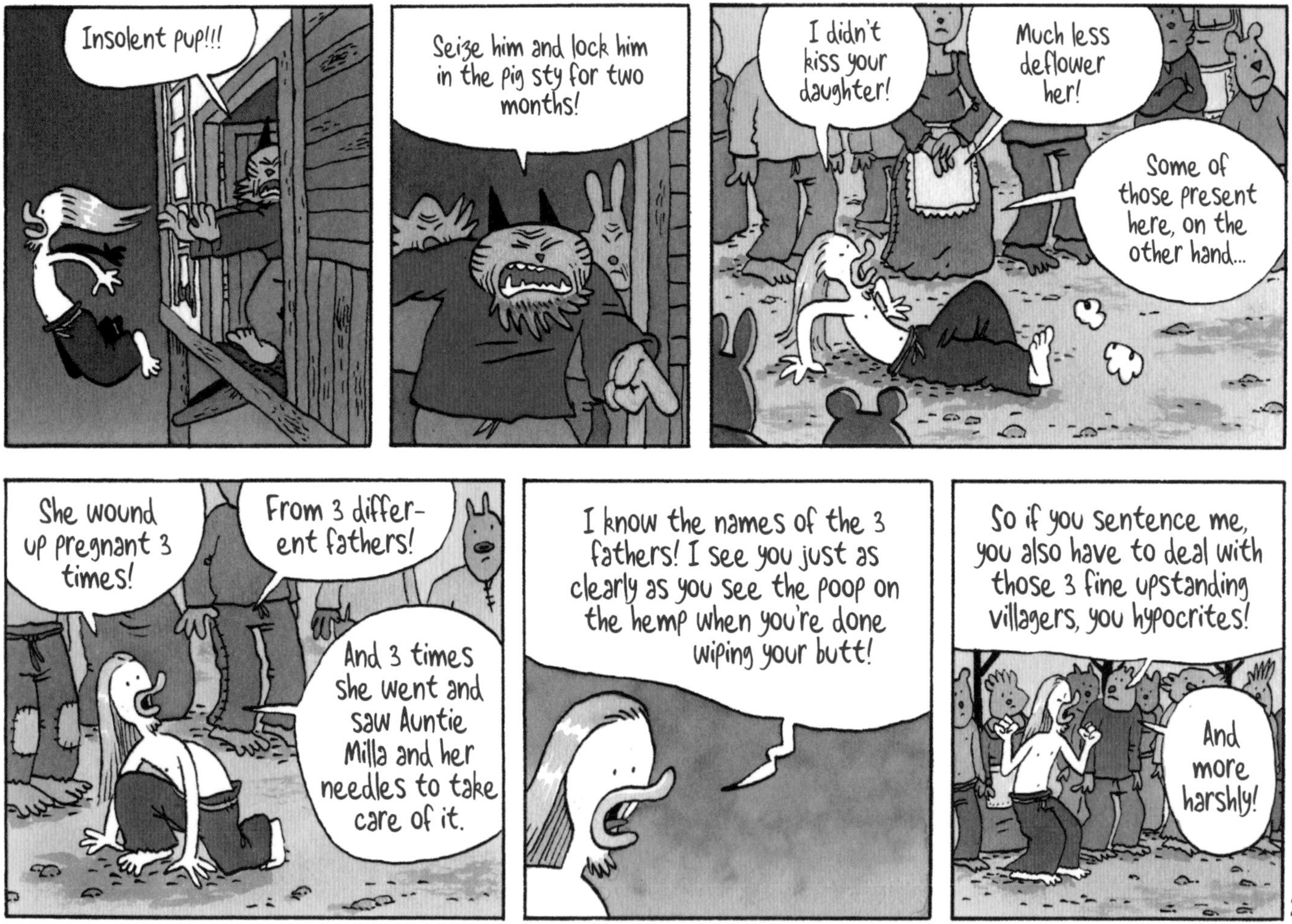
Insolent pup!!!
Seize him and lock him in the pig sty for two months!
I didn't kiss your daughter!
Much less deflower her!
Some of those present here, on the other hand...
She wound up pregnant 3 times!
From 3 different fathers!
And 3 times she went and saw Auntie Milla and her needles to take care of it.
I know the names of the 3 fathers! I see you just as clearly as you see the poop on the hemp when you're done wiping your butt!
So if you sentence me, you also have to deal with those 3 fine upstanding villagers, you hypocrites!
And more harshly!

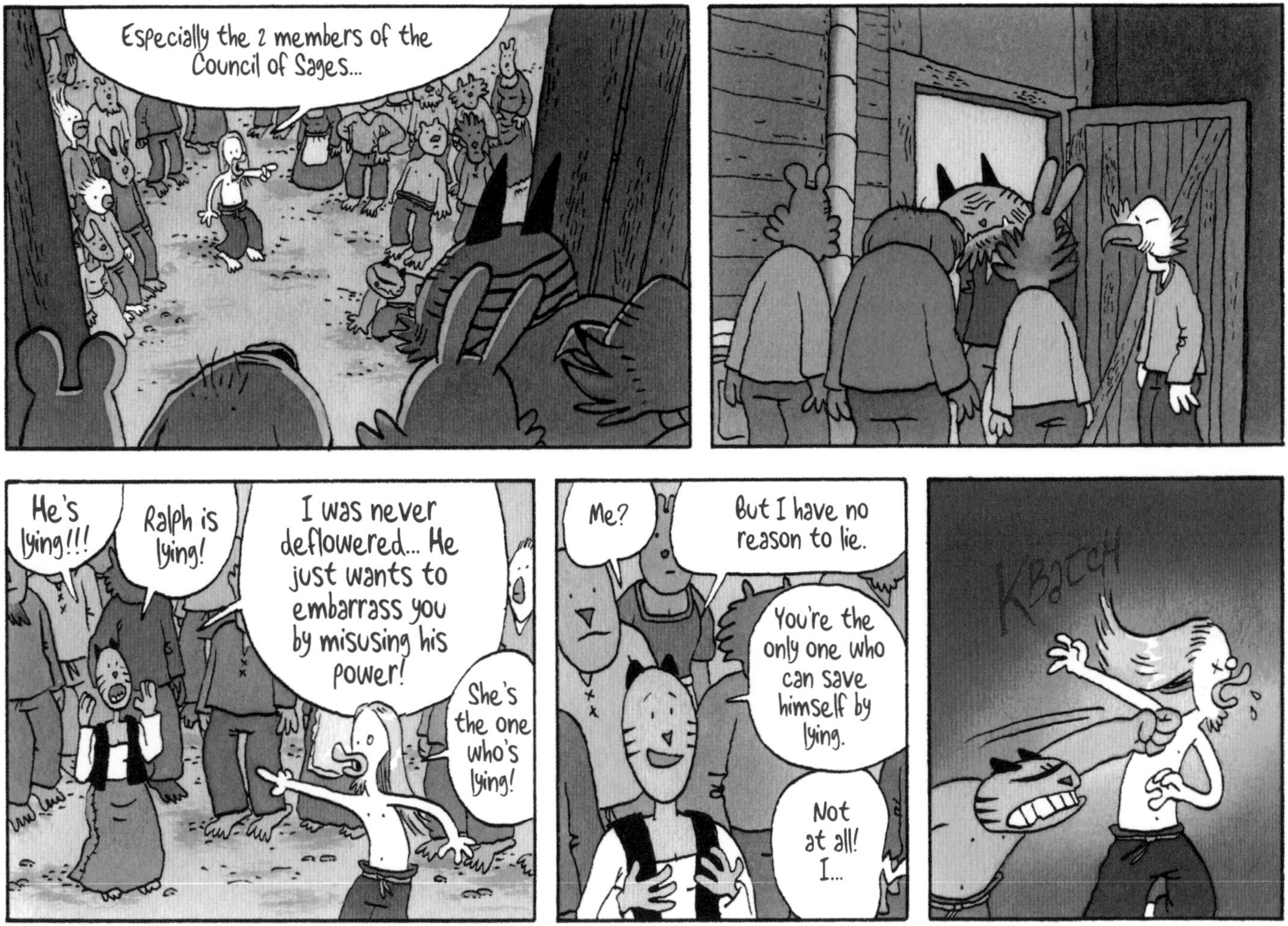
Especially the 2 members of the Council of Sages...
He's lying!!!
Ralph is lying!
I was never deflowered... He just wants to embarrass you by misusing his power!
She's the one who's lying!
Me?
But I have no reason to lie.
You're the only one who can save himself by lying.
Not at all! I...
KBATCH

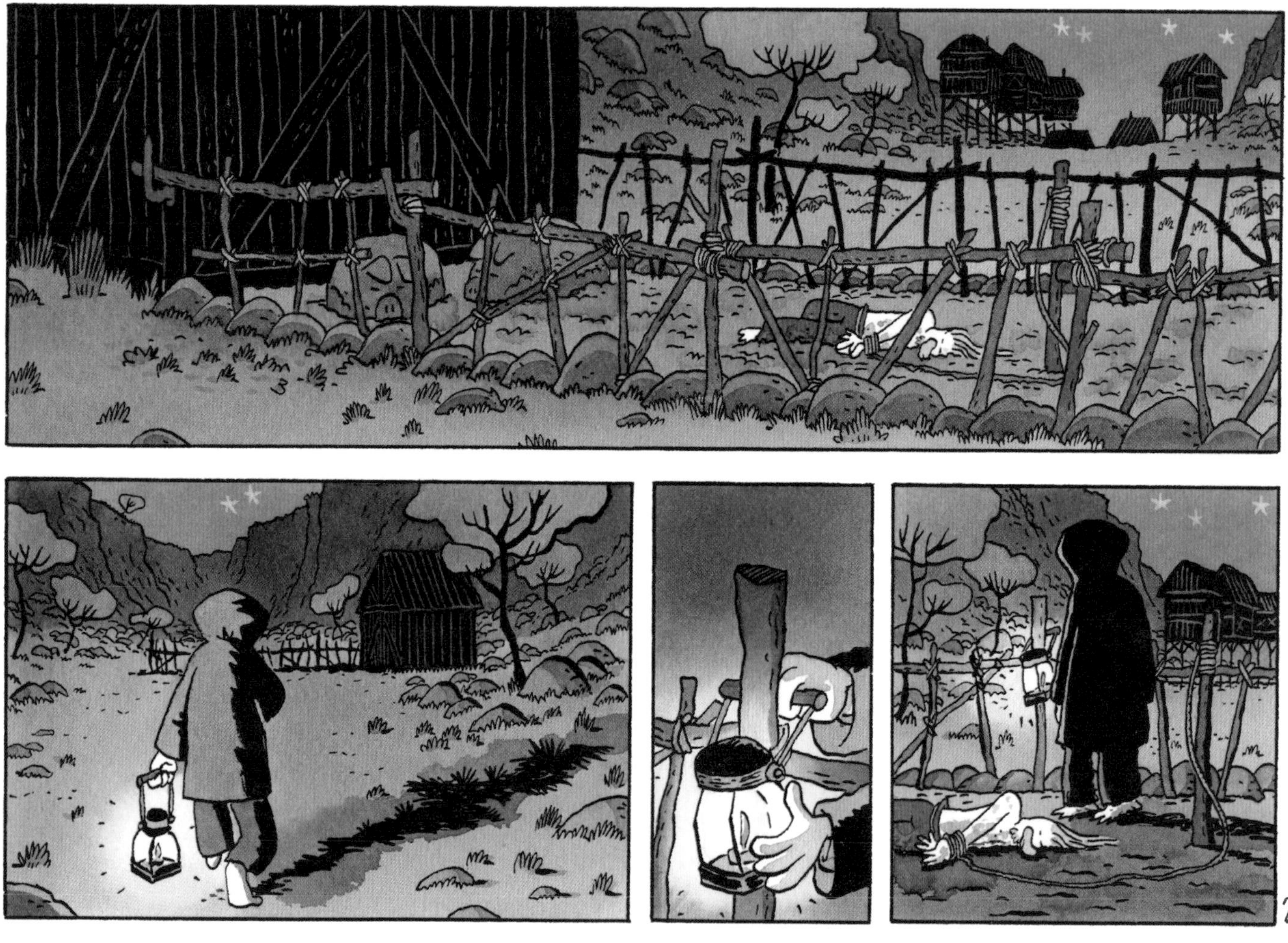

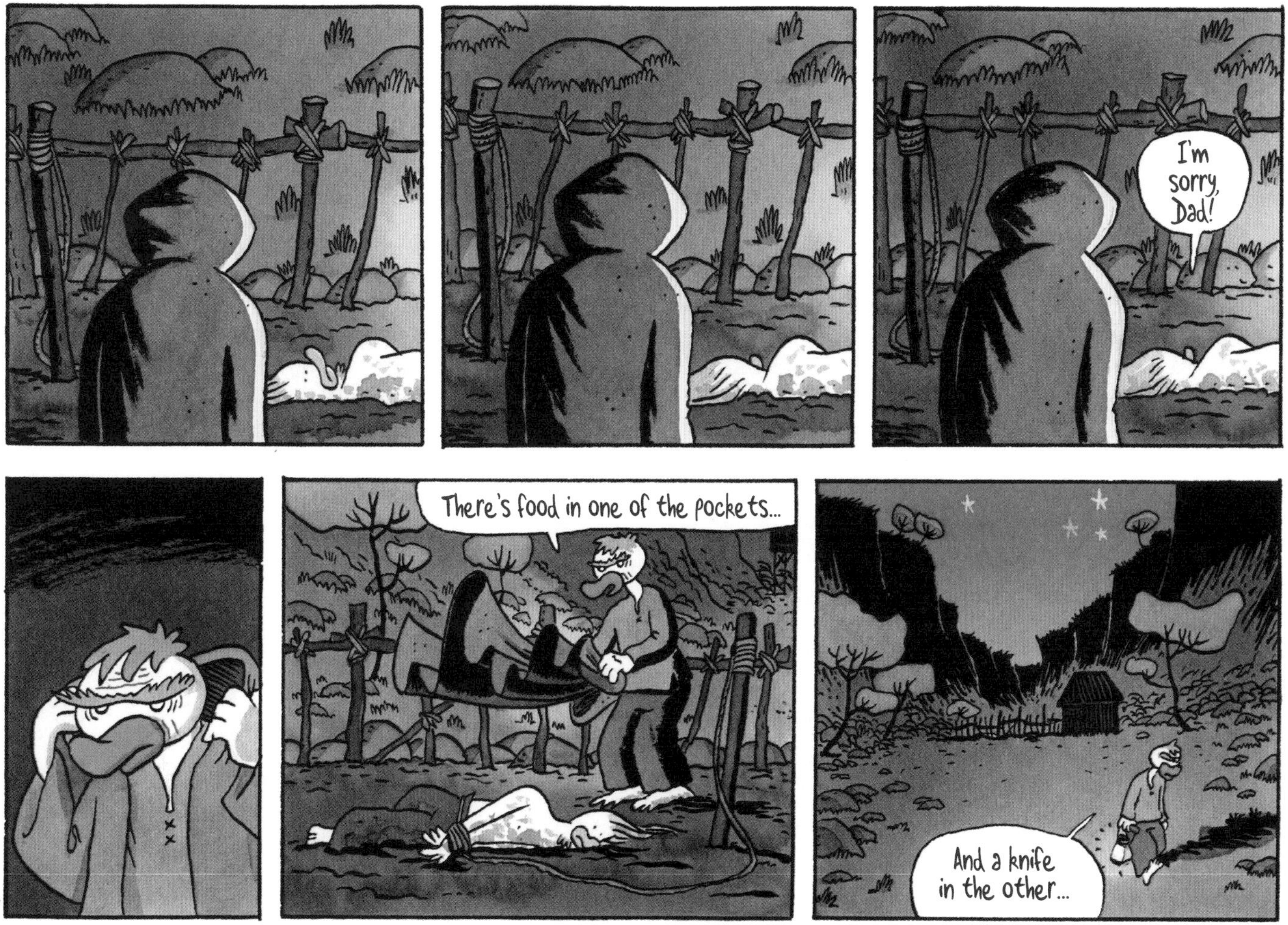
I'm sorry, Dad!
There's food in one of the pockets...
And a knife in the other...

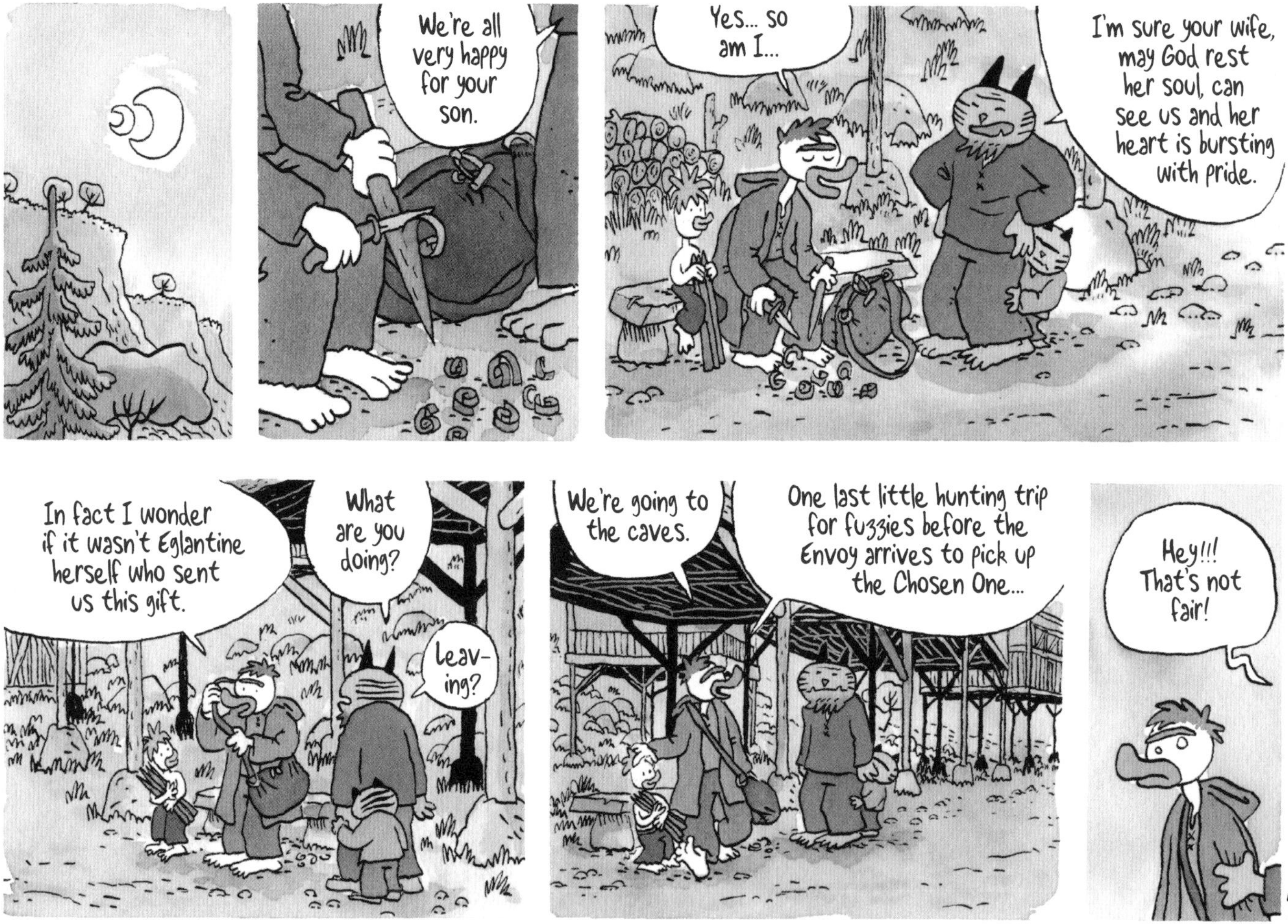
We're all very happy for your son.
Yes... so am I...
I'm sure your wife, may God rest her soul, can see us and her heart is bursting with pride.
In fact I wonder if it wasn't Eglantine herself who sent us this gift.
What are you doing?
Leav-ing?
We're going to the caves.
One last little hunting trip for fuzzies before the Envoy arrives to pick up the Chosen One...
Hey!!! That's not fair!

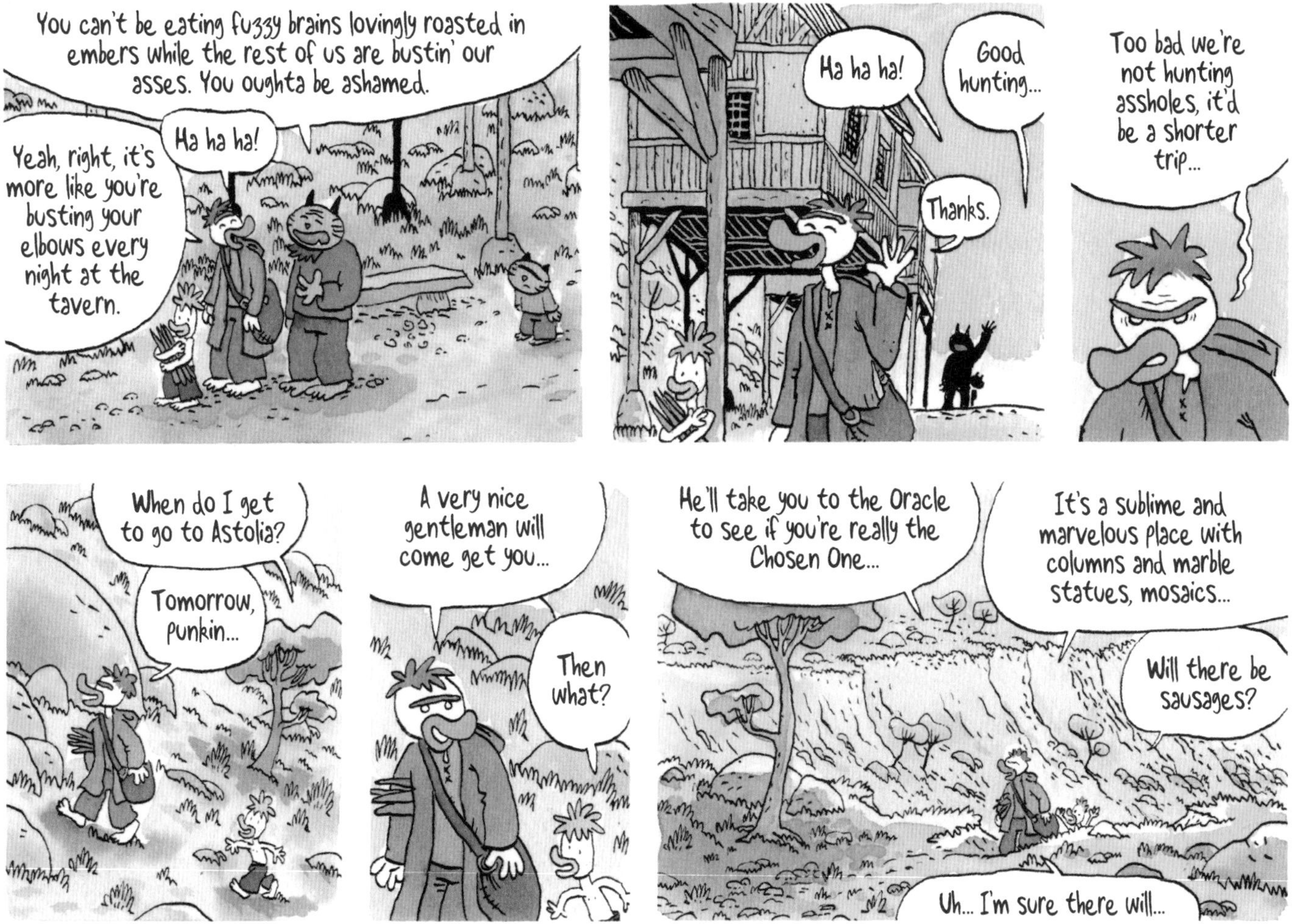

You can't be eating fuzzy brains lovingly roasted in embers while the rest of us are bustin' our asses. You oughta be ashamed.
Yeah, right, it's more like you're busting your elbows every night at the tavern.
Ha ha ha!
Ha ha ha!
Good hunting...
Thanks.
Too bad we're not hunting assholes, it'd be a shorter trip...
When do I get to go to Astolia?
Tomorrow, punkin...
A very nice gentleman will come get you...
Then what?
He'll take you to the Oracle to see if you're really the Chosen One...
It's a sublime and marvelous place with columns and marble statues, mosaics...
Will there be sausages?
Uh... I'm sure there will...

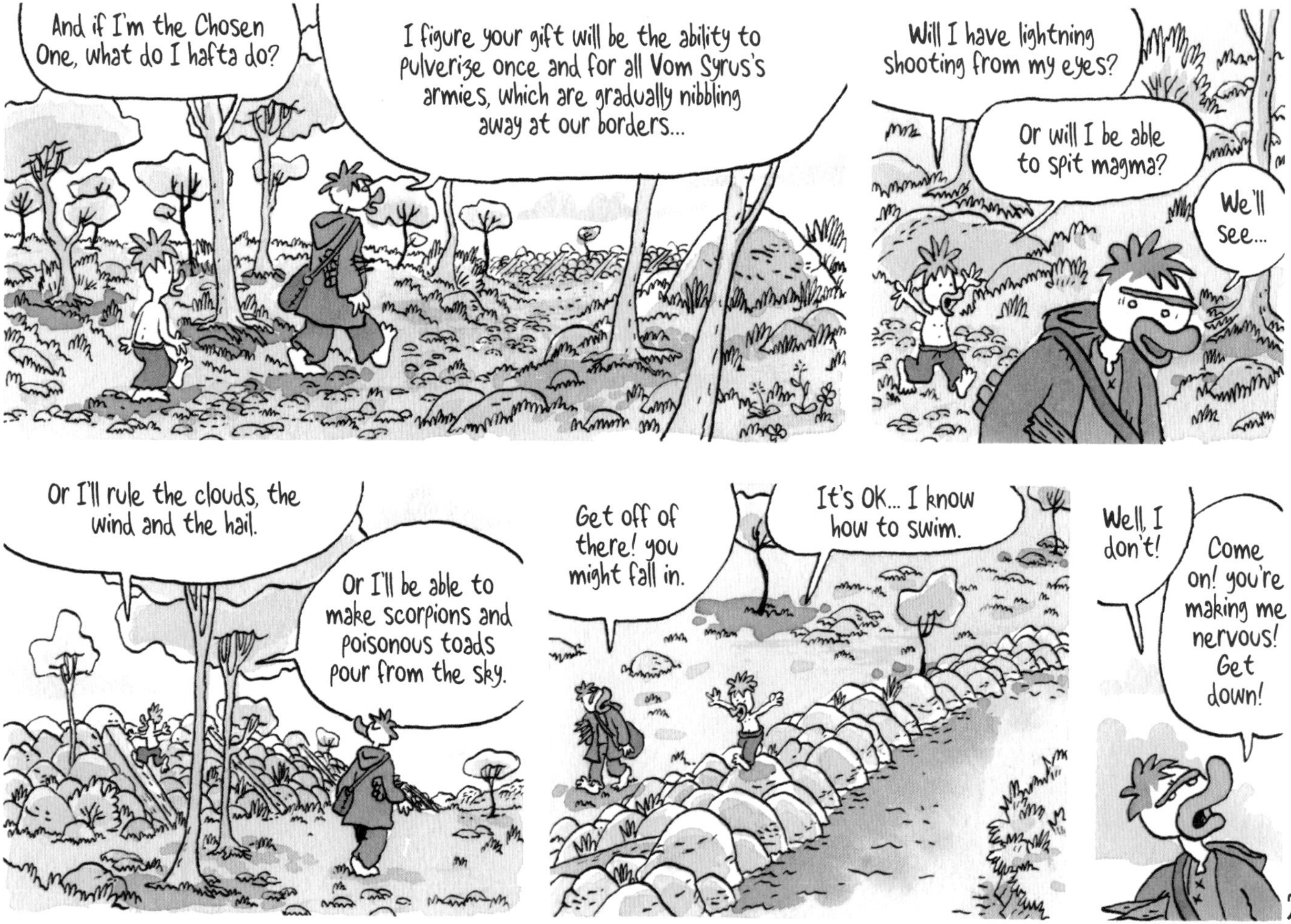
And if I'm the Chosen One, what do I hafta do?
I figure your gift will be the ability to pulverize once and for all Vom Syrus's armies, which are gradually nibbling away at our borders...
Will I have lightning shooting from my eyes?
Or will I be able to spit magma?
We'll see...
Or I'll rule the clouds, the wind and the hail.
Or I'll be able to make scorpions and poisonous toads pour from the sky.
Get off of there! you might fall in.
It's OK... I know how to swim.
Well, I don't!
Come on! you're making me nervous! Get down!

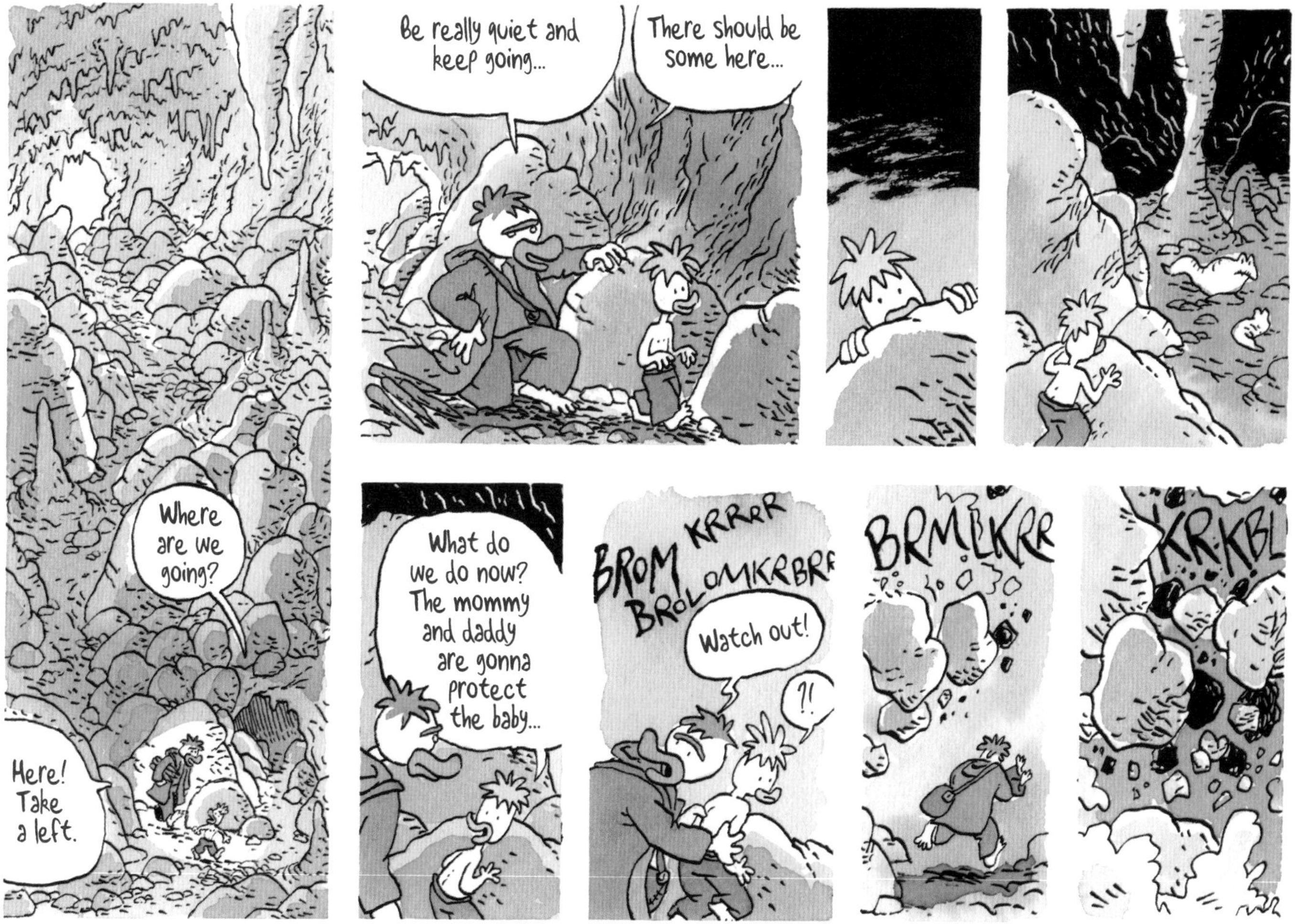

Where are we going?
Here! Take a left.
Be really quiet and keep going...
There should be some here...
What do we do now? The mommy and daddy are gonna protect the baby...
KRRRR
BROM
BROLOMKRBRR
Watch out!
?!
BRMLKRR
KRKBL

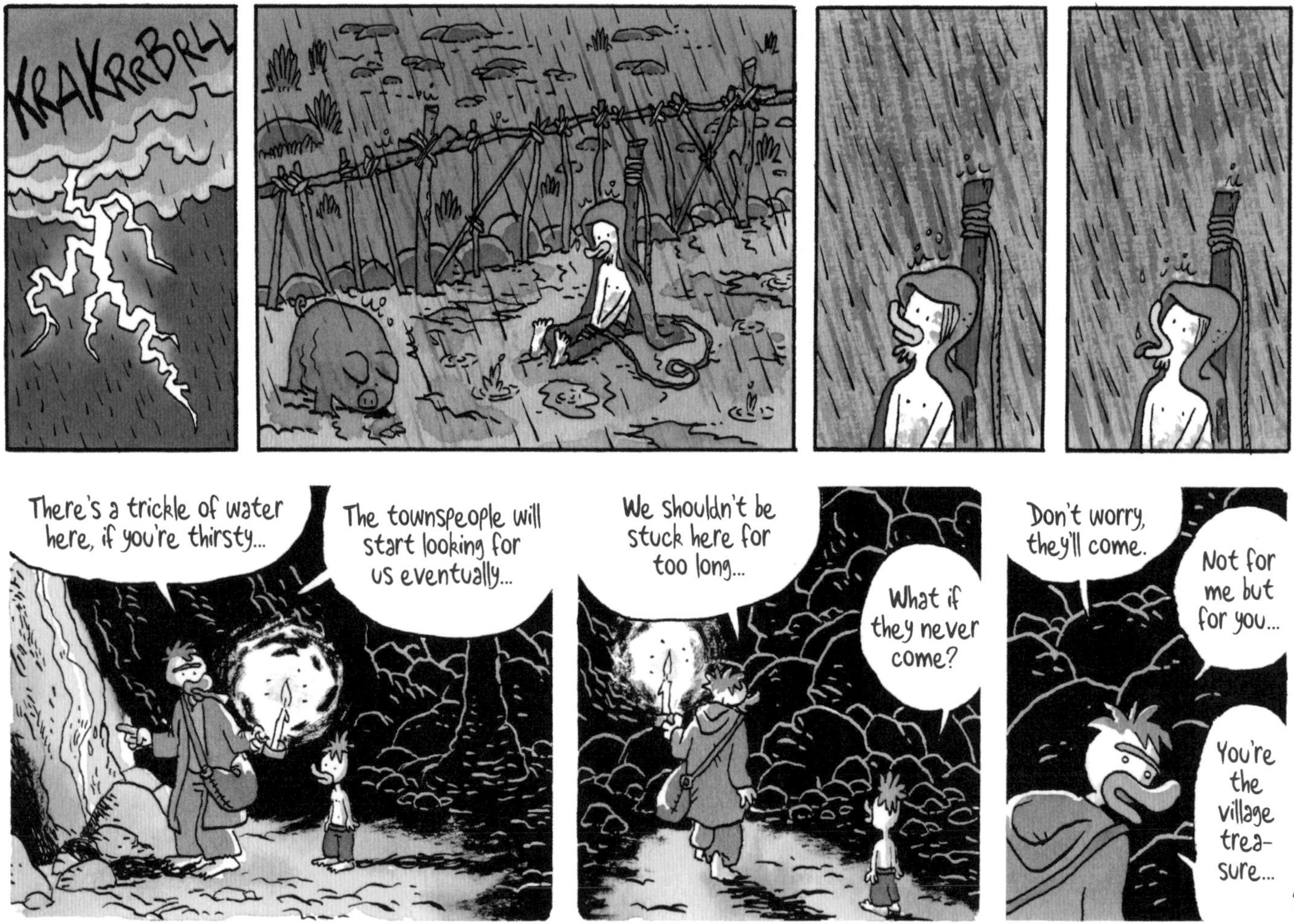
KRAKRRBRLL
There's a trickle of water here, if you're thirsty...
The townspeople will start looking for us eventually...
We shouldn't be stuck here for too long...
What if they never come?
Don't worry, they'll come.
Not for me but for you...
You're the village trea-sure...

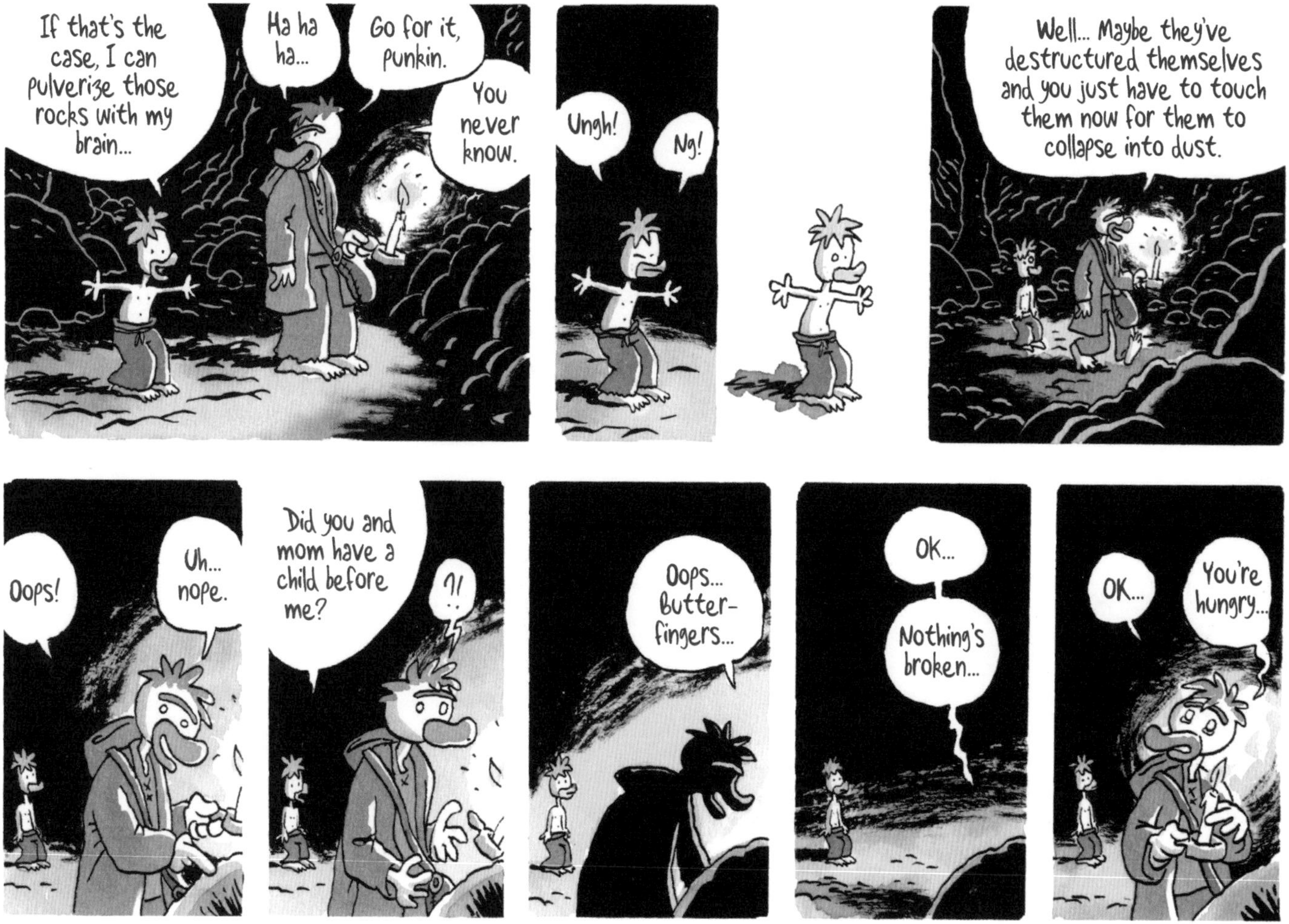
If that's the case, I can pulverize those rocks with my brain...
Ha ha ha...
Go for it, punkin.
You never know.
Ungh!
Ng!
Well... Maybe they've destructured themselves and you just have to touch them now for them to collapse into dust.
Oops!
Uh... nope.
Did you and mom have a child before me?
?!
Oops... Butter-fingers...
OK...
Nothing's broken...
OK...
You're hungry...

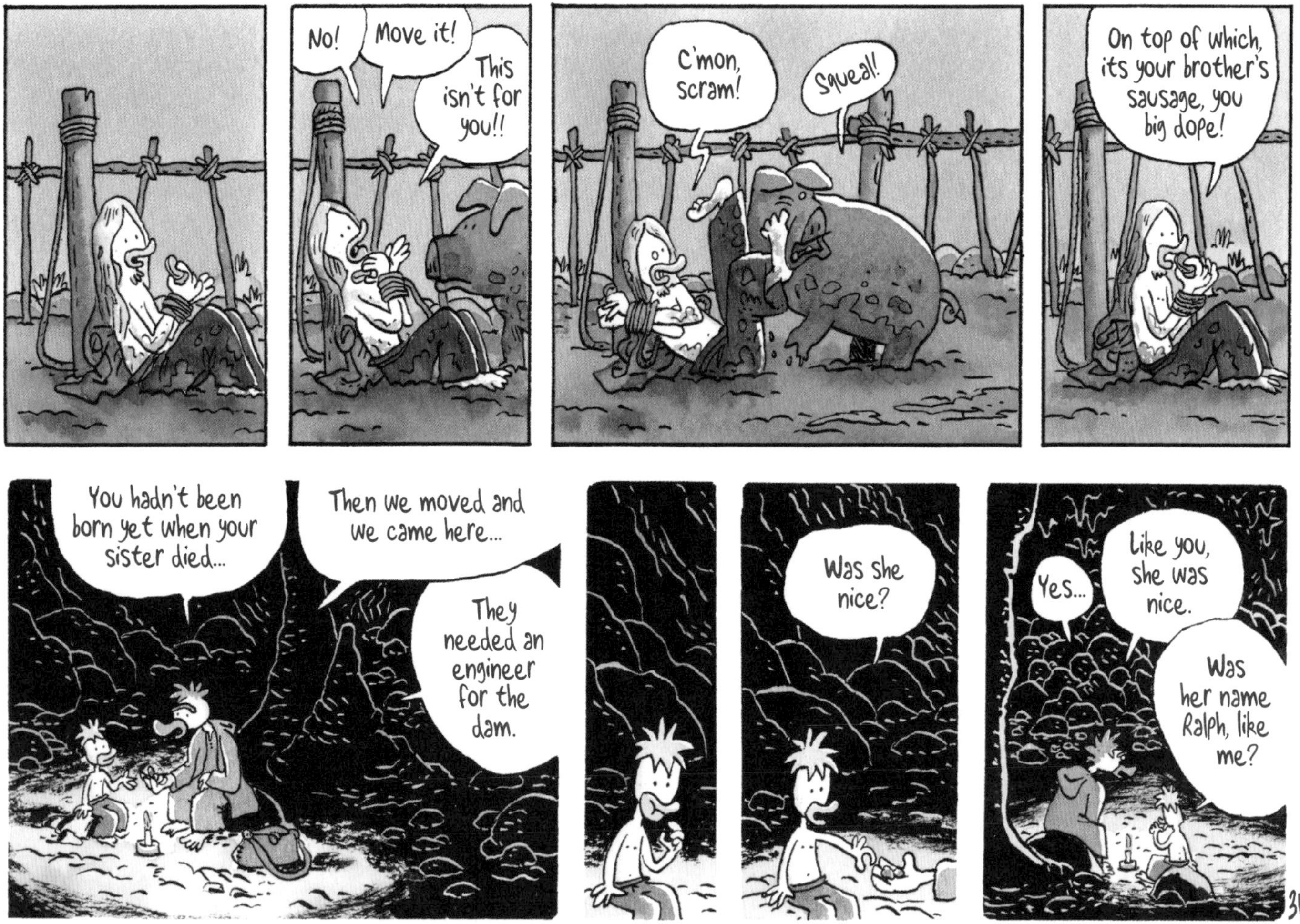
No!
Move it!
This isn't for you!!
C'mon, scram!
Squeal!
On top of which, its your brother's sausage, you big dope!
You hadn't been born yet when your sister died...
Then we moved and we came here...
They needed an engineer for the dam.
Was she nice?
Yes...
Like you, she was nice.
Was her name Ralph, like me?

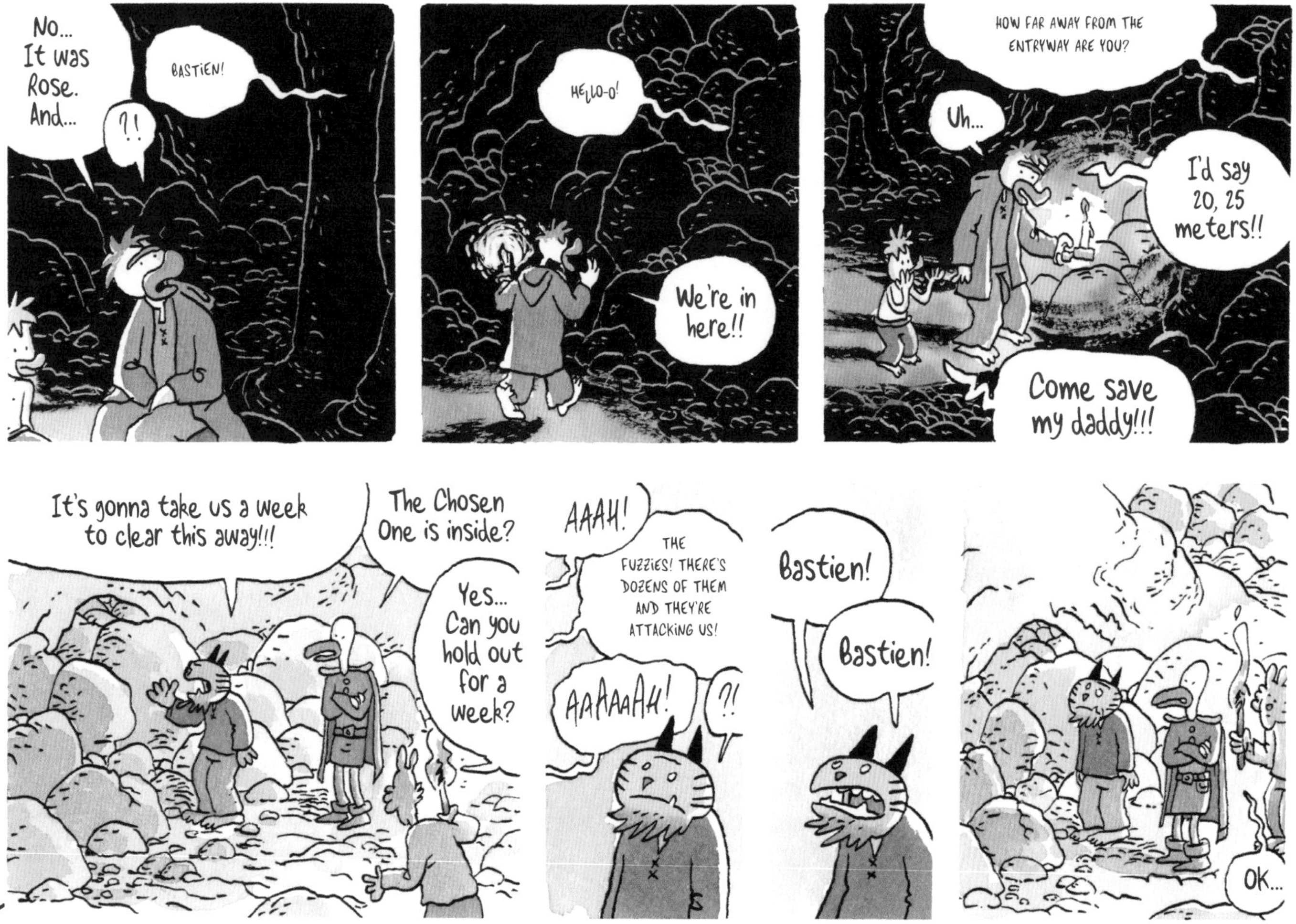
No... It was Rose. And...
?!
BASTIEN!
HELLO-O!
We're in here!!
HOW FAR AWAY FROM THE ENTRYWAY ARE YOU?
Uh...
I'd say 20, 25 meters!!
Come save my daddy!!!
It's gonna take us a week to clear this away!!!
The Chosen One is inside?
Yes... Can you hold out for a week?
AAAH!
THE FUZZIES! THERE'S DOZENS OF THEM AND THEY'RE ATTACKING US!
AAAAAAH!
?!
Bastien!
Bastien!
OK...

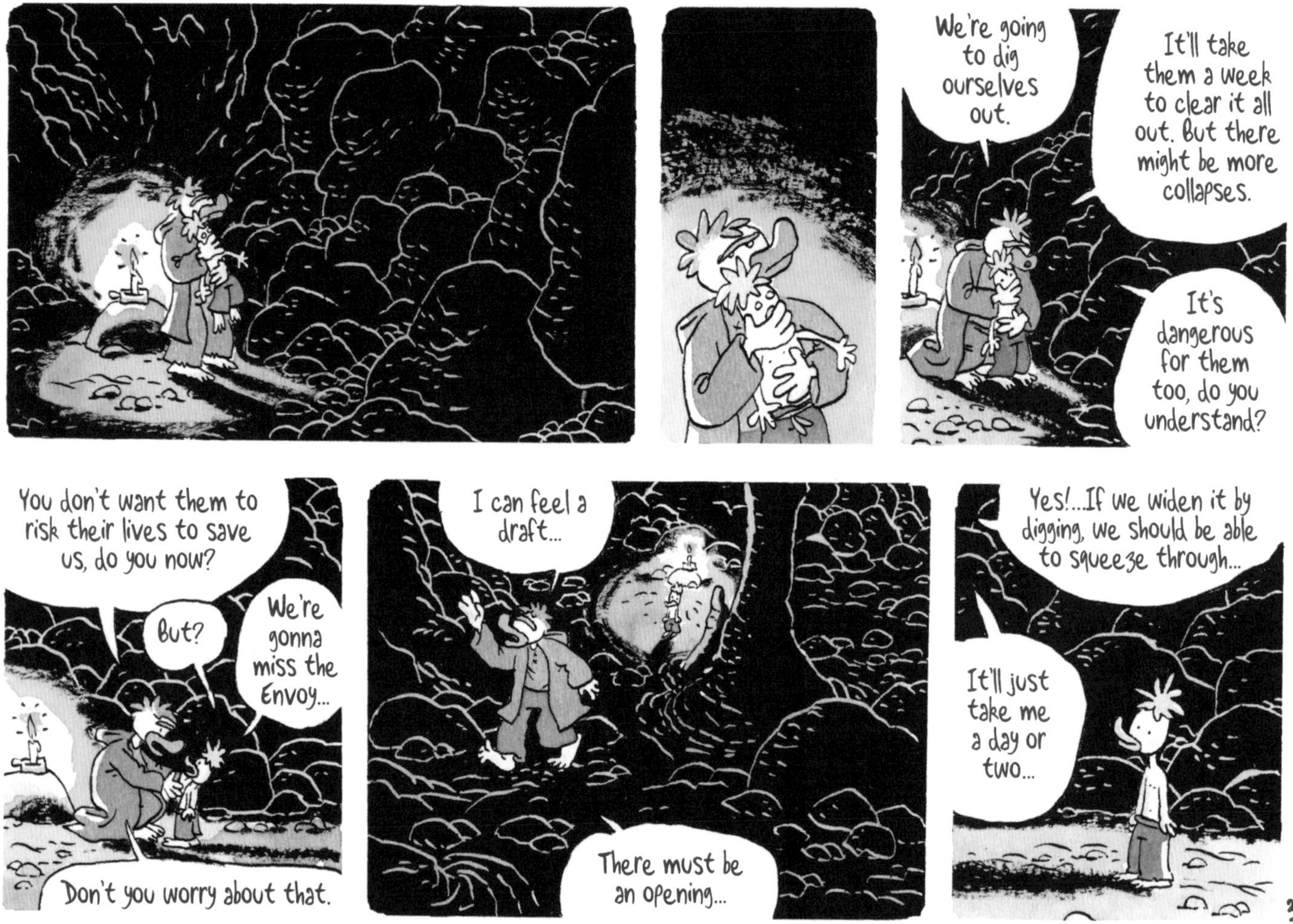
We're going to dig ourselves out.
It'll take them a week to clear it all out. But there might be more collapses.
It's dangerous for them too, do you understand?
You don't want them to risk their lives to save us, do you now?
But?
We're gonna miss the Envoy...
Don't you worry about that.
I can feel a draft...
There must be an opening...
Yes!...If we widen it by digging, we should be able to squeeze through...
It'll just take me a day or two...

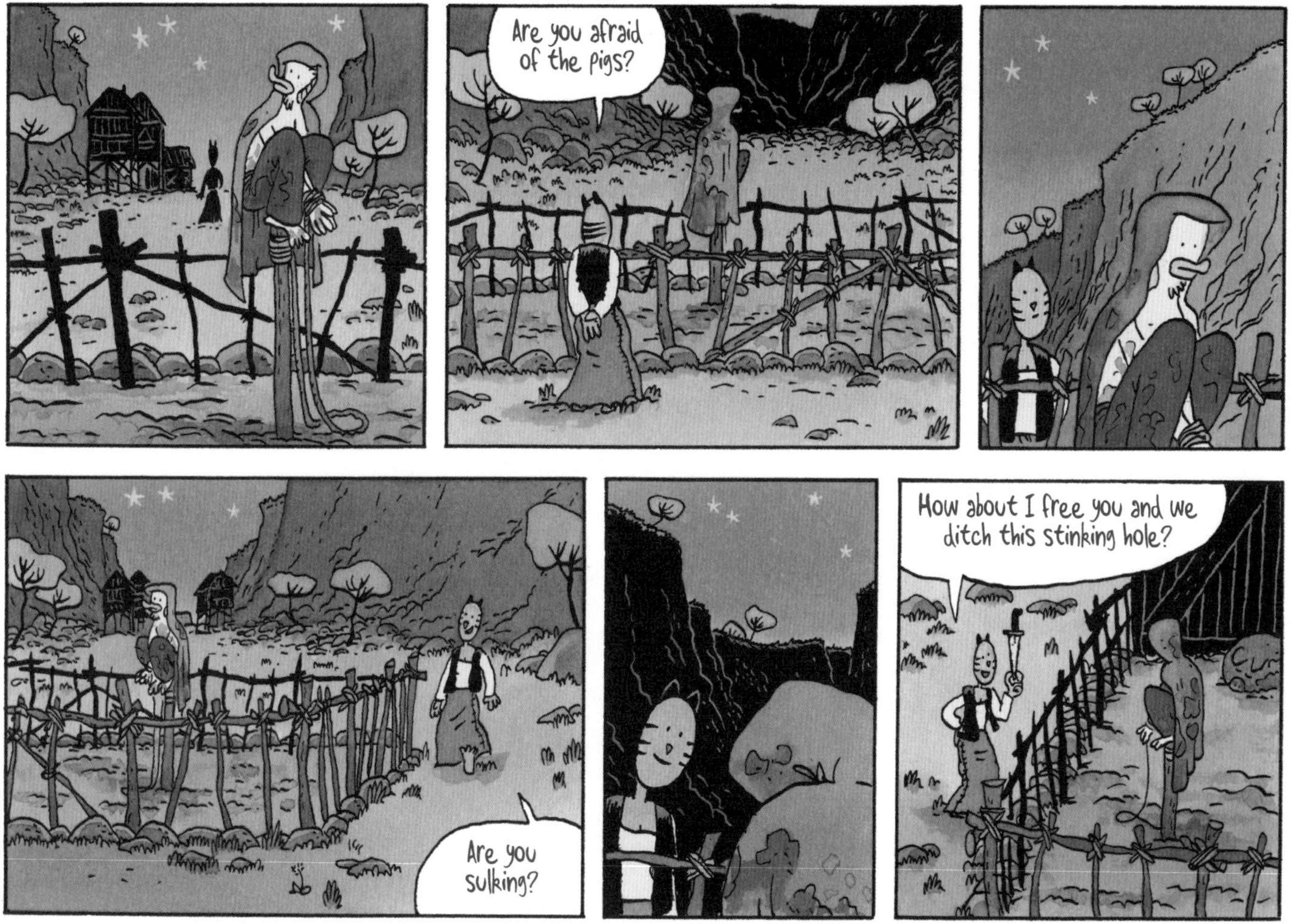
Are you afraid of the pigs?
Are you sulking?
How about I free you and we ditch this stinking hole?

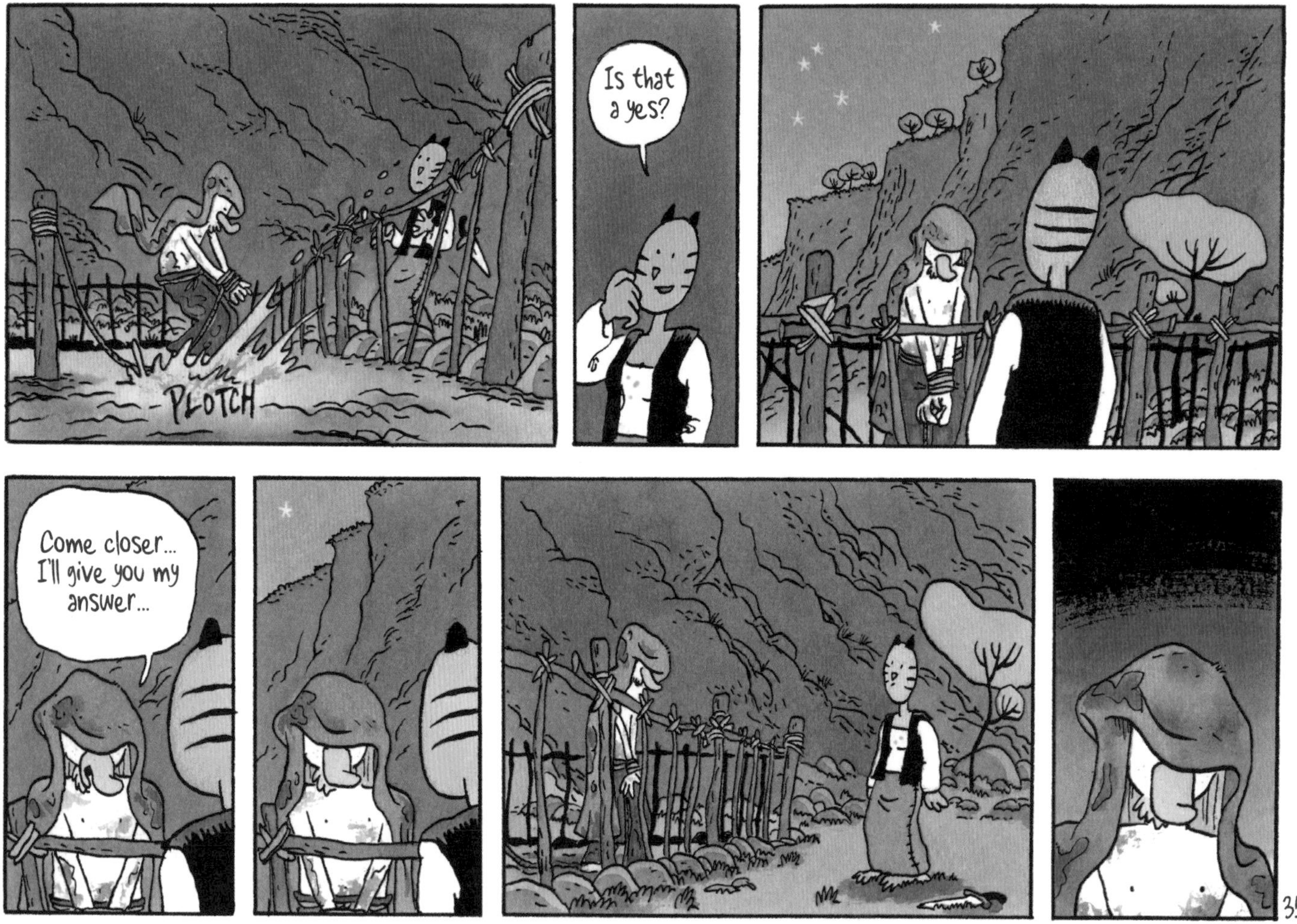
PLOTCH
Is that a yes?
Come closer... I'll give you my answer...

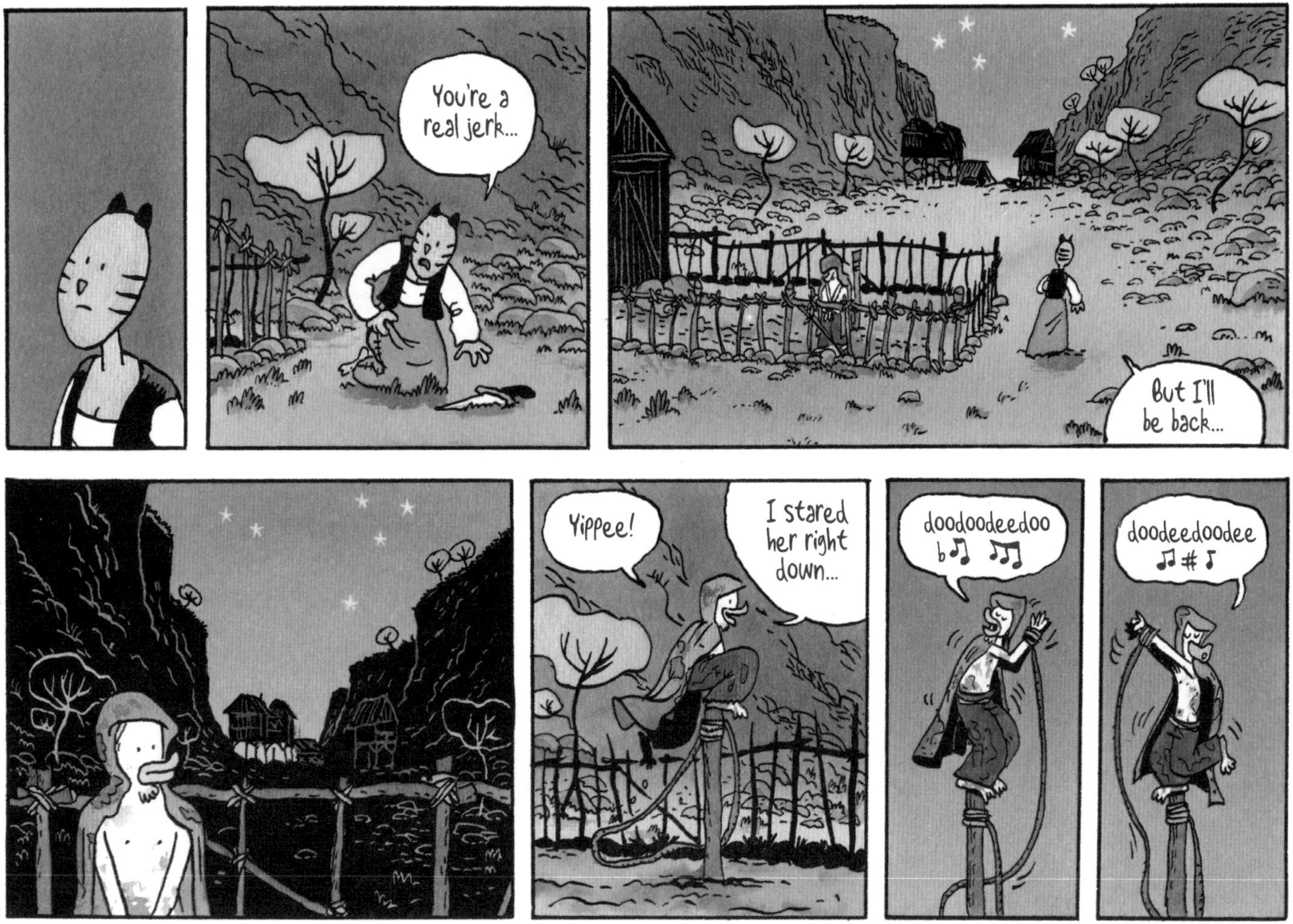
You're a real jerk...
But I'll be back...
Yippee!
I stared her right down...
doodoodeedoo
doodeedoodee

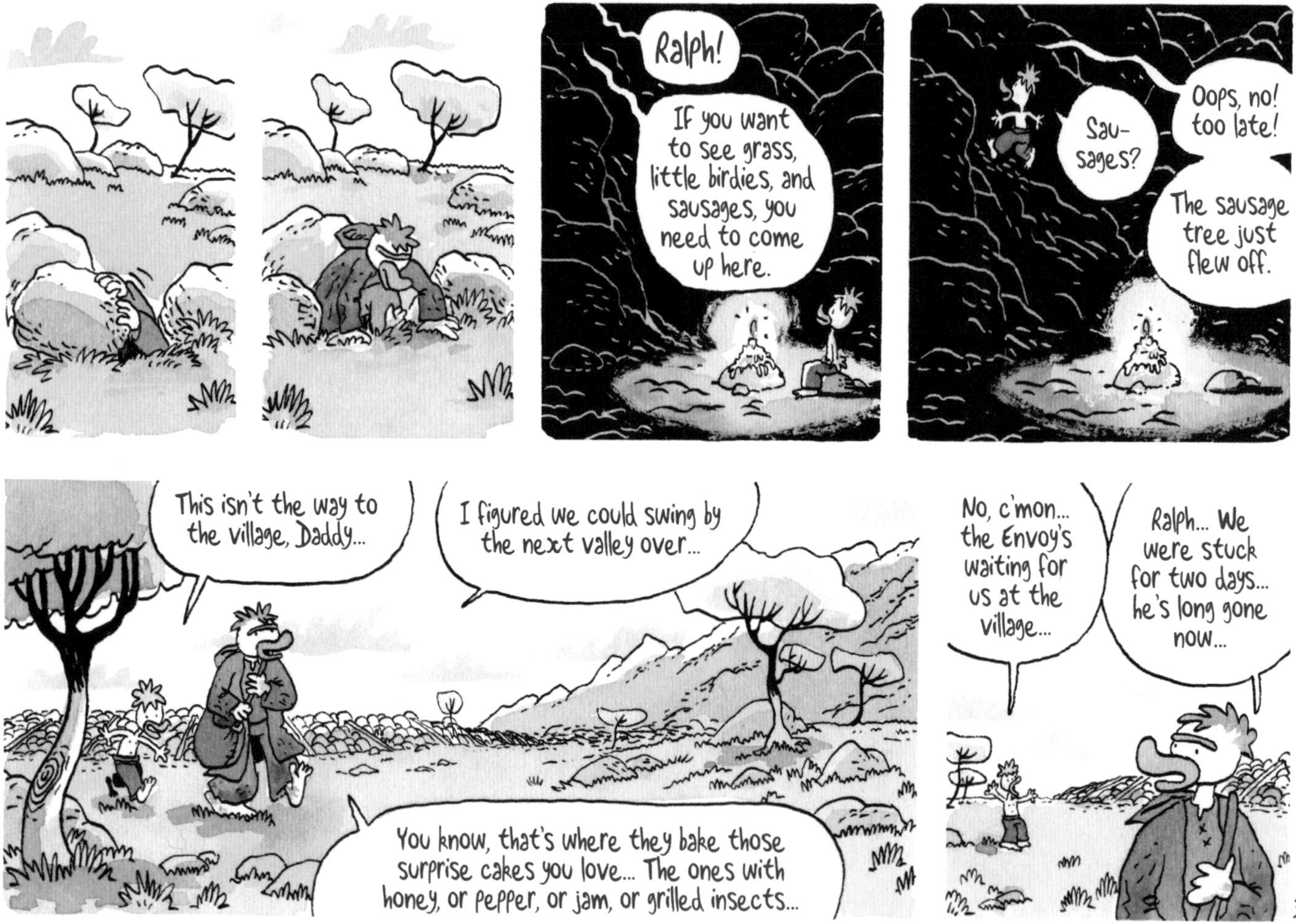

Ralph!
If you want to see grass, little birdies, and sausages, you need to come up here.
Sau-sages?
Oops, no! too late!
The sausage tree just flew off.
This isn't the way to the village, Daddy...
I figured we could swing by the next valley over...
You know, that's where they bake those surprise cakes you love... The ones with honey, or pepper, or jam, or grilled insects...
No, c'mon... the Envoy's waiting for us at the village...
Ralph... We were stuck for two days... he's long gone now...

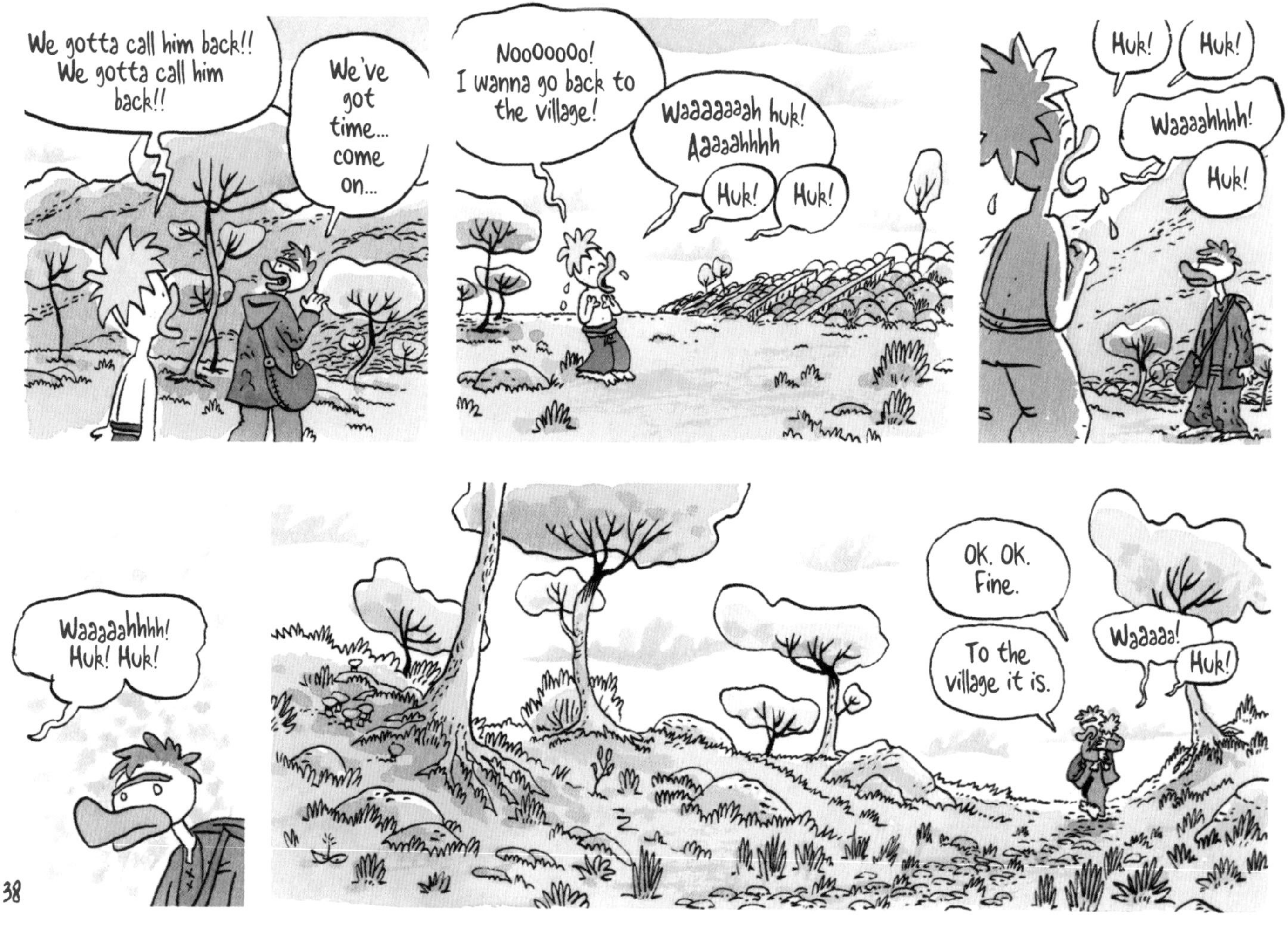
We gotta call him back!! We gotta call him back!!
We've got time... come on...
NoOooooo! I wanna go back to the village!
Waaaaaaah huk! Aaaaahhhh
Huk!
Huk!
Huk!
Huk!
Waaaahhhh!
Huk!
Waaaaahhhh! Huk! Huk!
OK. OK. Fine.
To the village it is.
Waaaaa!
Huk!

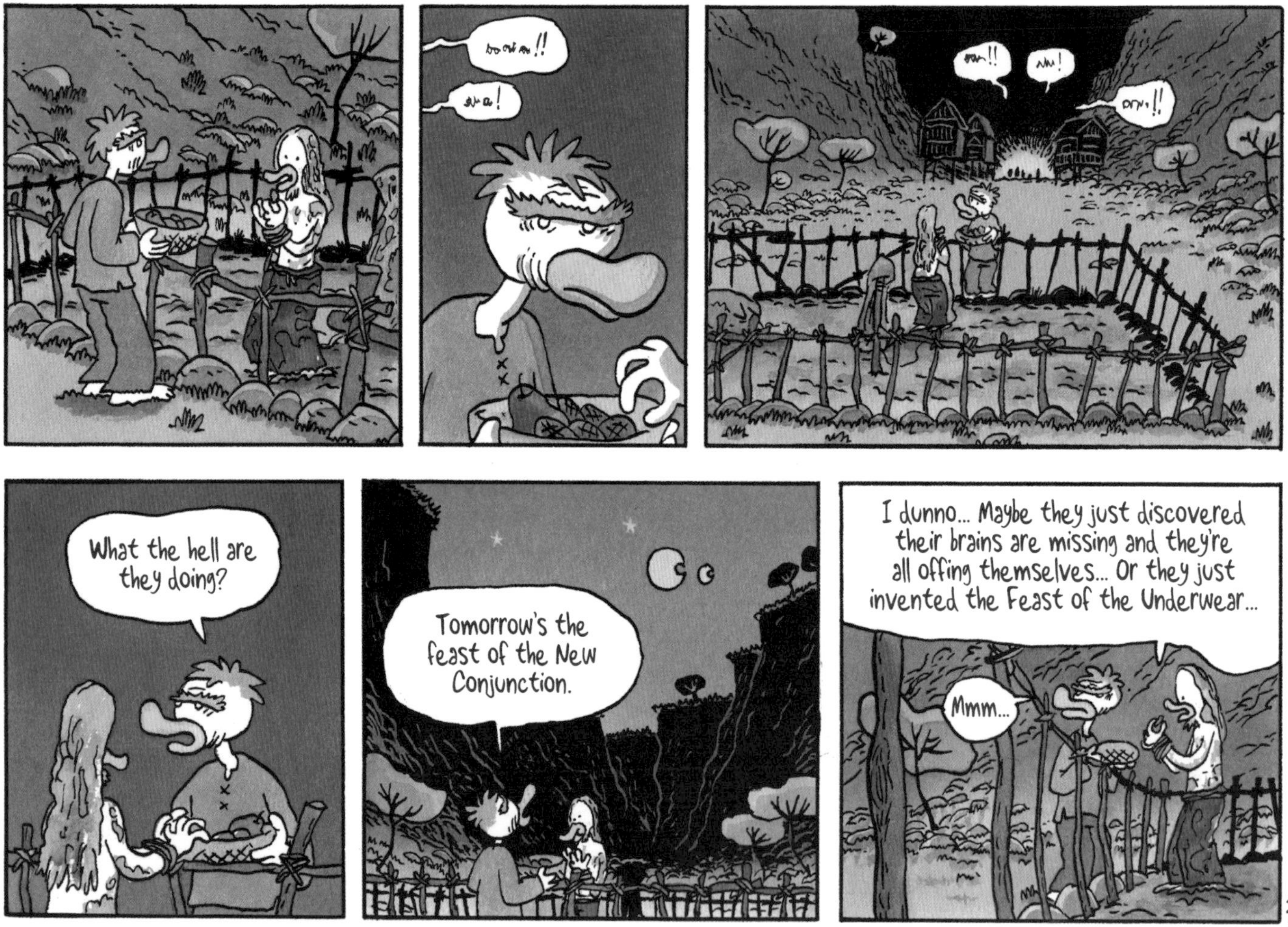
What the hell are they doing?
Tomorrow's the feast of the New Conjunction.
I dunno... Maybe they just discovered their brains are missing and they're all offing themselves... Or they just invented the Feast of the Underwear...
Mmm...

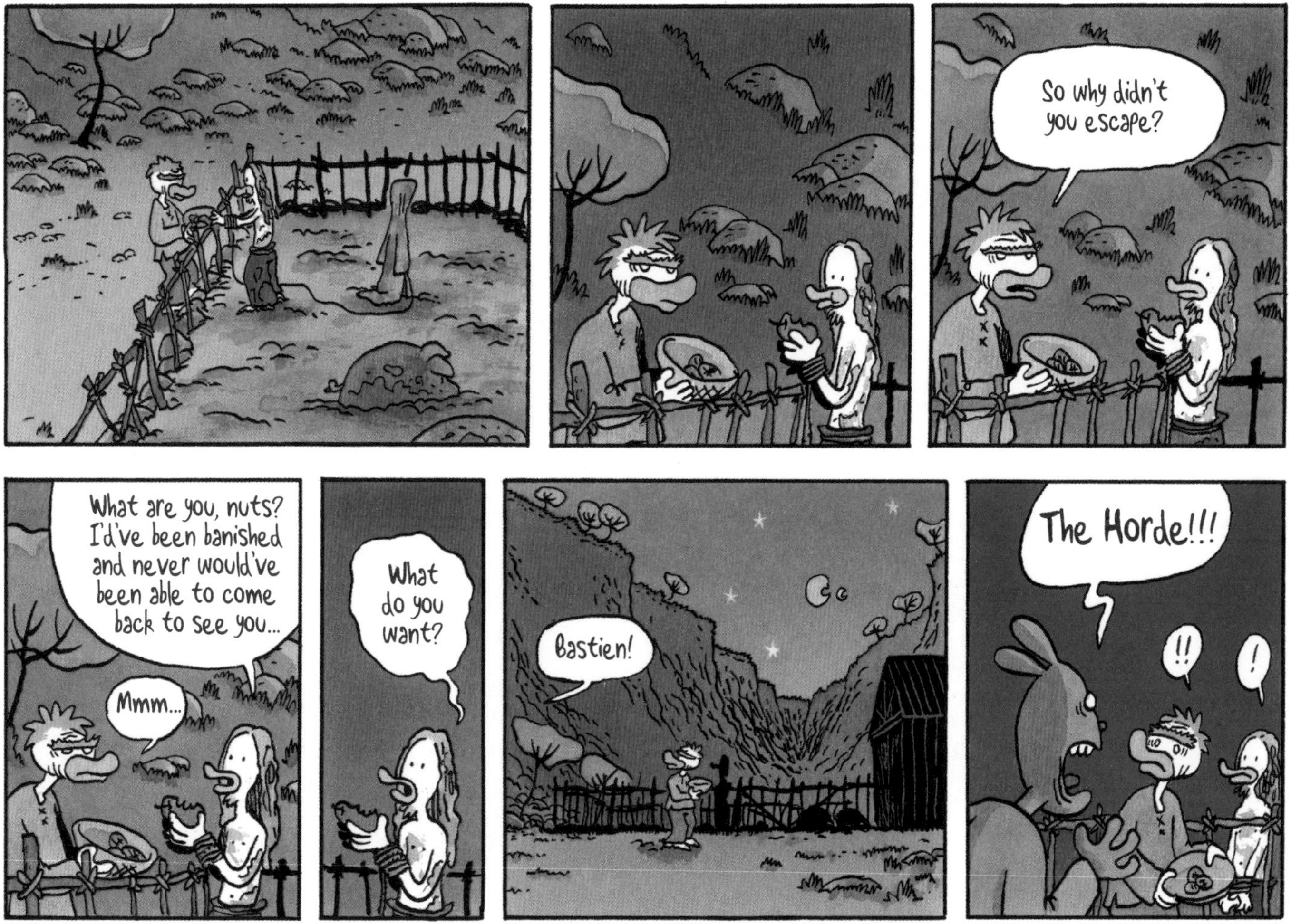
So why didn't you escape?
What are you, nuts? I'd've been banished and never would've been able to come back to see you...
Mmm...
What do you want?
Bastien!
The Horde!!!
!!
!

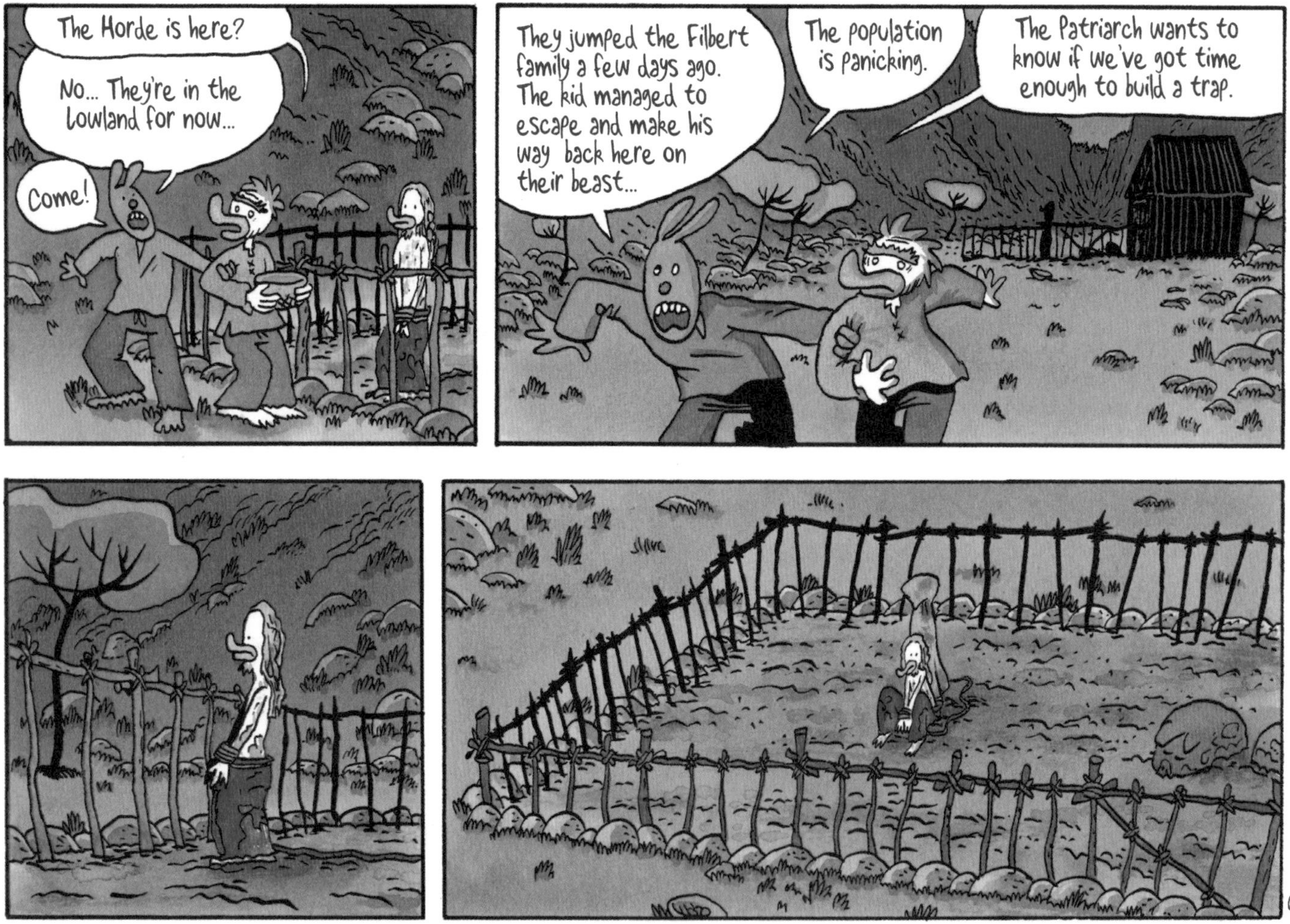
The Horde is here?
No... They're in the Lowland for now...
Come!
They jumped the Filbert family a few days ago. The kid managed to escape and make his way back here on their beast...
The population is panicking.
The Patriarch wants to know if we've got time enough to build a trap.

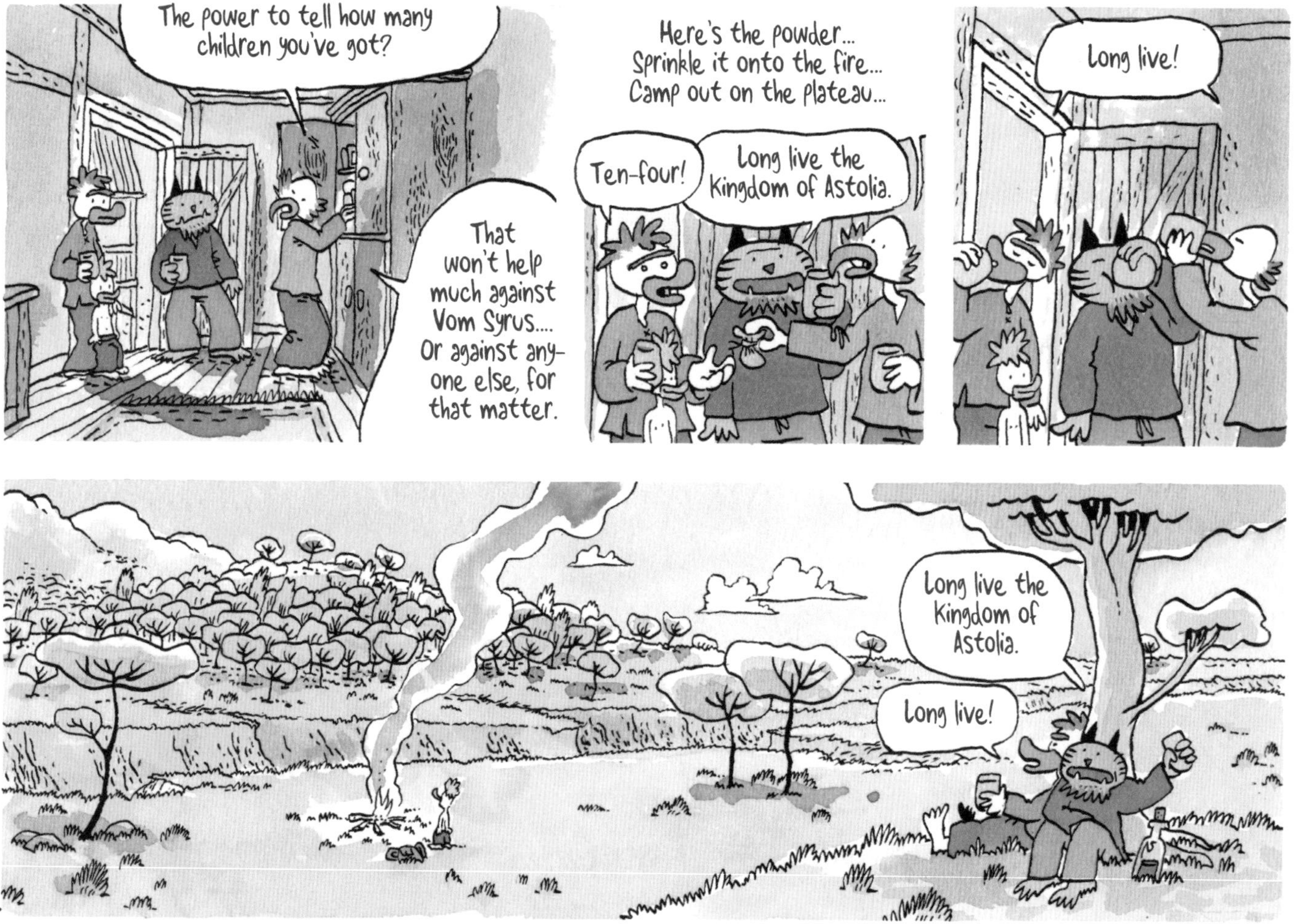
The power to tell how many children you've got?
That won't help much against Vom Syrus.... Or against anyone else, for that matter.
Here's the powder... Sprinkle it onto the fire... Camp out on the plateau...
Ten-four!
Long live the Kingdom of Astolia.
Long live!
Long live the Kingdom of Astolia.
Long live!

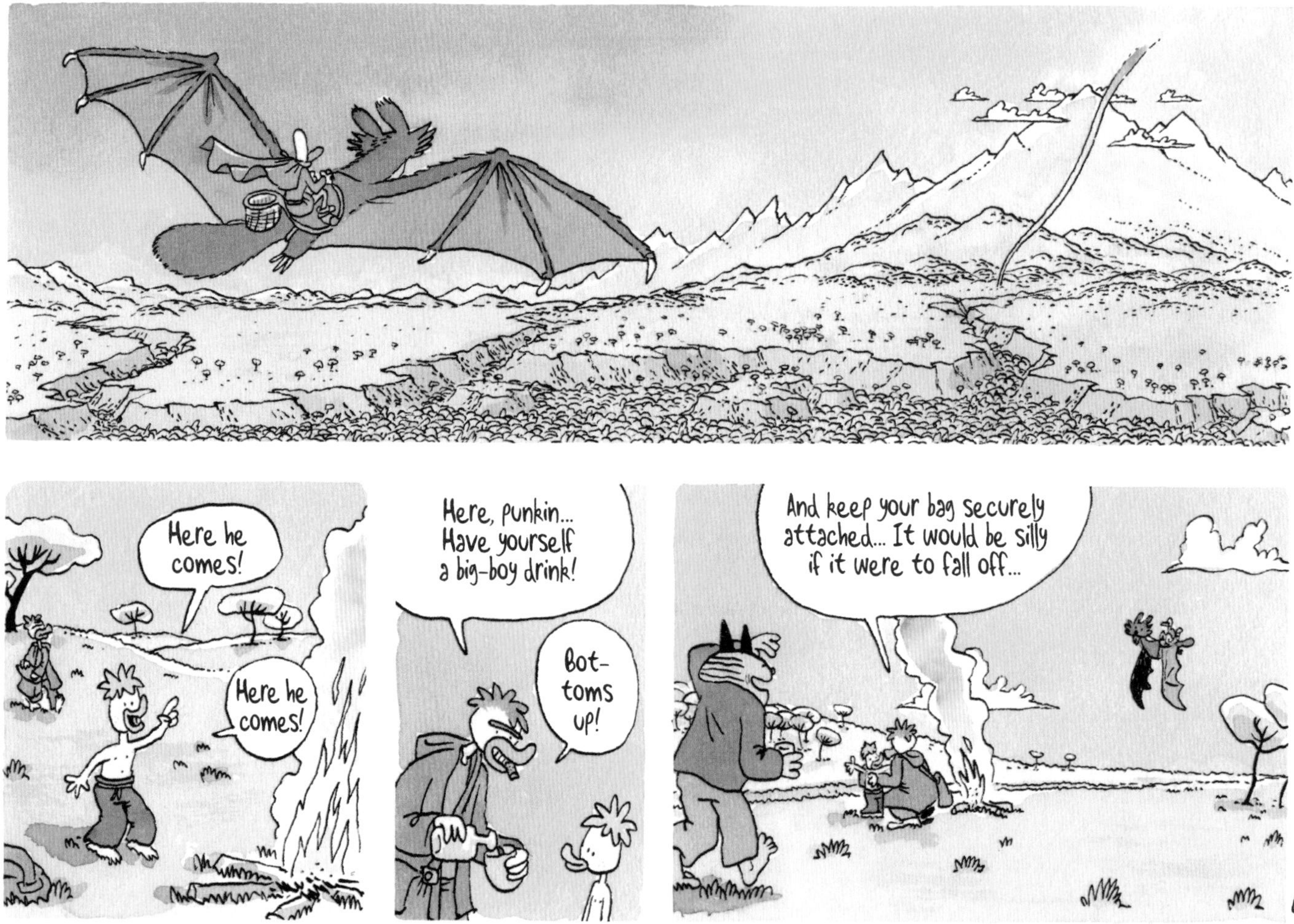
Here he comes!
Here he comes!
Here, punkin... Have yourself a big-boy drink!
Bot-toms up!
And keep your bag securely attached... It would be silly if it were to fall off...

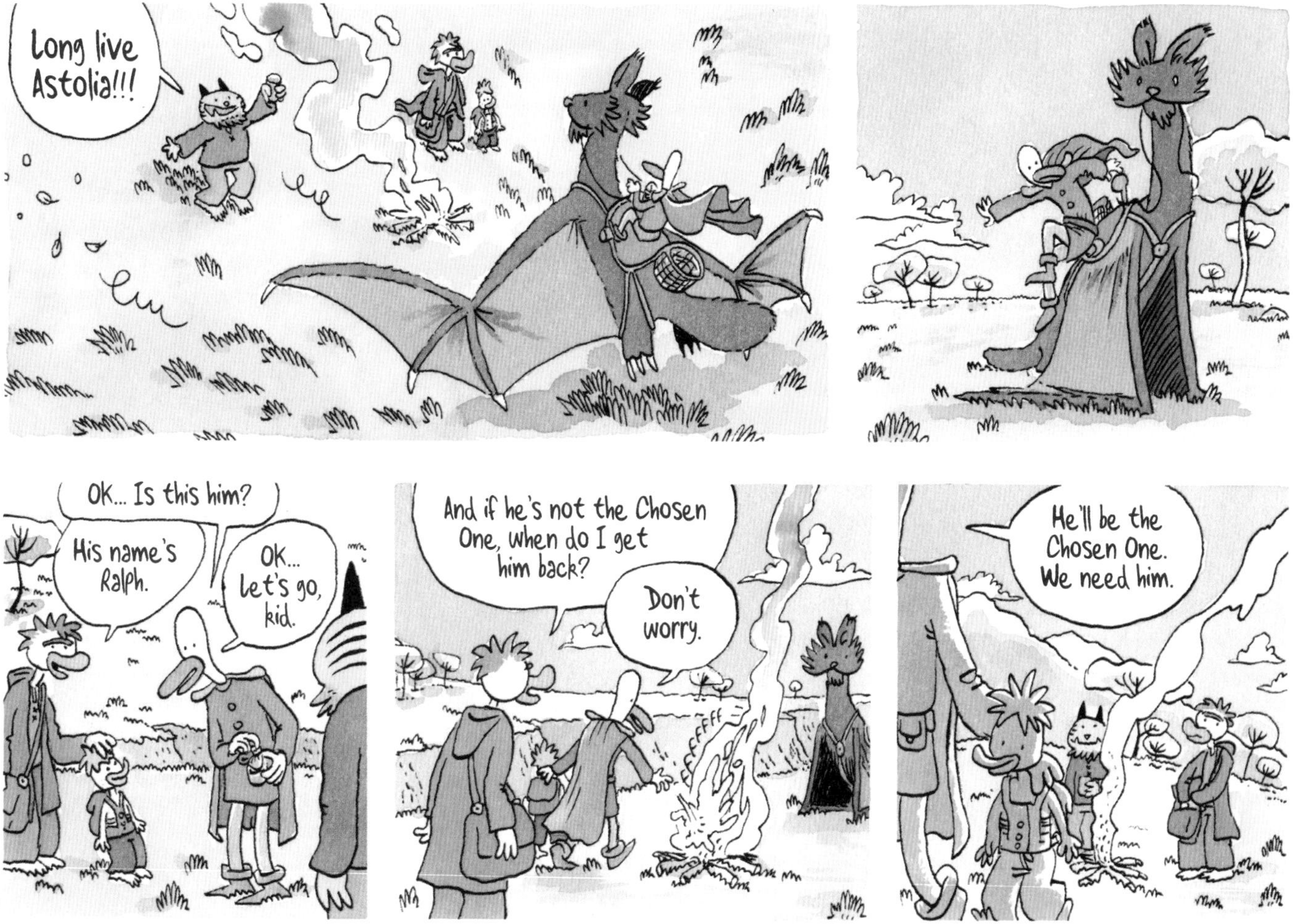
Long live Astolia!!!
OK... Is this him?
His name's Ralph.
OK... Let's go, kid.
And if he's not the Chosen One, when do I get him back?
Don't worry.
He'll be the Chosen One. We need him.

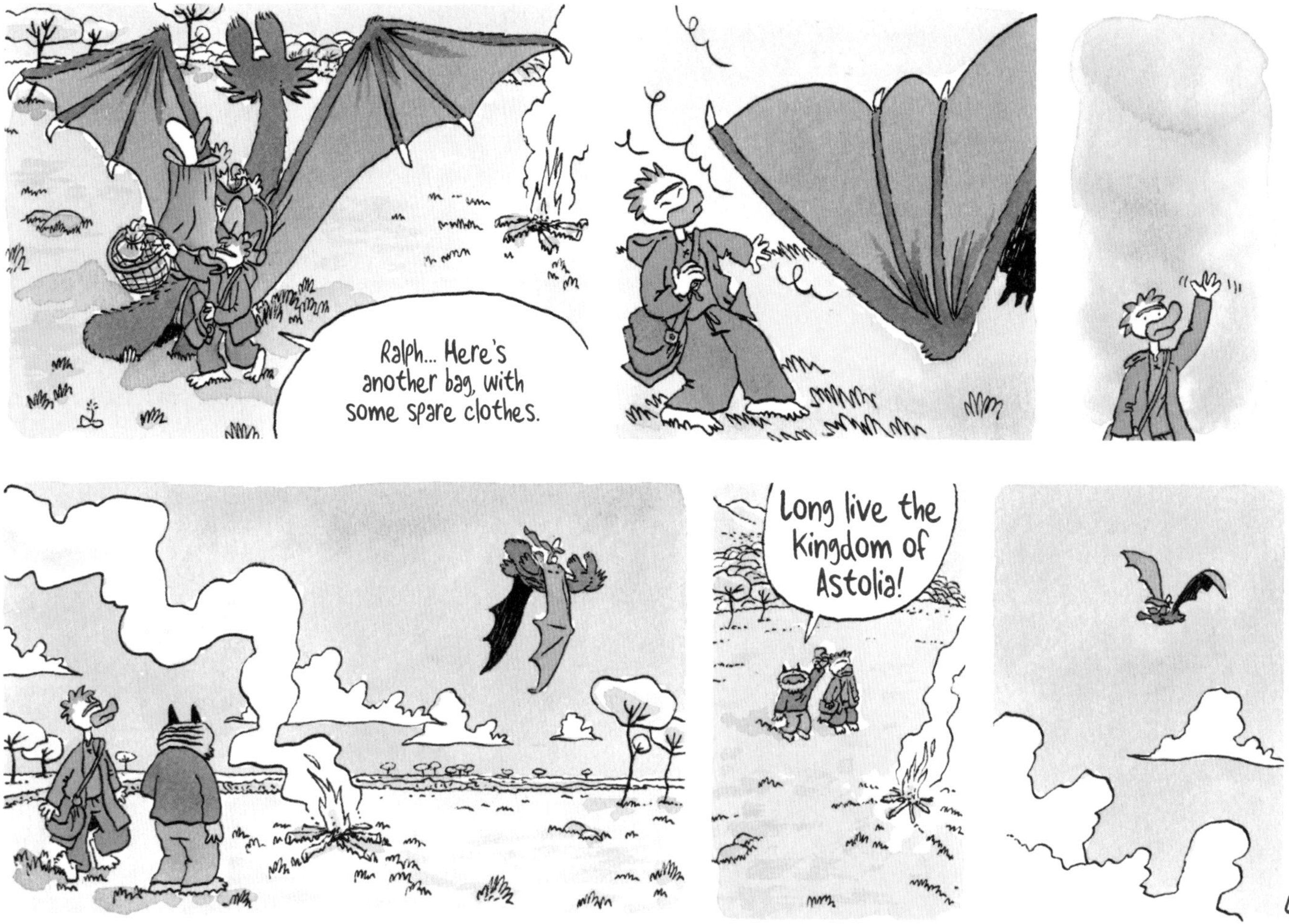
Ralph... Here's another bag, with some spare clothes.
Long live the Kingdom of Astolia!

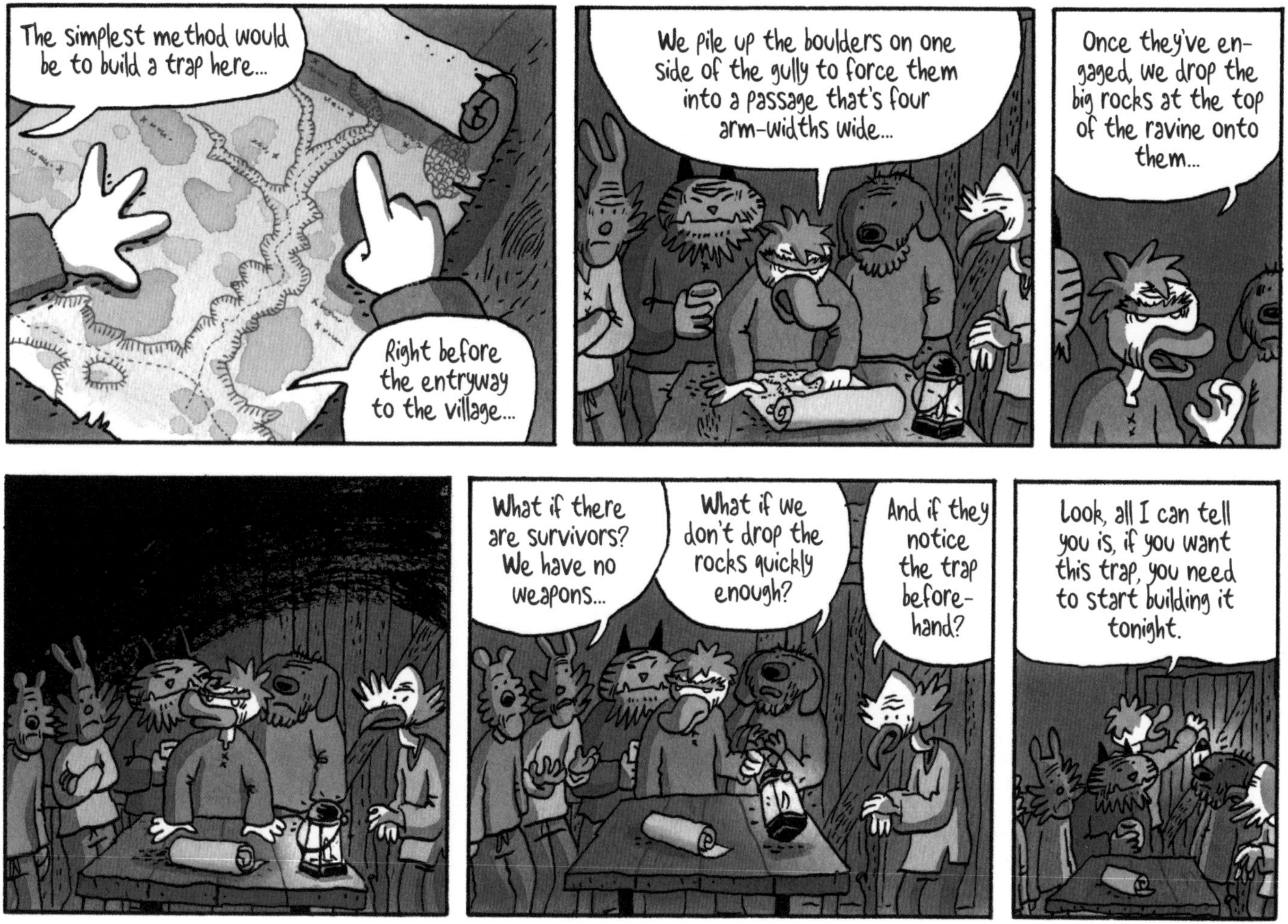
The simplest method would be to build a trap here...
Right before the entryway to the village...
We pile up the boulders on one side of the gully to force them into a passage that's four arm-widths wide...
Once they've engaged, we drop the big rocks at the top of the ravine onto them...
What if there are survivors? We have no weapons...
What if we don't drop the rocks quickly enough?
And if they notice the trap beforehand?
Look, all I can tell you is, if you want this trap, you need to start building it tonight.

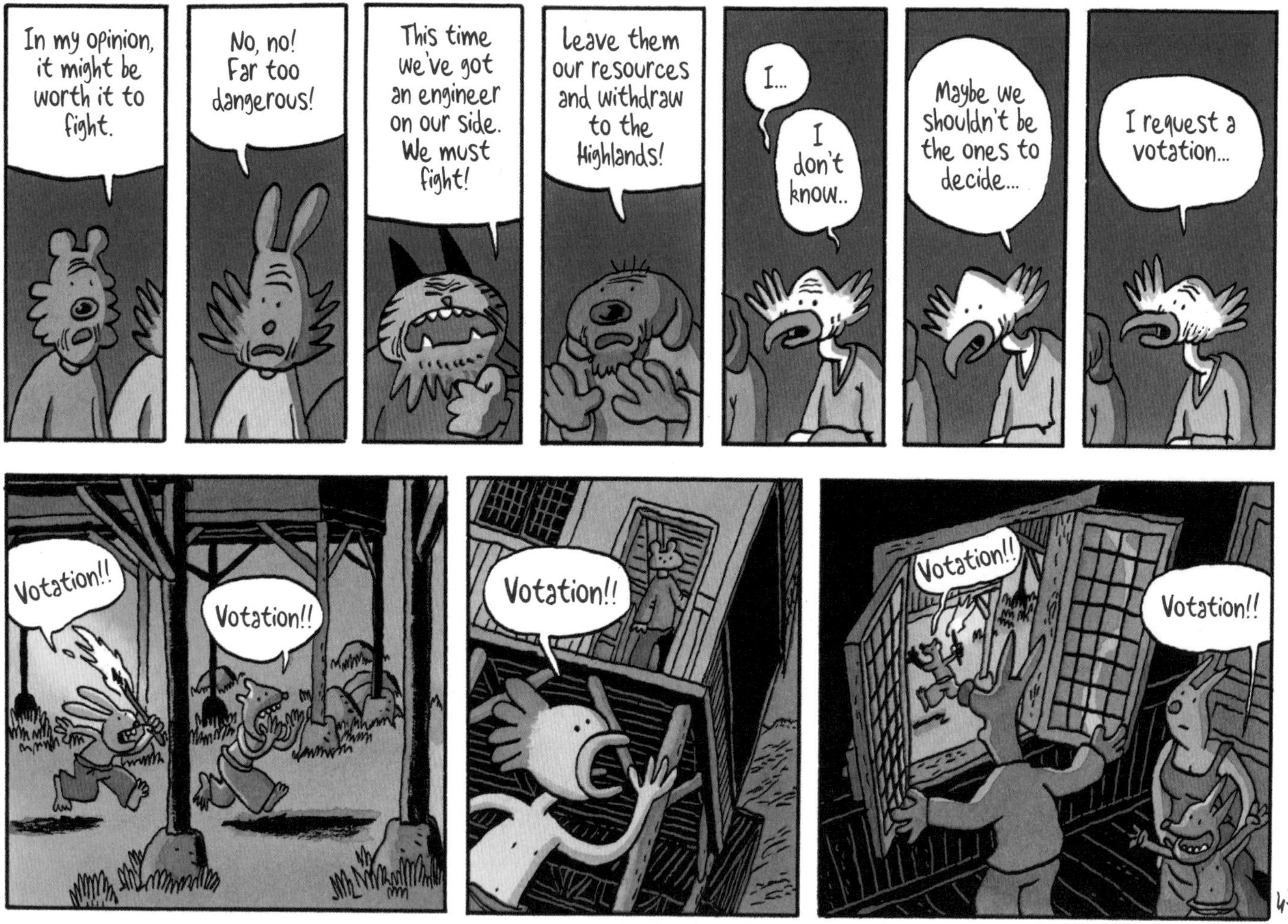
In my opinion, it might be worth it to fight.
No, no! Far too dangerous!
This time we've got an engineer on our side. We must fight!
Leave them our resources and withdraw to the Highlands!
I...
I don't know..
Maybe we shouldn't be the ones to decide...
I request a votation...
Votation!!
Votation!!
Votation!!
Votation!!
Votation!!

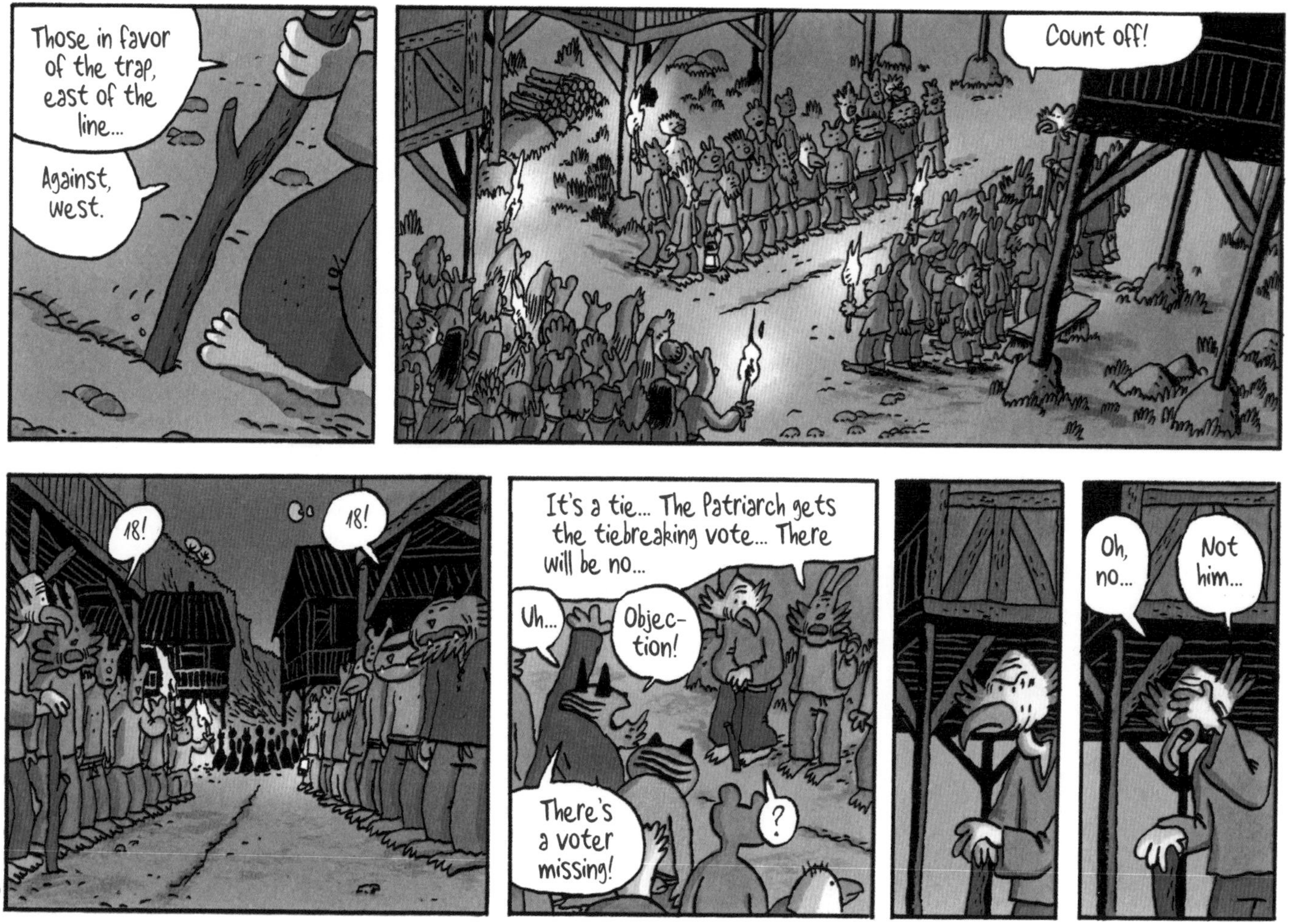
Those in favor of the trap, east of the line...
Against, west.
Count off!
18!
18!
It's a tie... The Patriarch gets the tiebreaking vote... There will be no...
Uh...
Objec-tion!
There's a voter missing!
?
Oh, no...
Not him...

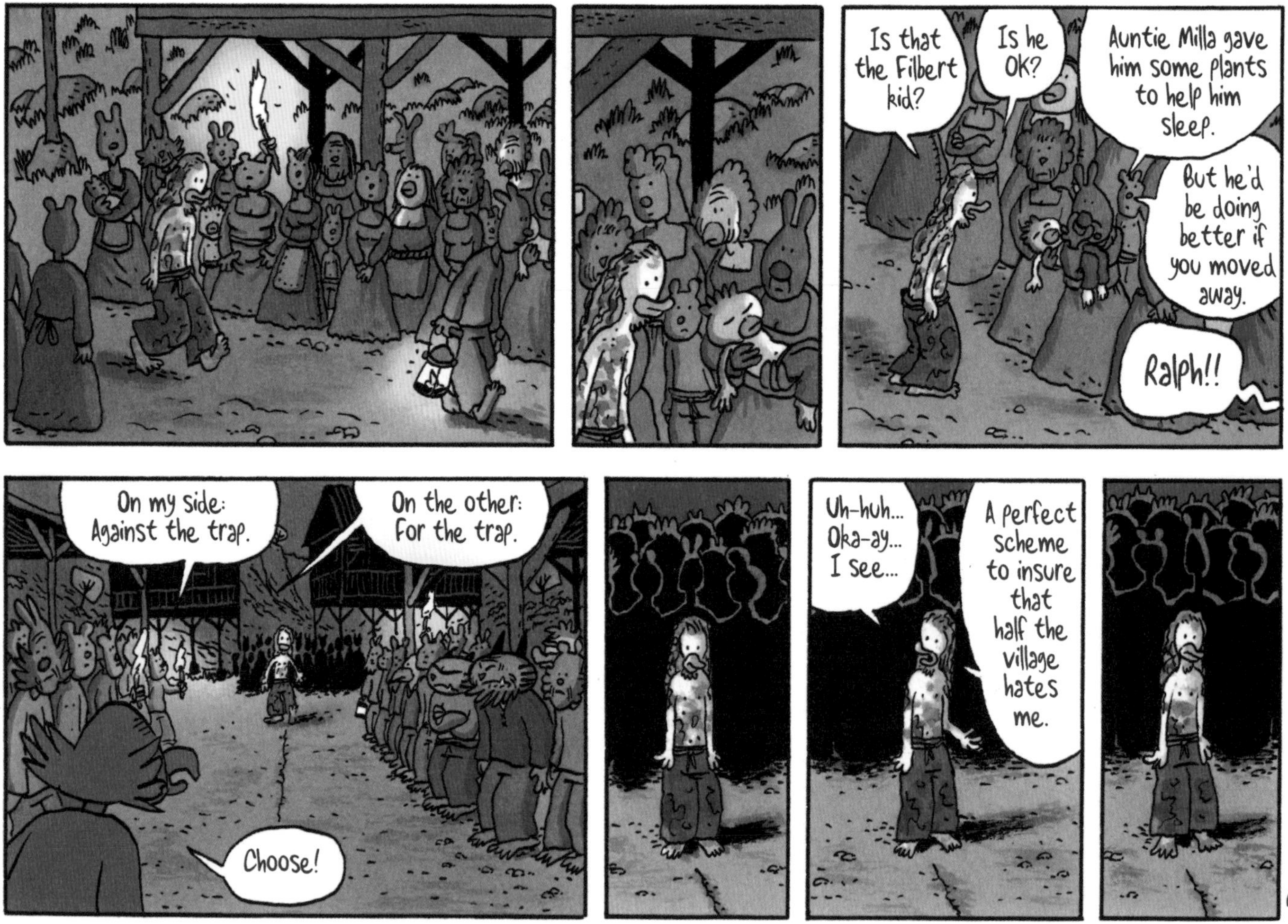
Is that the Filbert kid?
Is he OK?
Auntie Milla gave him some plants to help him sleep.
But he'd be doing better if you moved away.
Ralph!!
On my side: Against the trap.
On the other: For the trap.
Choose!
Uh-huh... Oka-ay... I see...
A perfect scheme to insure that half the village hates me.

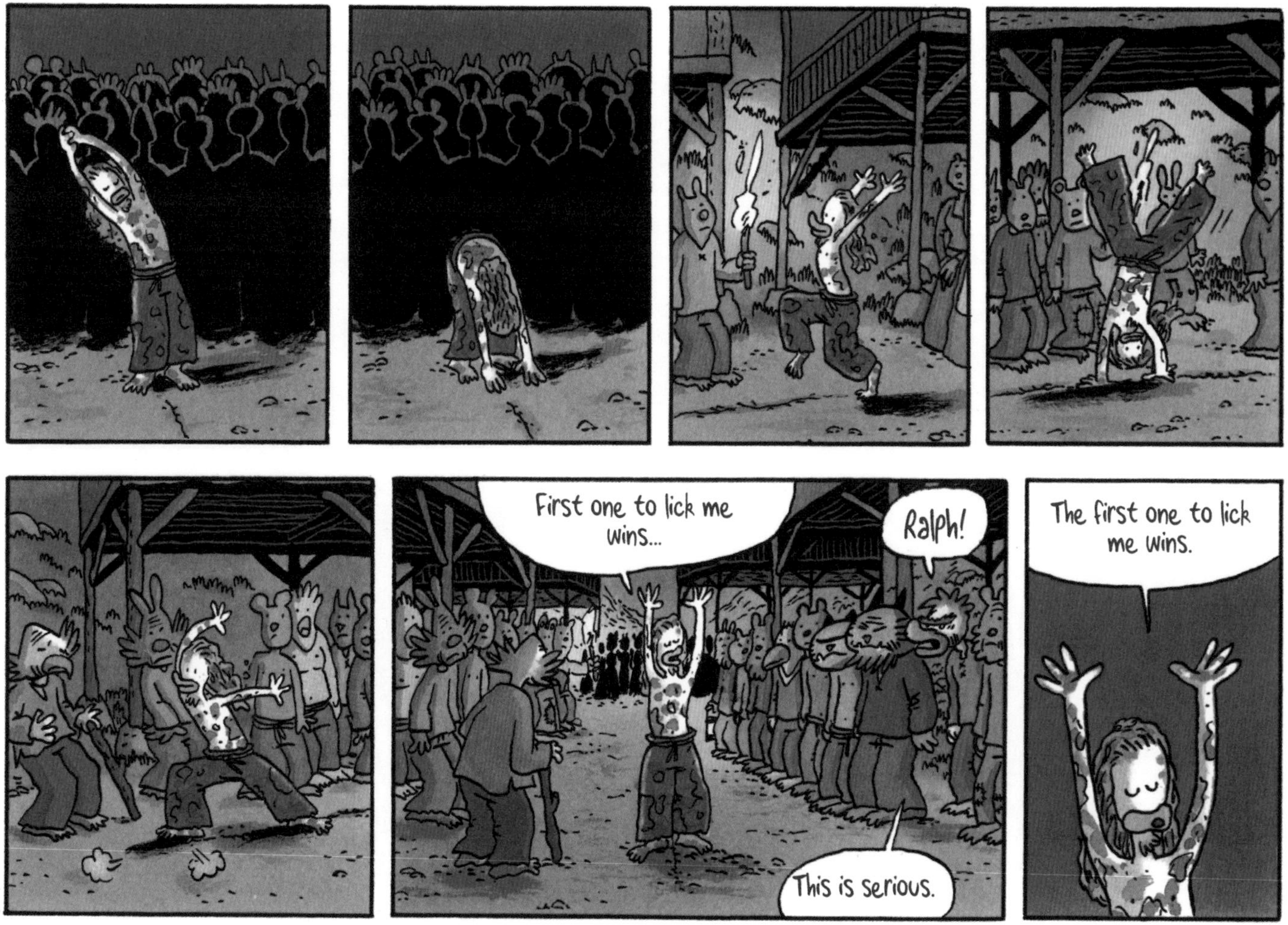
First one to lick me wins...
Ralph!
This is serious.
The first one to lick me wins.

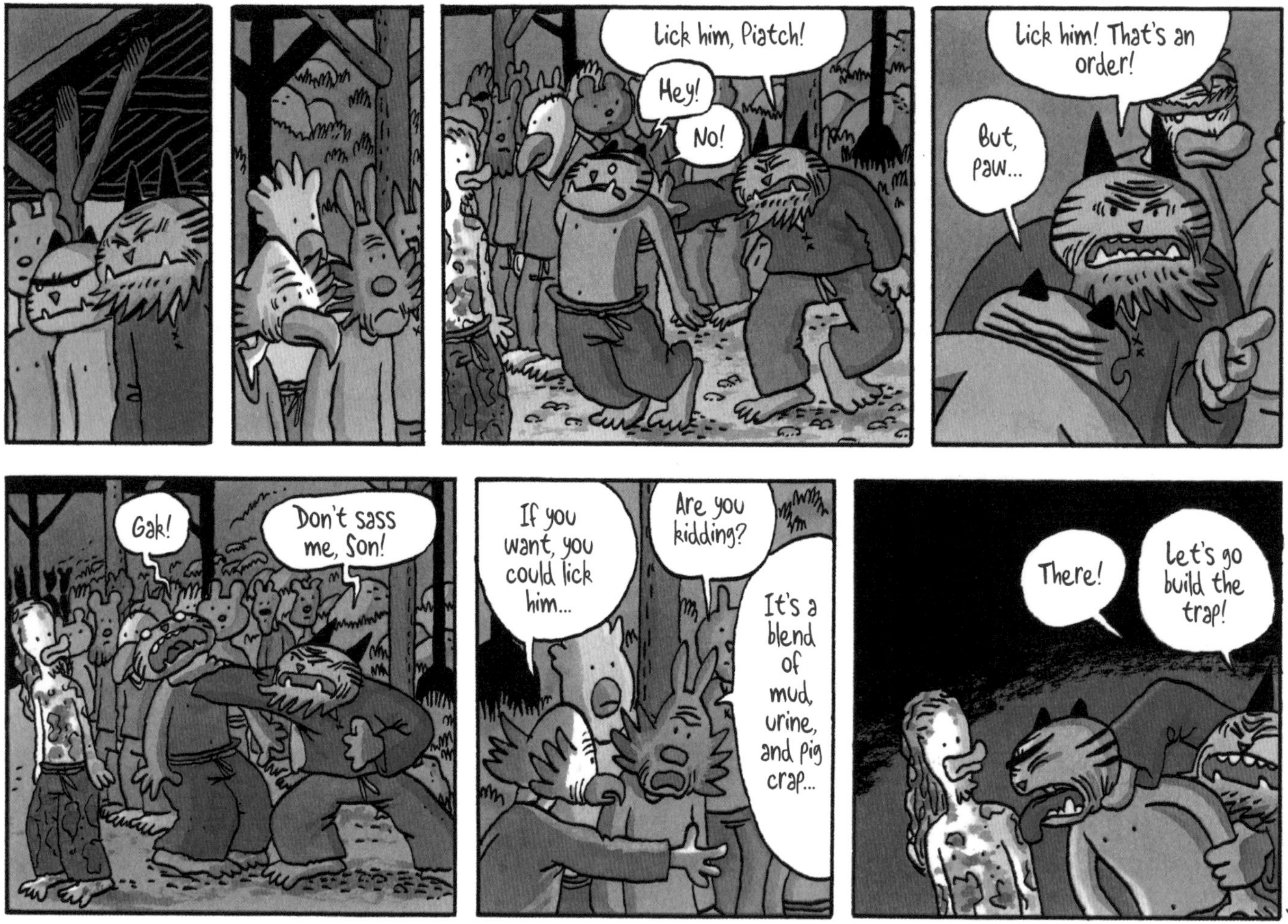

Lick him, Piatch!
Hey!
No!
But, paw...
Lick him! That's an order!
Gak!
Don't sass me, Son!
If you want, you could lick him...
Are you kidding?
It's a blend of mud, urine, and pig crap...
There!
Let's go build the trap!

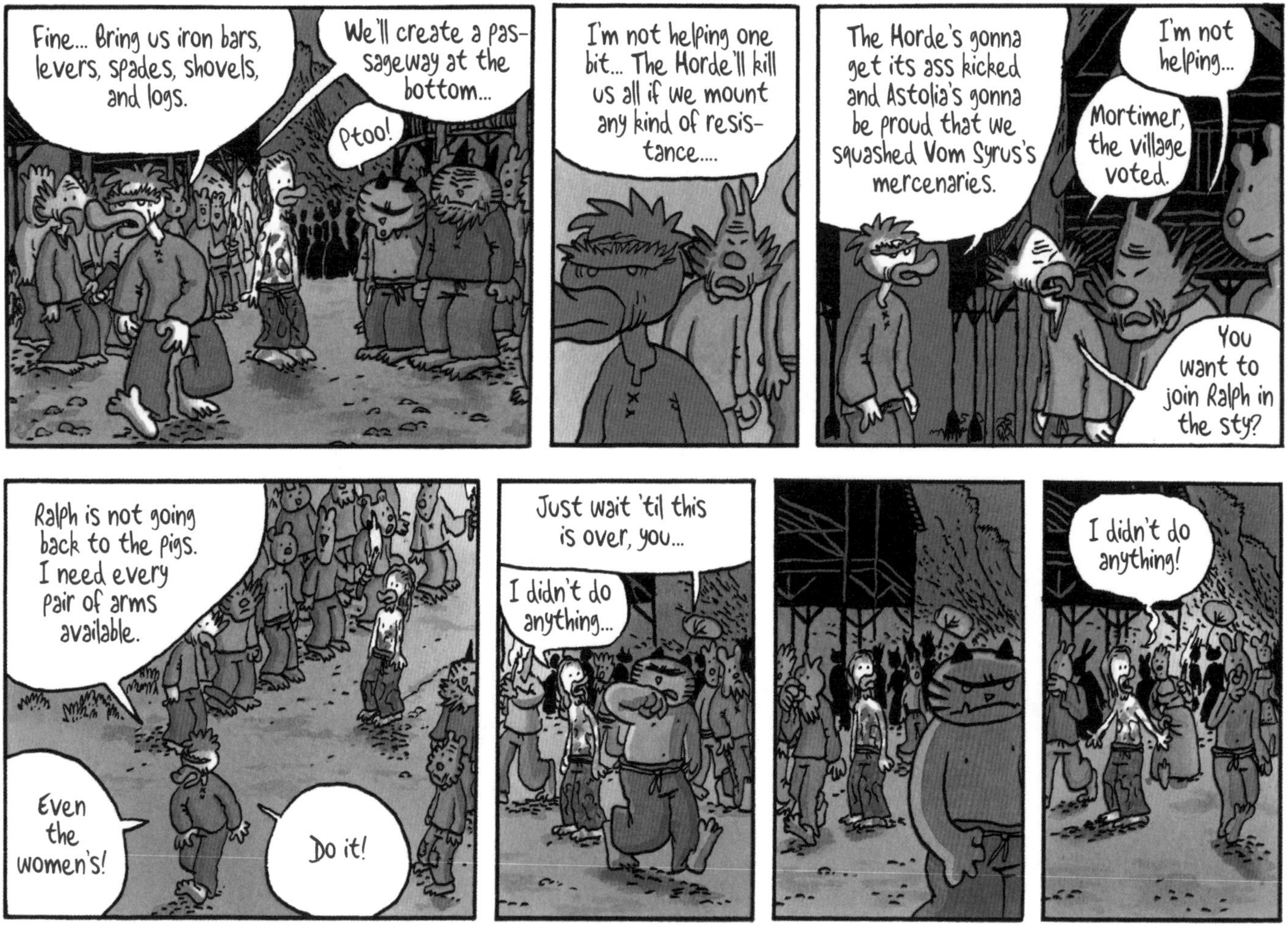
Fine... Bring us iron bars, levers, spades, shovels, and logs.
We'll create a passageway at the bottom...
Ptoo!
I'm not helping one bit... The Horde'll kill us all if we mount any kind of resistance....
The Horde's gonna get its ass kicked and Astolia's gonna be proud that we squashed Vom Syrus's mercenaries.
I'm not helping...
Mortimer, the village voted.
You want to join Ralph in the sty?
Ralph is not going back to the pigs. I need every pair of arms available.
Even the women's!
Do it!
Just wait 'til this is over, you...
I didn't do anything...
I didn't do anything!

Thanks... that'll be the last one...

Yo! Down below!

Chop down some trees and stick them among the boulders... and make it look natural...

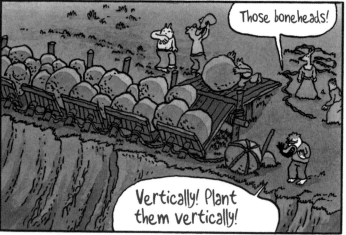

Those boneheads!

Vertically! Plant them vertically!

53

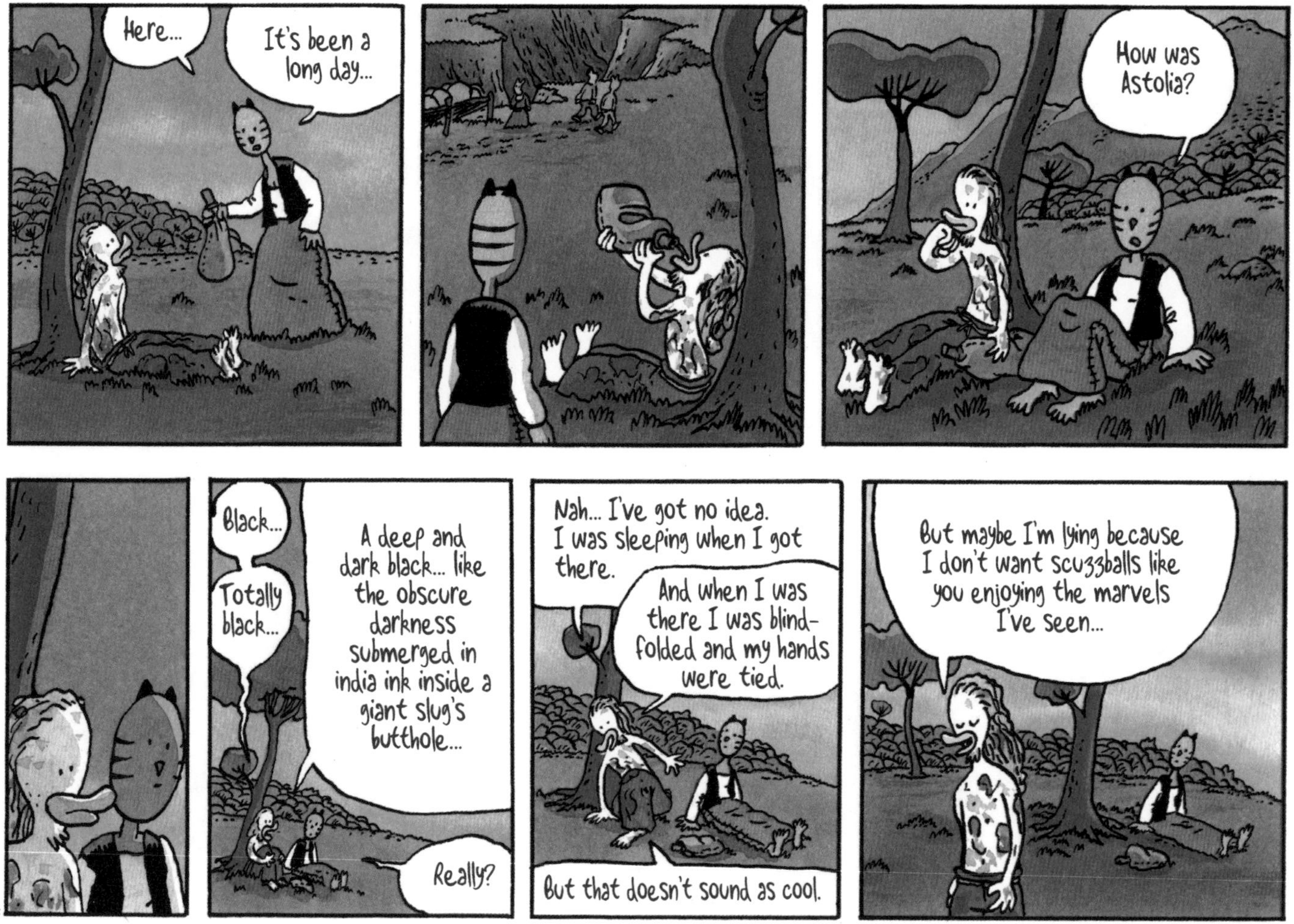
Here...
It's been a long day...
How was Astolia?
Black...
Totally black...
A deep and dark black... like the obscure darkness submerged in india ink inside a giant slug's butthole...
Really?
Nah... I've got no idea. I was sleeping when I got there.
And when I was there I was blind-folded and my hands were tied.
But that doesn't sound as cool.
But maybe I'm lying because I don't want scuzzballs like you enjoying the marvels I've seen...

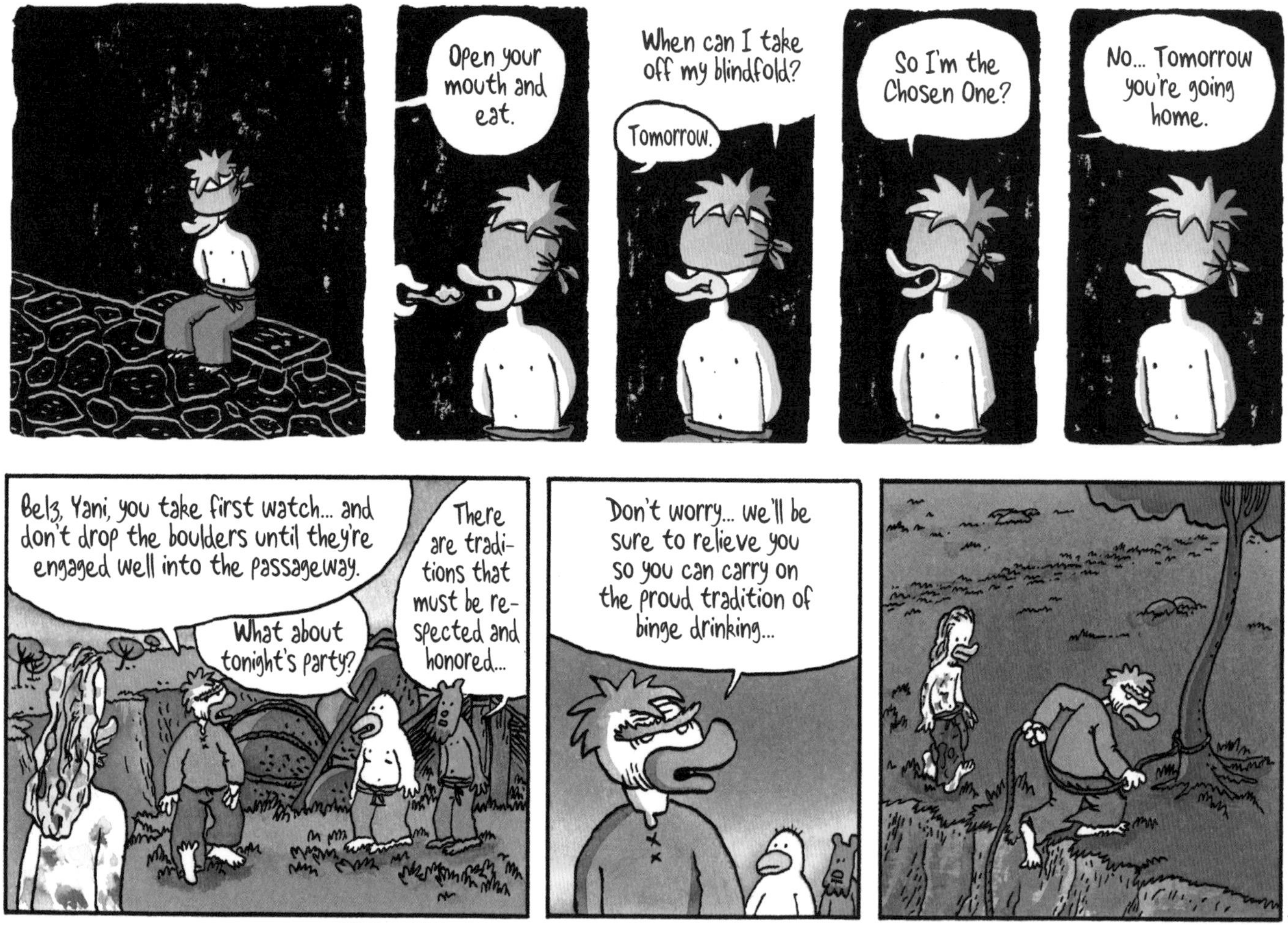
Open your mouth and eat.
When can I take off my blindfold?
Tomorrow.
So I'm the Chosen One?
No... Tomorrow you're going home.
Belz, Yani, you take first watch... and don't drop the boulders until they're engaged well into the passageway.
What about tonight's party?
There are traditions that must be respected and honored...
Don't worry... we'll be sure to relieve you so you can carry on the proud tradition of binge drinking...

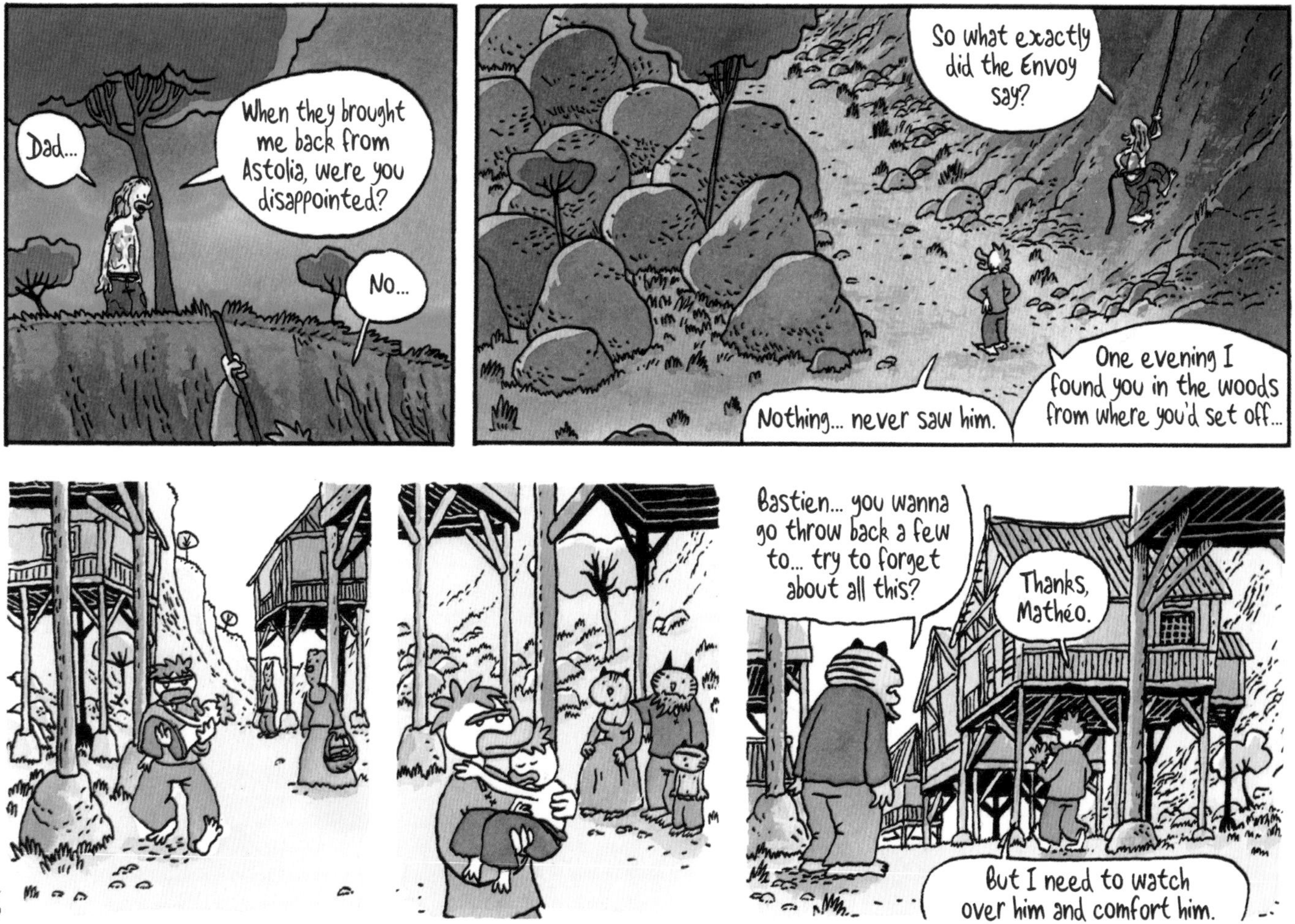
Dad...
When they brought me back from Astolia, were you disappointed?
No...
So what exactly did the Envoy say?
Nothing... never saw him.
One evening I found you in the woods from where you'd set off...
Bastien... you wanna go throw back a few to... try to forget about all this?
Thanks, Mathéo.
But I need to watch over him and comfort him.

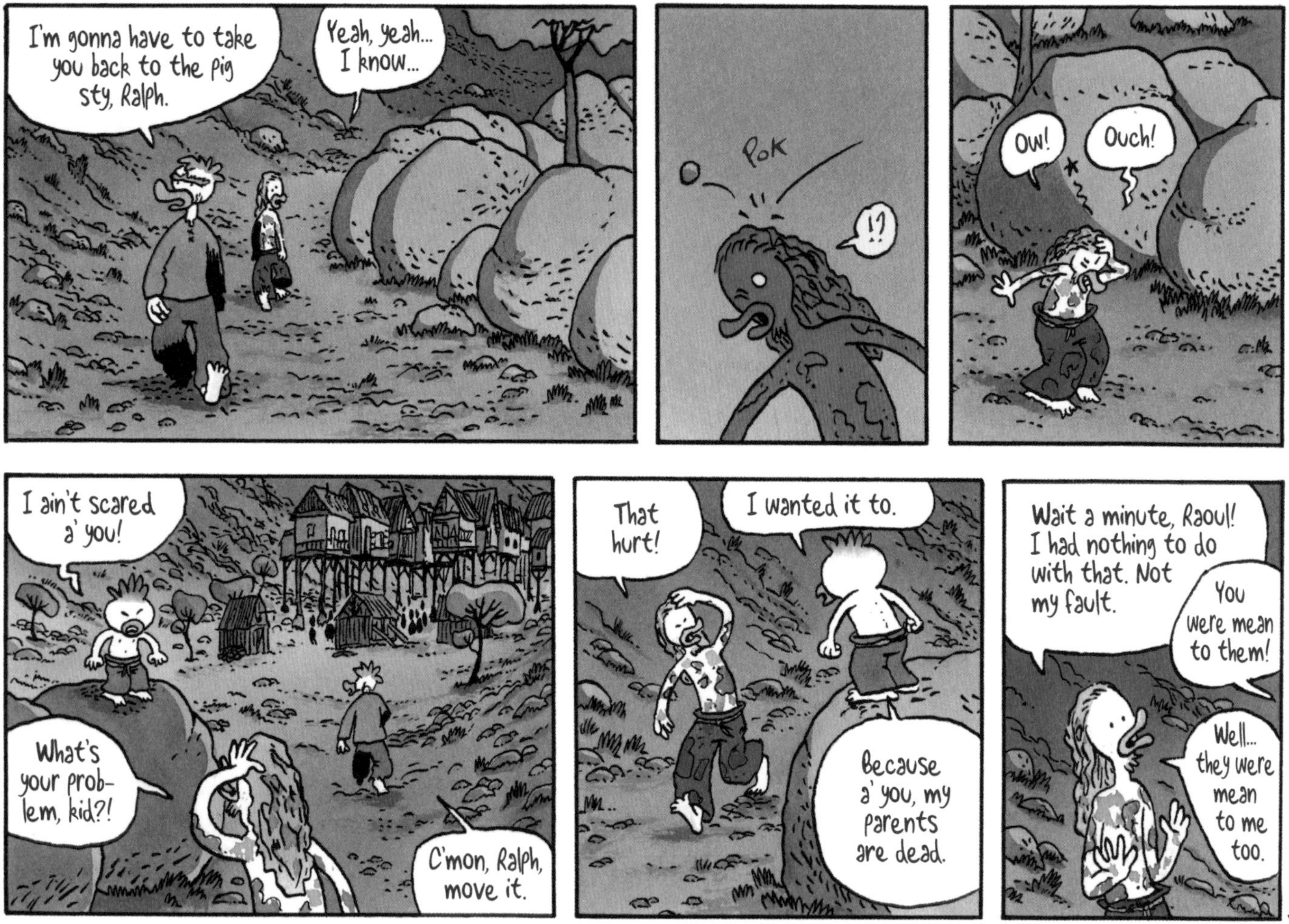
I'm gonna have to take you back to the pig sty, Ralph.
Yeah, yeah... I know...
POK
!?
Ow!
Ouch!
I ain't scared a' you!
What's your prob-lem, kid?!
C'mon, Ralph, move it.
That hurt!
I wanted it to.
Because a' you, my parents are dead.
Wait a minute, Raoul! I had nothing to do with that. Not my fault.
You were mean to them!
Well... they were mean to me too.

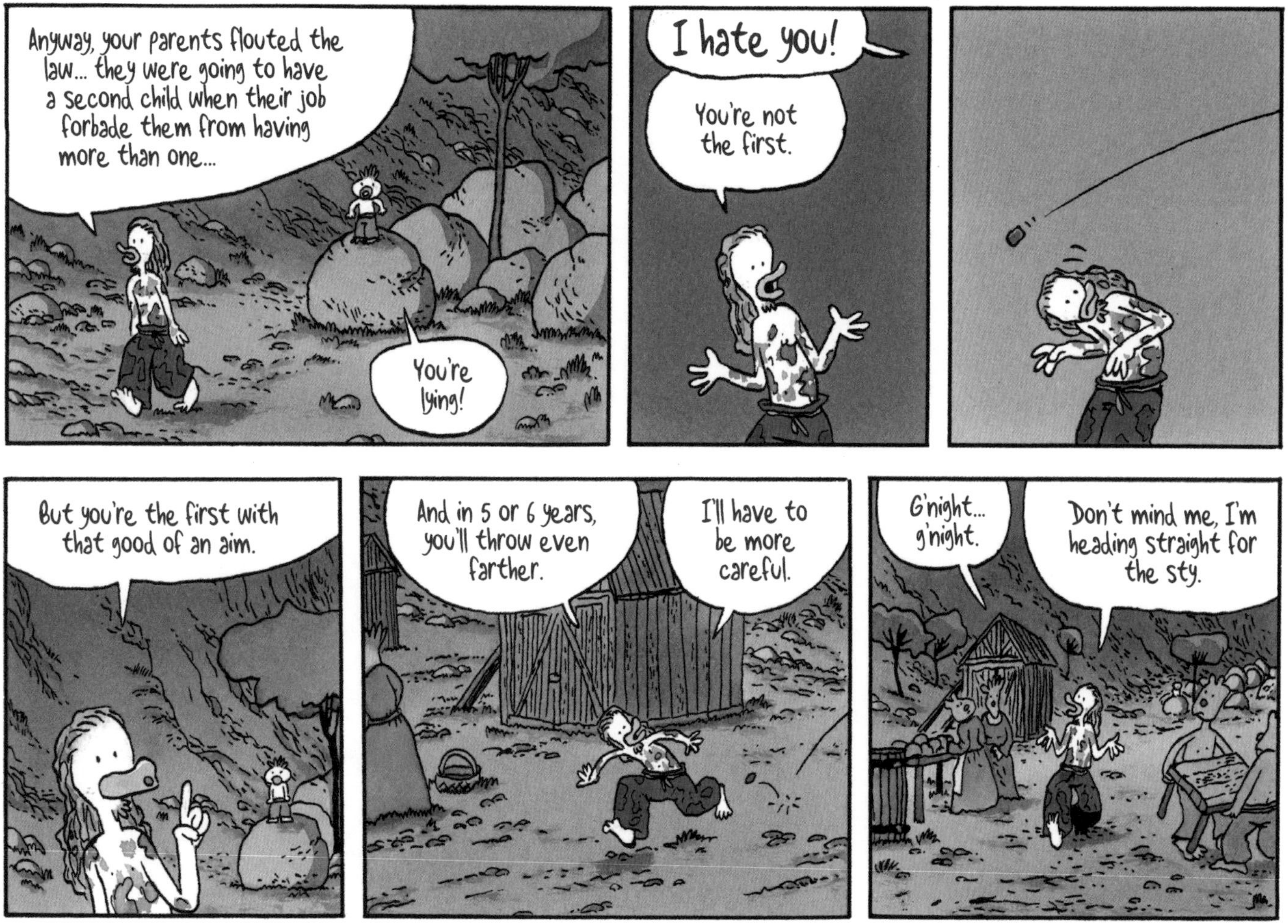

Anyway, your parents flouted the law... they were going to have a second child when their job forbade them from having more than one...
You're lying!
I hate you!
You're not the first.
But you're the first with that good of an aim.
And in 5 or 6 years, you'll throw even farther.
I'll have to be more careful.
G'night... g'night.
Don't mind me, I'm heading straight for the sty.

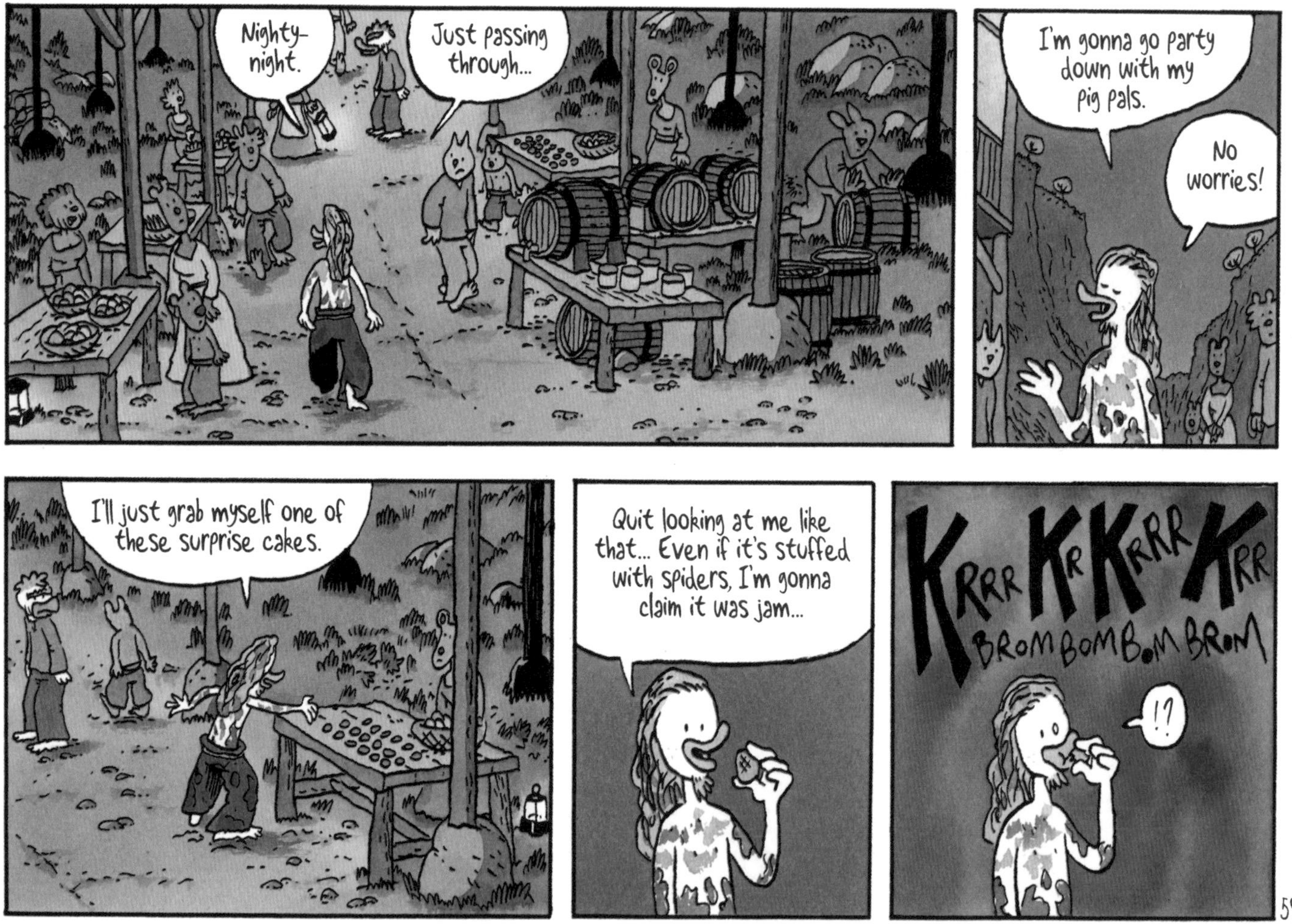
Nighty-night.
Just passing through...
I'm gonna go party down with my pig pals.
No worries!
I'll just grab myself one of these surprise cakes.
Quit looking at me like that... Even if it's stuffed with spiders, I'm gonna claim it was jam...
KRRR KR KRRR KRR
BROM BOM BOM BROM
!?

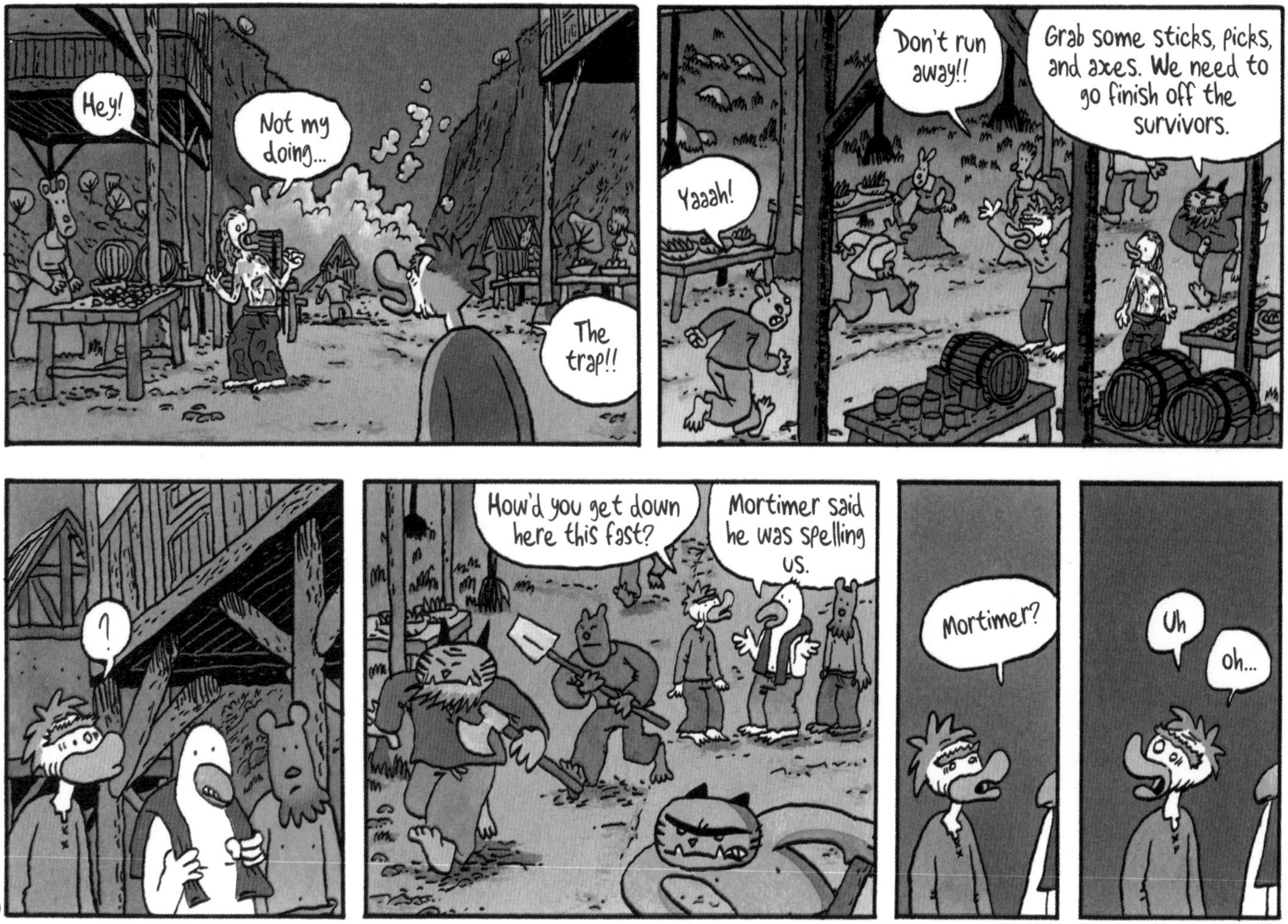
Hey!
Not my doing...
The trap!!
Don't run away!!
Grab some sticks, picks, and axes. We need to go finish off the survivors.
Yaaah!
?
How'd you get down here this fast?
Mortimer said he was spelling us.
Mortimer?
Uh
Oh...

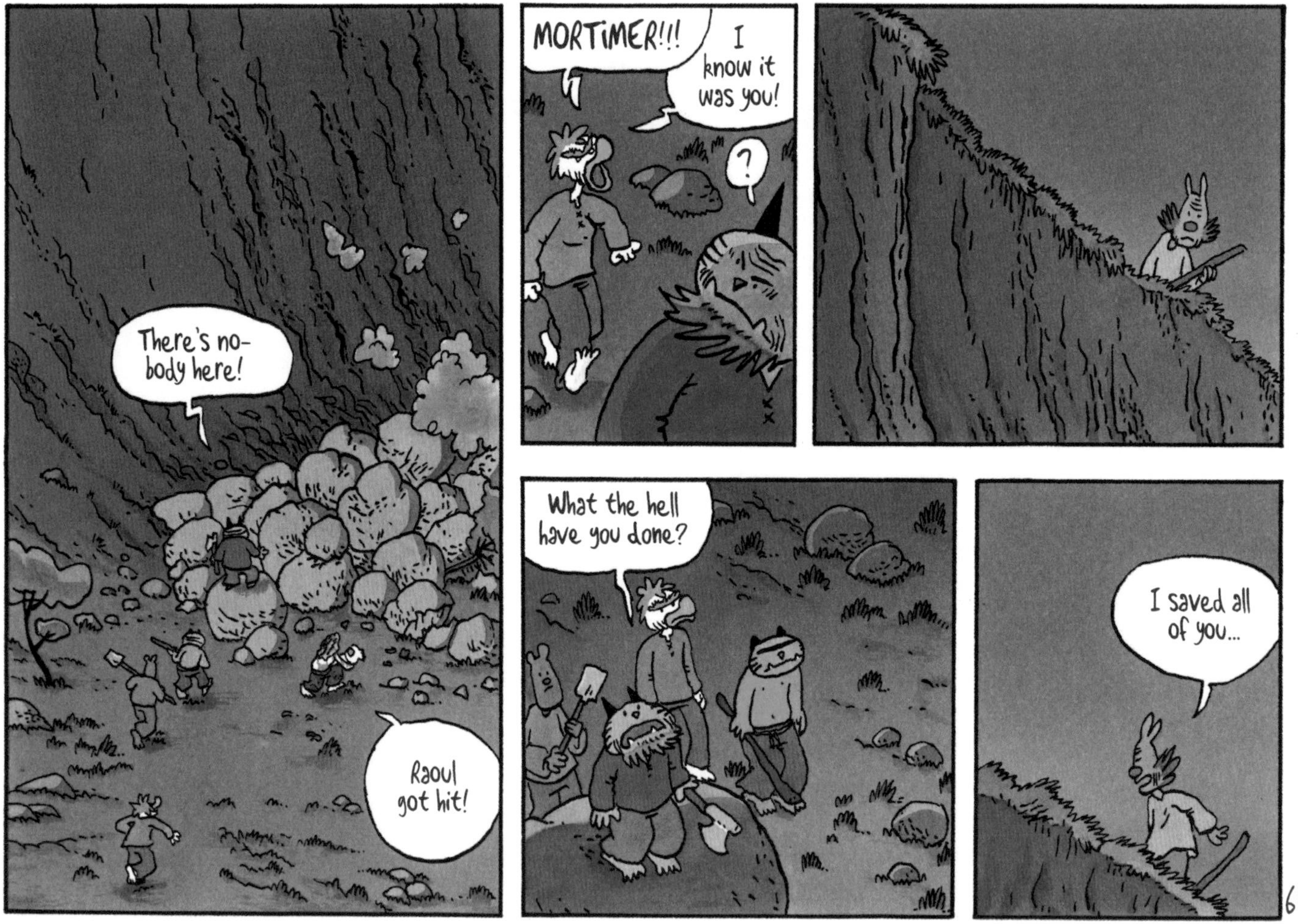
There's nobody here!
Raoul got hit!
MORTIMER!!!
I know it was you!
?
What the hell have you done?
I saved all of you...

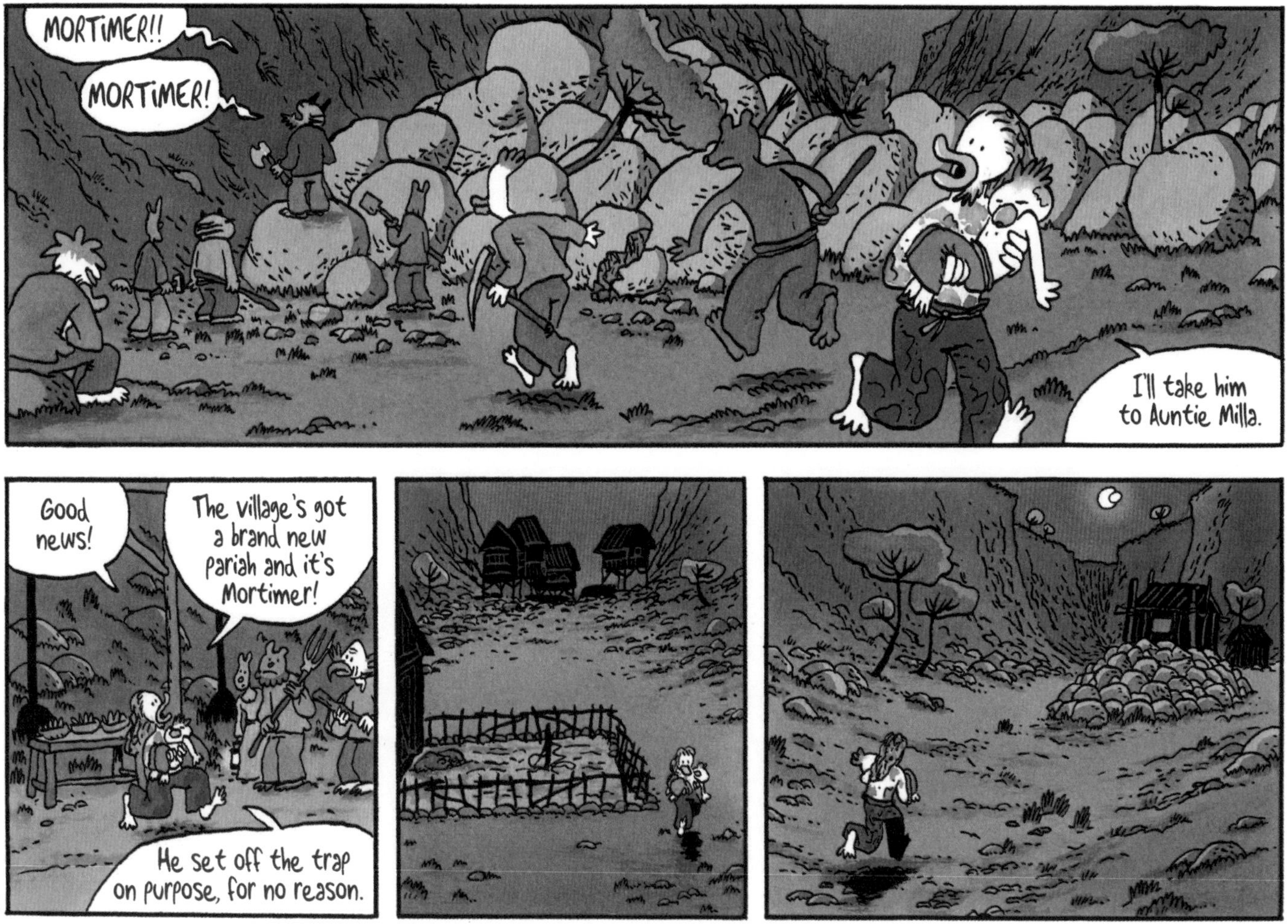
MORTIMER!!
MORTIMER!
I'll take him to Auntie Milla.
Good news!
The village's got a brand new pariah and it's Mortimer!
He set off the trap on purpose, for no reason.

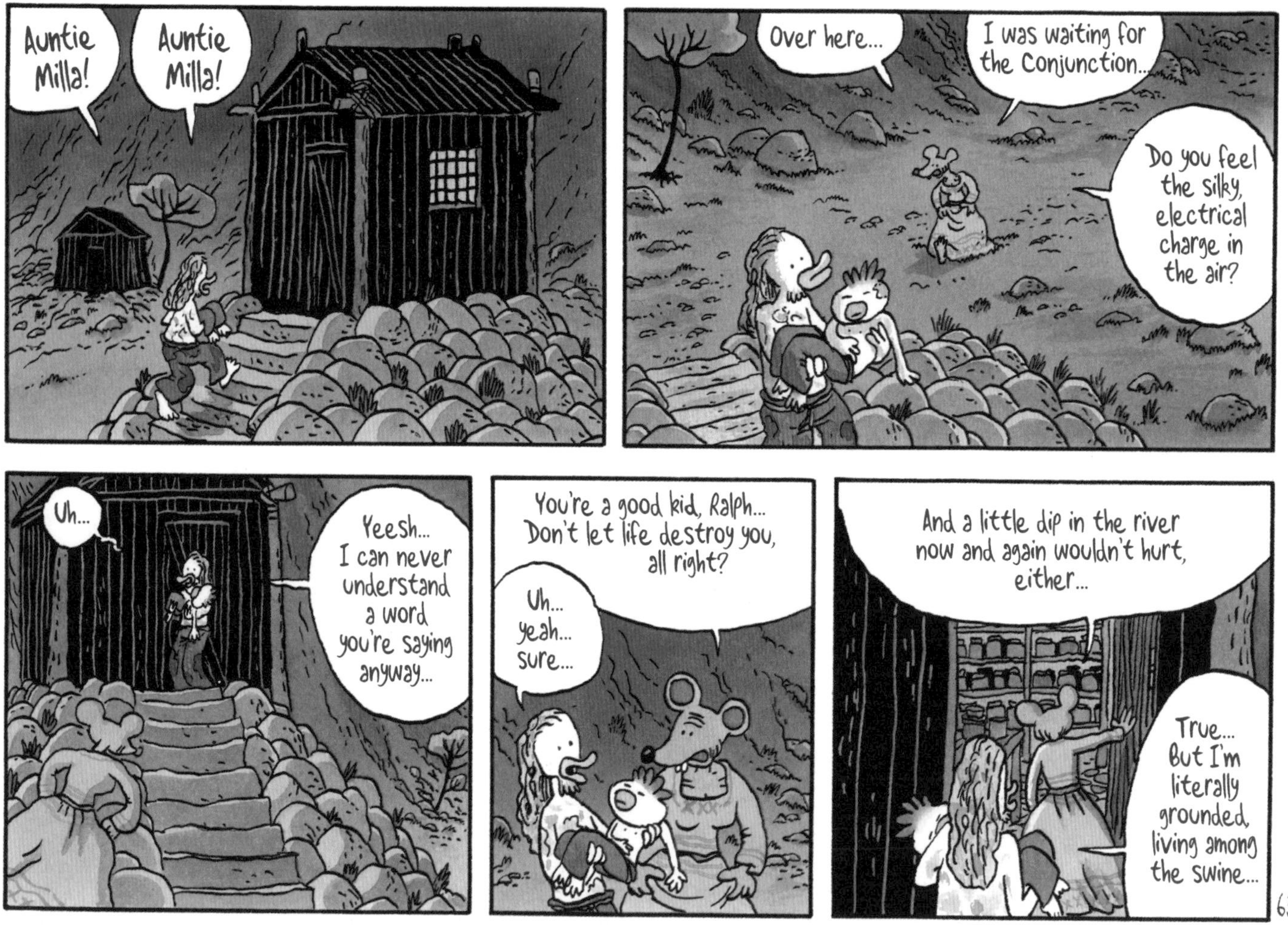
Auntie Milla!
Auntie Milla!
Over here...
I was waiting for the Conjunction...
Do you feel the silky, electrical charge in the air?
Uh...
Yeesh... I can never understand a word you're saying anyway...
You're a good kid, Ralph... Don't let life destroy you, all right?
Uh... yeah... sure...
And a little dip in the river now and again wouldn't hurt, either...
True... But I'm literally grounded, living among the swine...

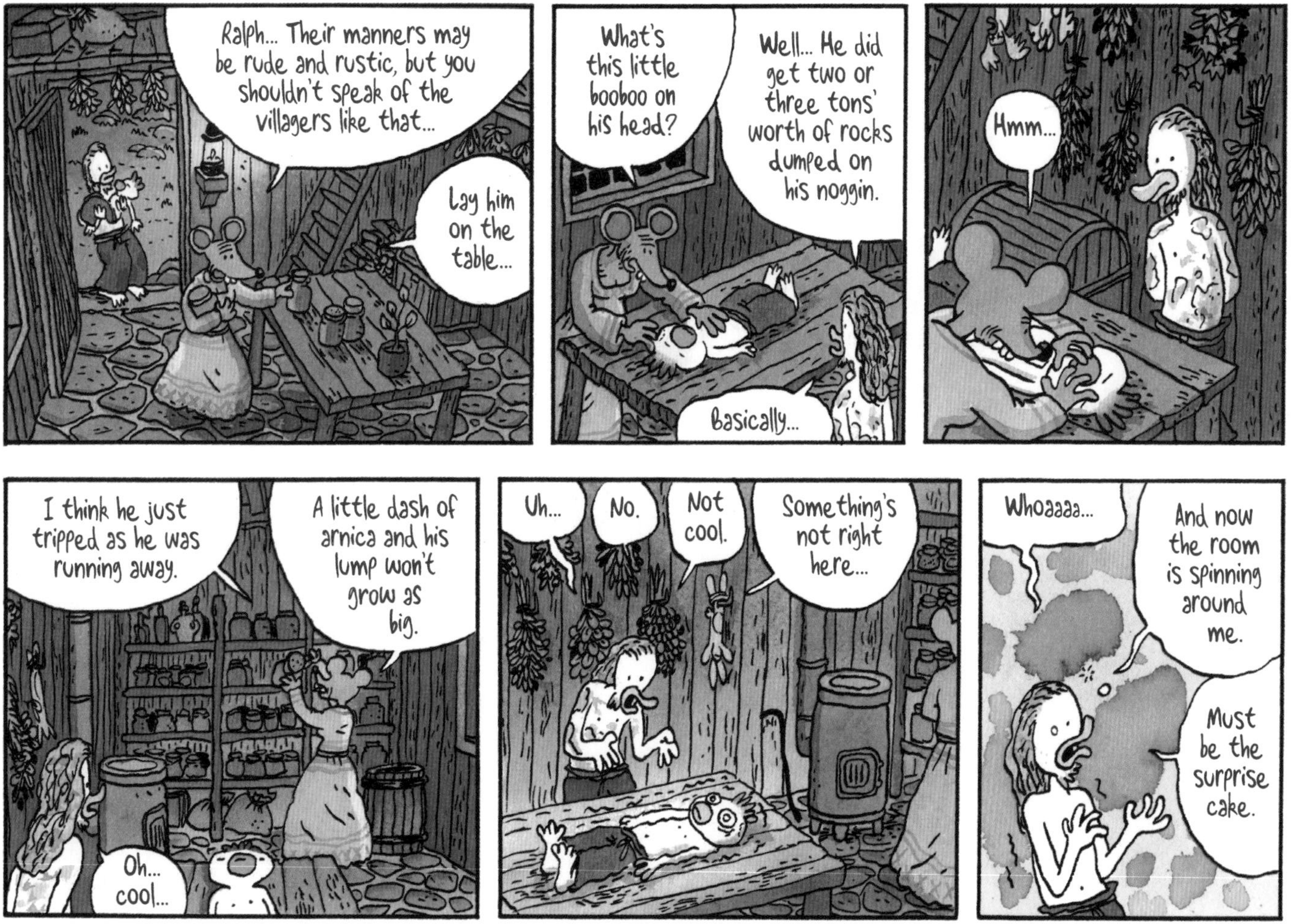

Ralph... Their manners may be rude and rustic, but you shouldn't speak of the villagers like that...
Lay him on the table...
What's this little booboo on his head?
Well... He did get two or three tons' worth of rocks dumped on his noggin.
Basically...
Hmm...
I think he just tripped as he was running away.
A little dash of arnica and his lump won't grow as big.
Oh... cool...
Uh...
No.
Not cool.
Something's not right here...
Whoaaaa...
And now the room is spinning around me.
Must be the surprise cake.

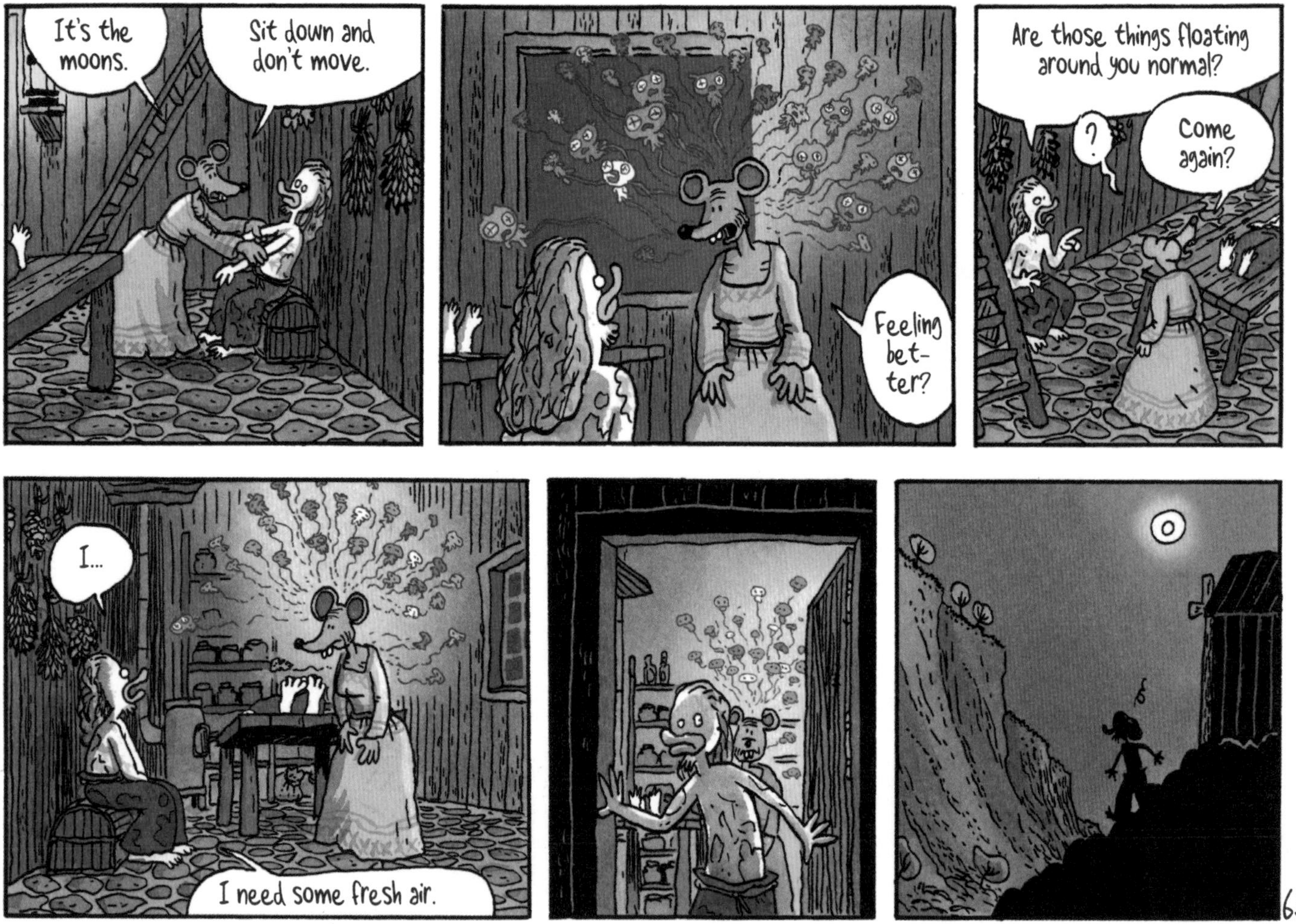
It's the moons.
Sit down and don't move.
Feeling bet-ter?
Are those things floating around you normal?
?
Come again?
I...
I need some fresh air.

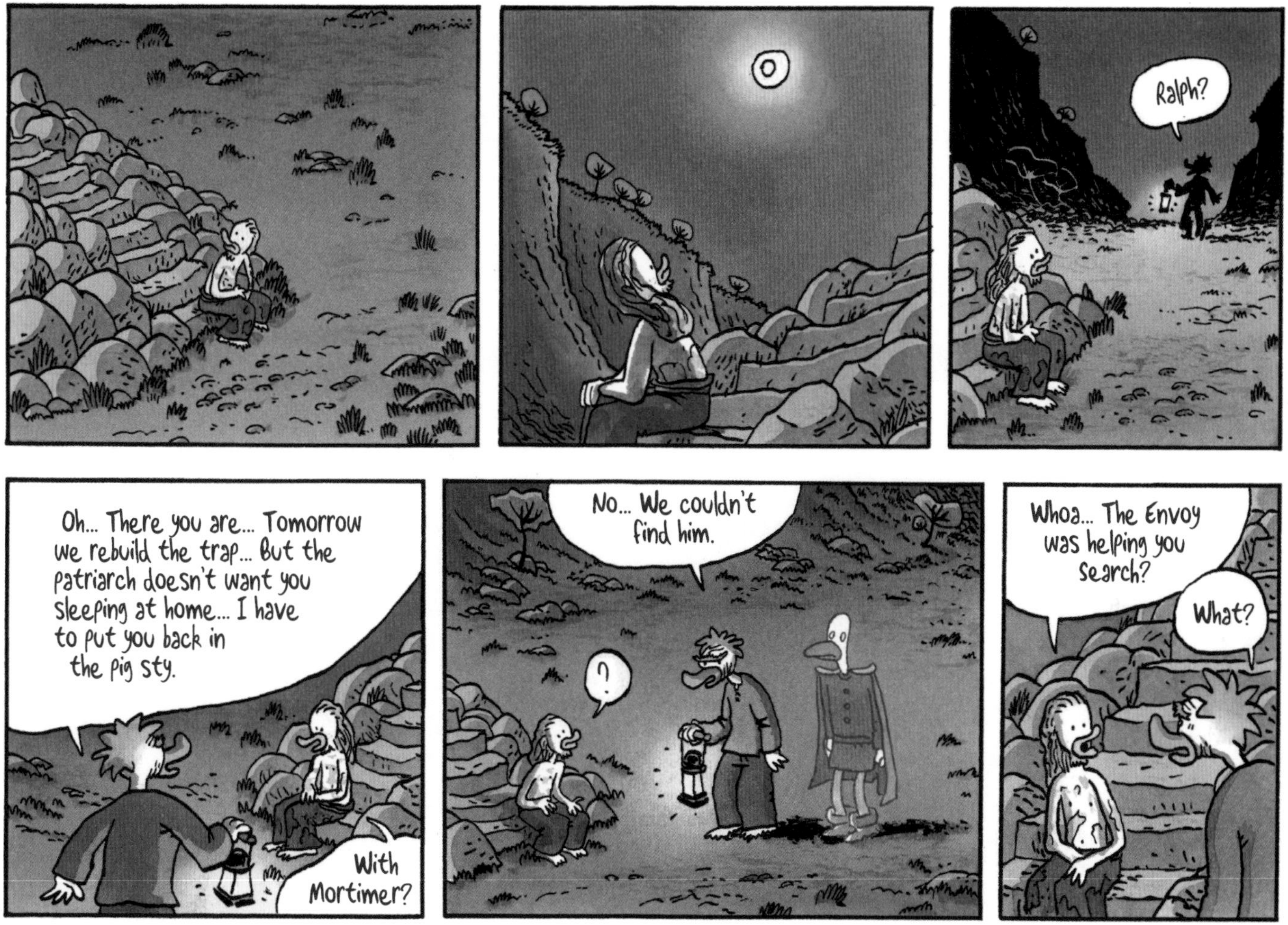
Ralph?
Oh... There you are... Tomorrow we rebuild the trap... But the patriarch doesn't want you sleeping at home... I have to put you back in the pig sty.
With Mortimer?
No... We couldn't find him.
?
Whoa... The Envoy was helping you search?
What?

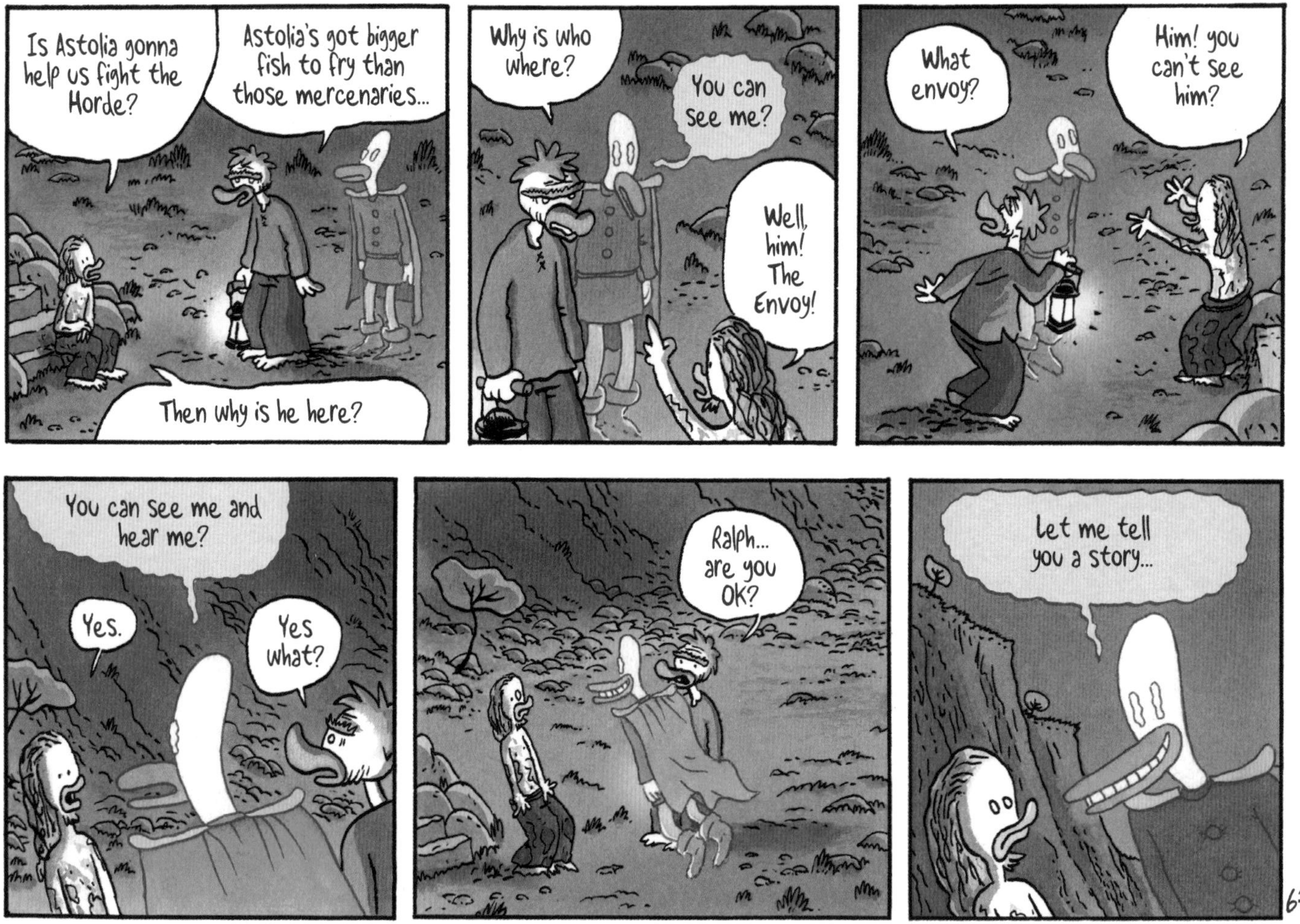
Is Astolia gonna help us fight the Horde?
Astolia's got bigger fish to fry than those mercenaries...
Then why is he here?
Why is who where?
You can see me?
Well, him! The Envoy!
What envoy?
Him! you can't see him?
You can see me and hear me?
Yes.
Yes what?
Ralph... are you OK?
Let me tell you a story...

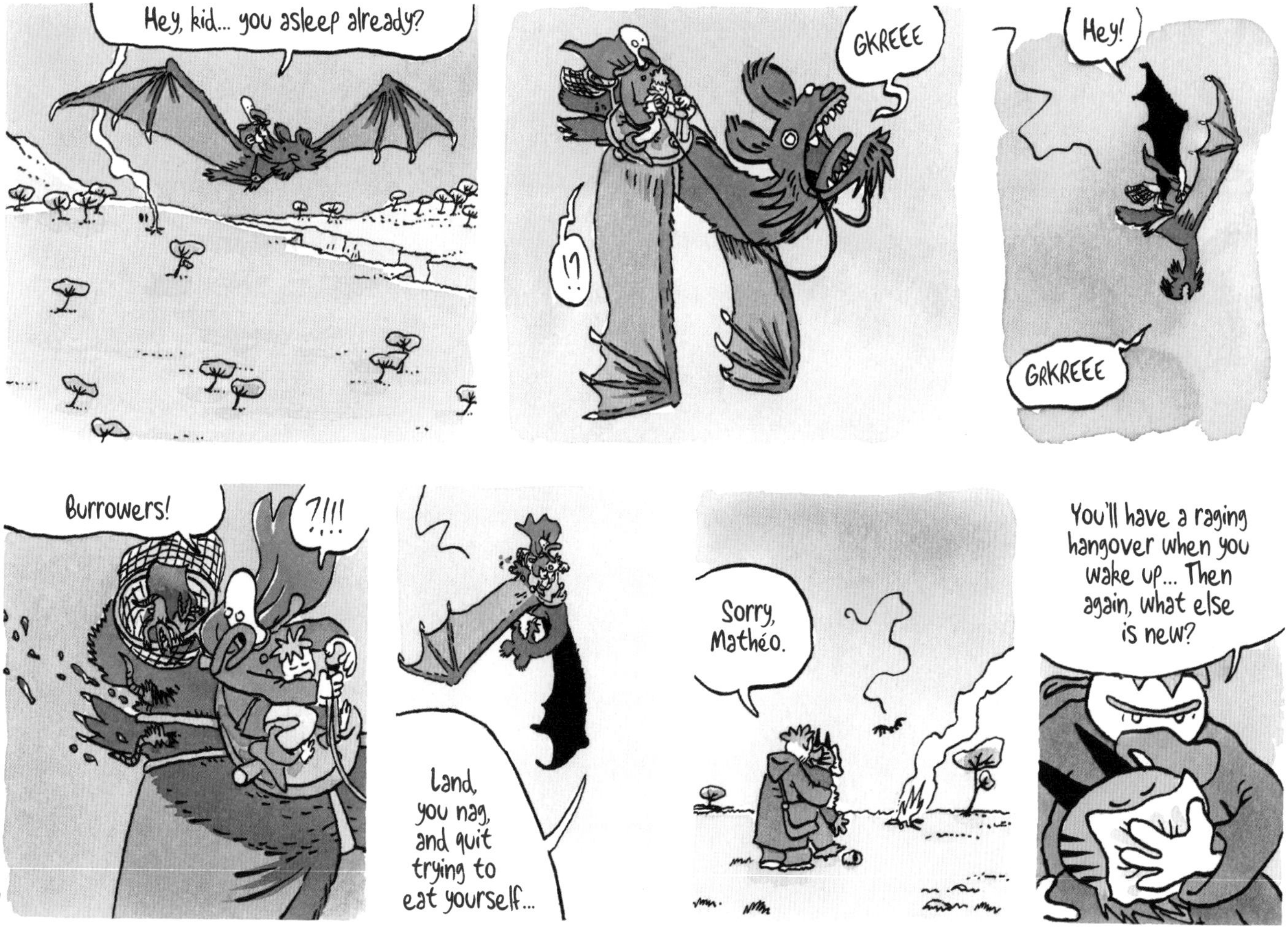
Hey, kid... you asleep already?
GKREEE
!?
Hey!
GRKREEE
Burrowers!
?!!!
Land, you nag, and quit trying to eat yourself...
Sorry, Mathéo.
You'll have a raging hangover when you wake up... Then again, what else is new?

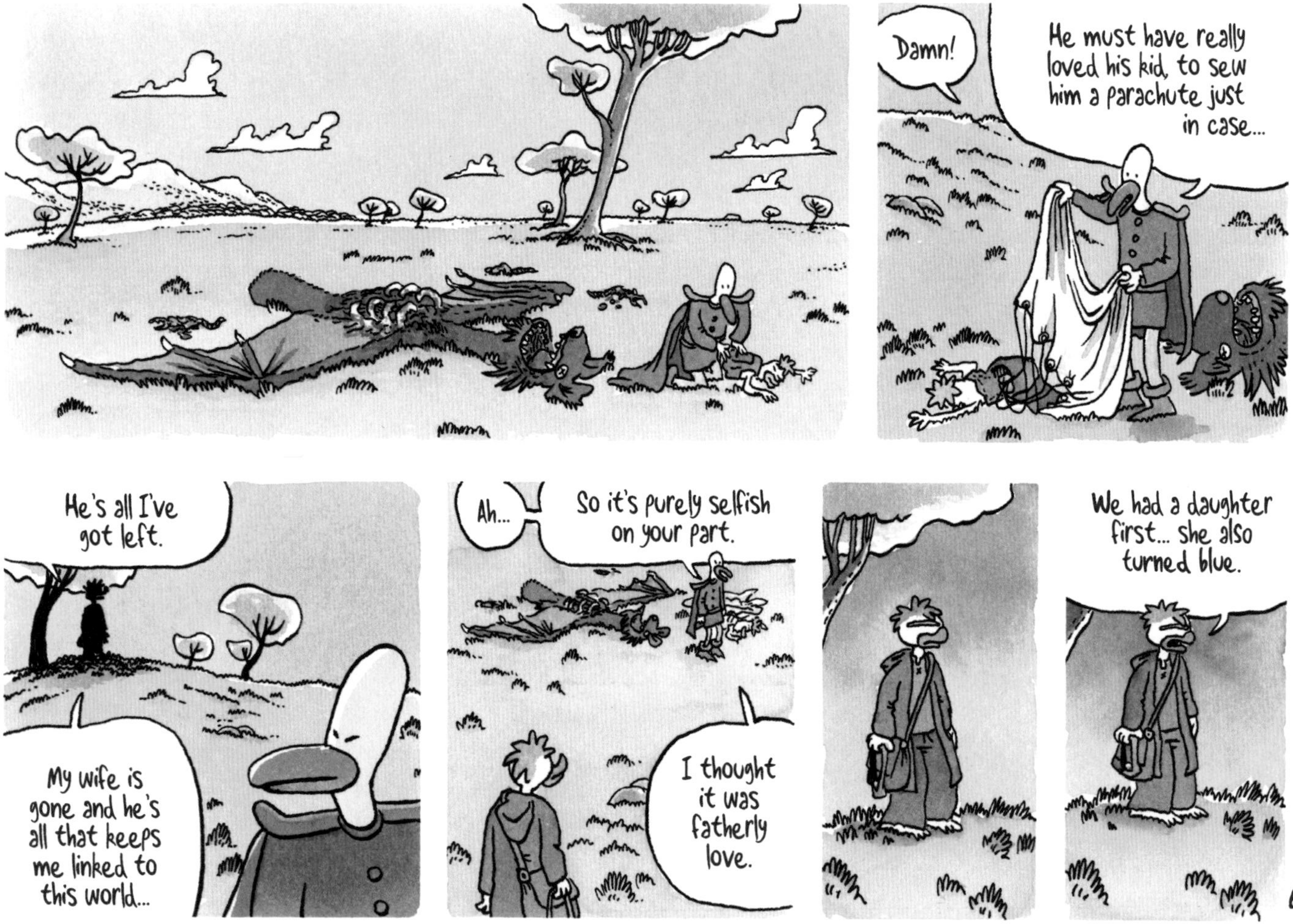

Damn!
He must have really loved his kid, to sew him a parachute just in case...
He's all I've got left.
My wife is gone and he's all that keeps me linked to this world...
Ah...
So it's purely selfish on your part.
I thought it was fatherly love.
We had a daughter first... she also turned blue.

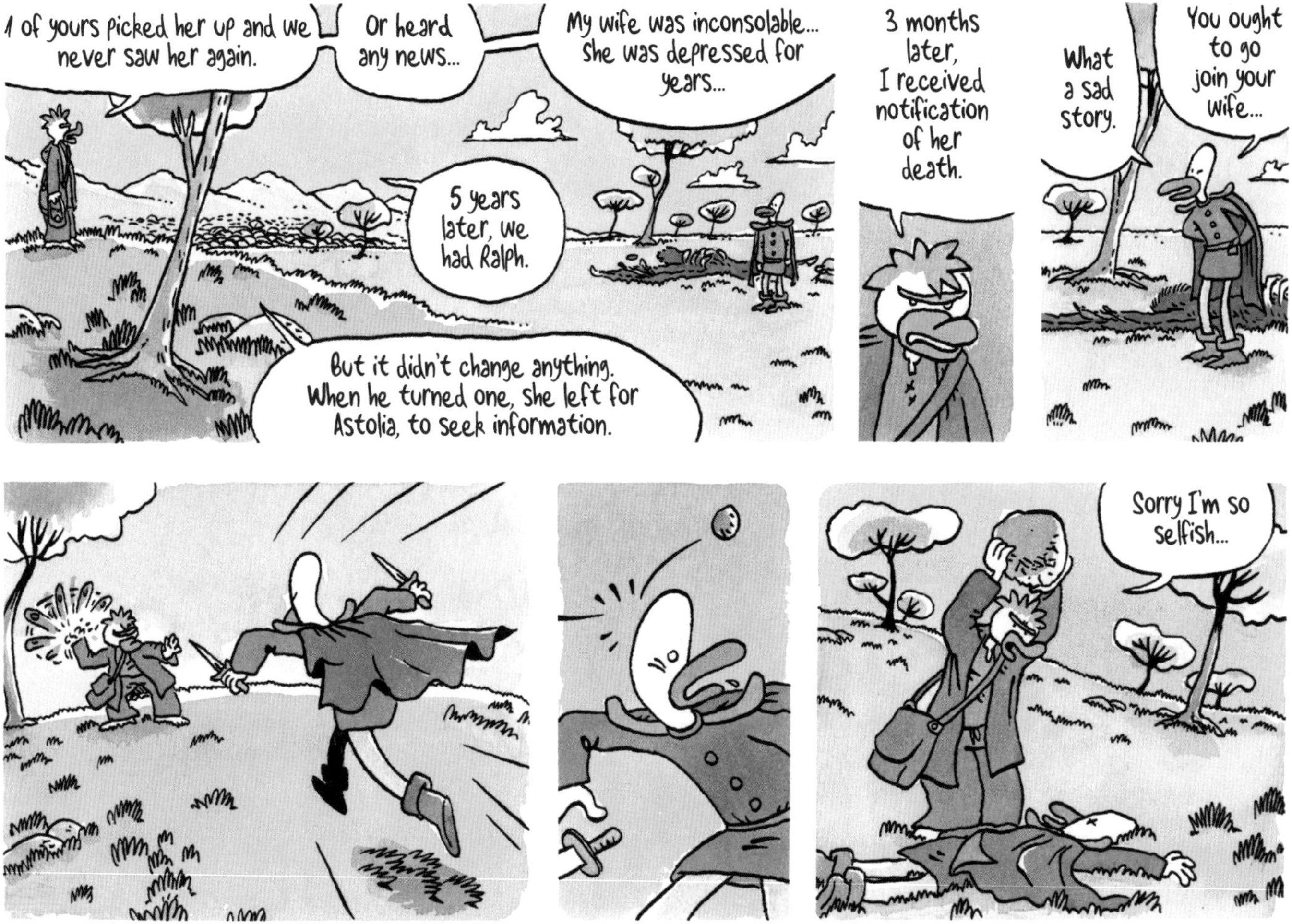
1 of yours picked her up and we never saw her again.
Or heard any news...
My wife was inconsolable... She was depressed for years...
5 years later, we had Ralph.
But it didn't change anything. When he turned one, she left for Astolia, to seek information.
3 months later, I received notification of her death.
What a sad story.
You ought to go join your wife...
Sorry I'm so selfish...

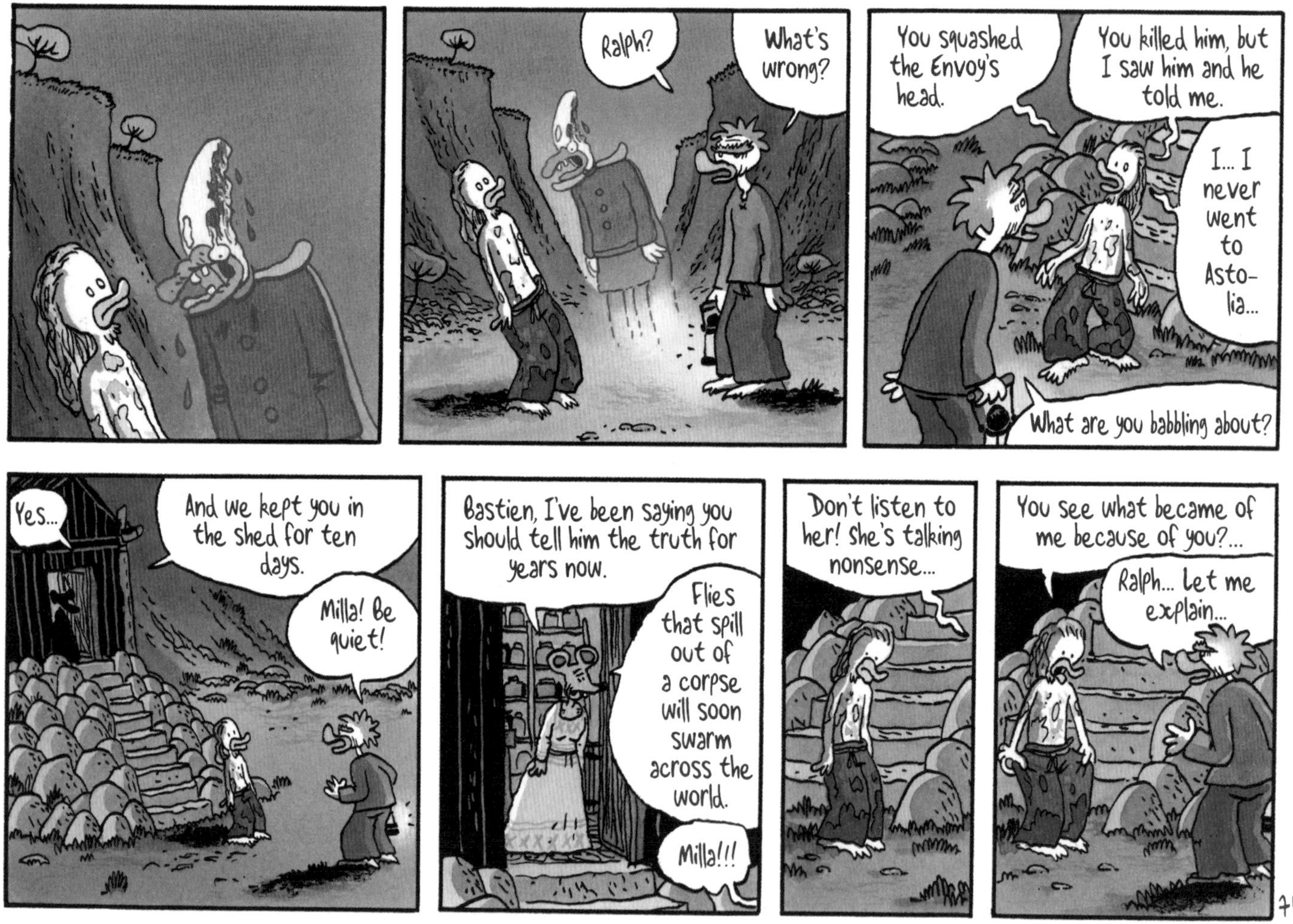
Ralph?
What's wrong?
You squashed the Envoy's head.
You killed him, but I saw him and he told me.
I... I never went to Asto-lia...
What are you babbling about?
Yes...
And we kept you in the shed for ten days.
Milla! Be quiet!
Bastien, I've been saying you should tell him the truth for years now.
Flies that spill out of a corpse will soon swarm across the world.
Milla!!!
Don't listen to her! She's talking nonsense...
You see what became of me because of you?...
Ralph... Let me explain...

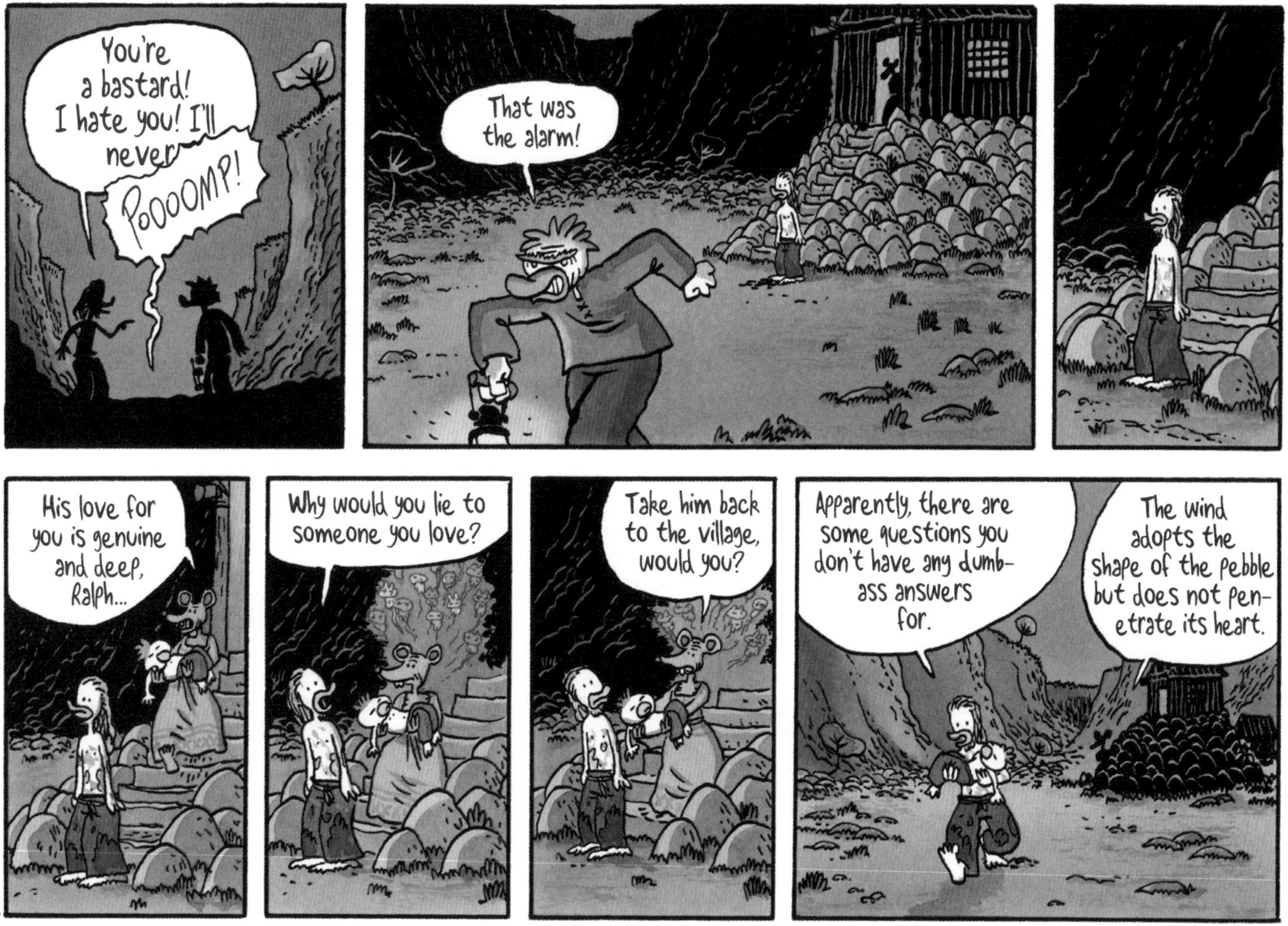
You're a bastard! I hate you! I'll never
POOOOMP!
That was the alarm!
His love for you is genuine and deep, Ralph...
Why would you lie to someone you love?
Take him back to the village, would you?
Apparently, there are some questions you don't have any dumb-ass answers for.
The wind adopts the shape of the pebble but does not pen-etrate its heart.

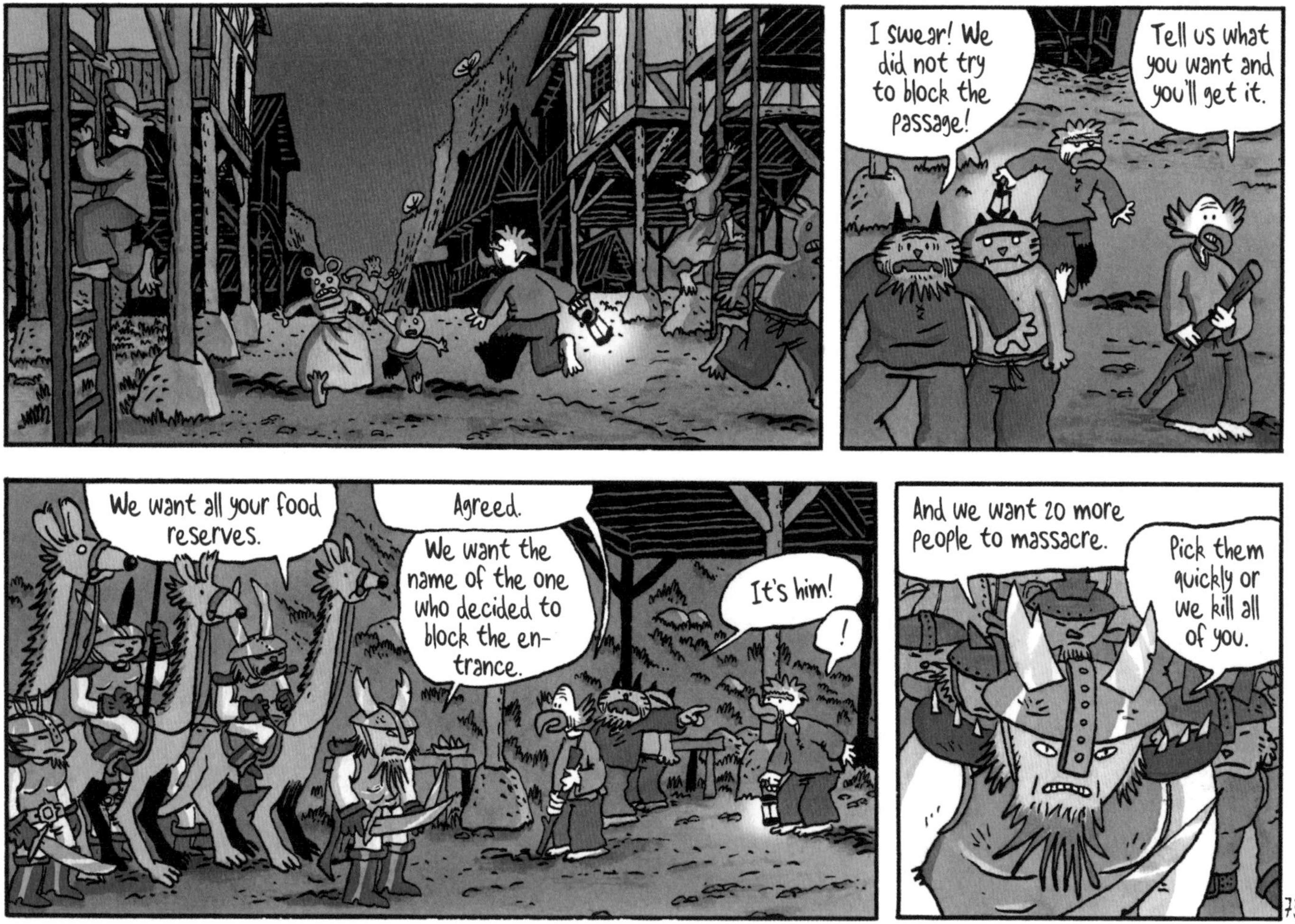
I swear! We did not try to block the passage!
Tell us what you want and you'll get it.
We want all your food reserves.
Agreed.
We want the name of the one who decided to block the entrance.
It's him!
!
And we want 20 more people to massacre.
Pick them quickly or we kill all of you.

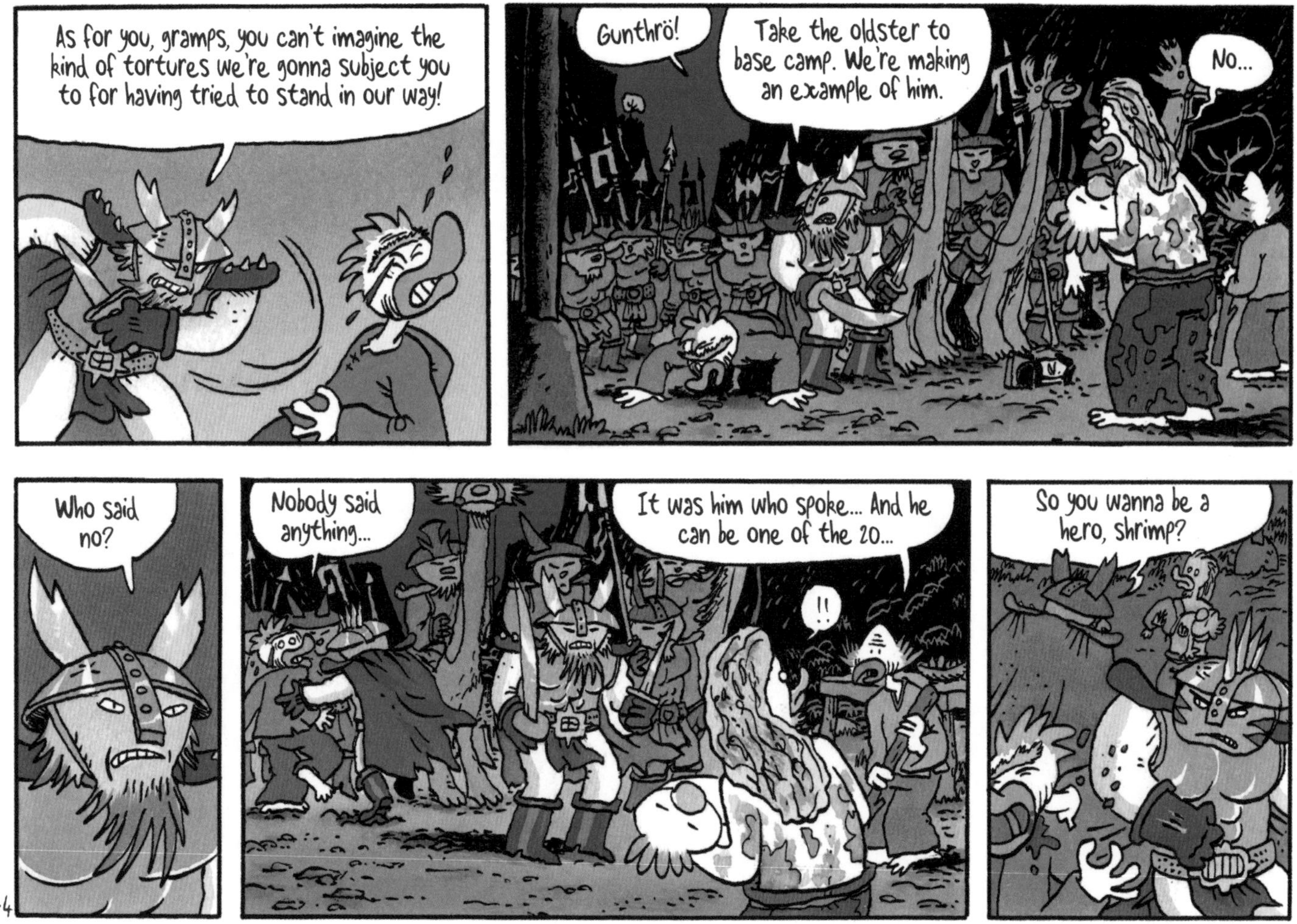
As for you, gramps, you can't imagine the kind of tortures we're gonna subject you to for having tried to stand in our way!
Gunthrö!
Take the oldster to base camp. We're making an example of him.
No...
Who said no?
Nobody said anything...
It was him who spoke... And he can be one of the 20...
!!
So you wanna be a hero, shrimp?

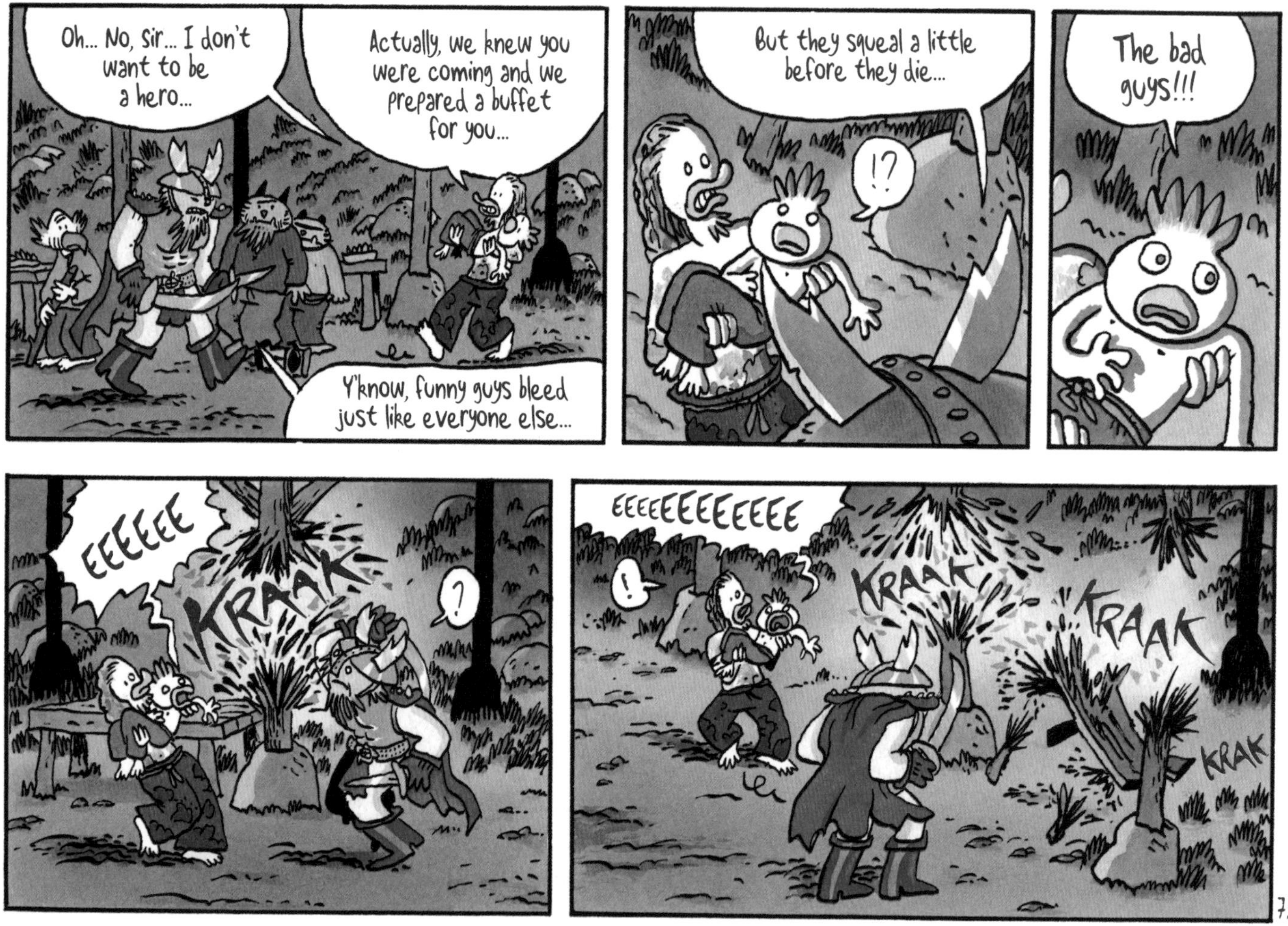
Oh... No, sir... I don't want to be a hero...
Actually, we knew you were coming and we prepared a buffet for you...
Y'know, funny guys bleed just like everyone else...
But they squeal a little before they die...
!?
The bad guys!!!
EEEEEE
KRAAK
?
EEEEEEEEEEEE
!
KRAAK
KRAAK
KRAK

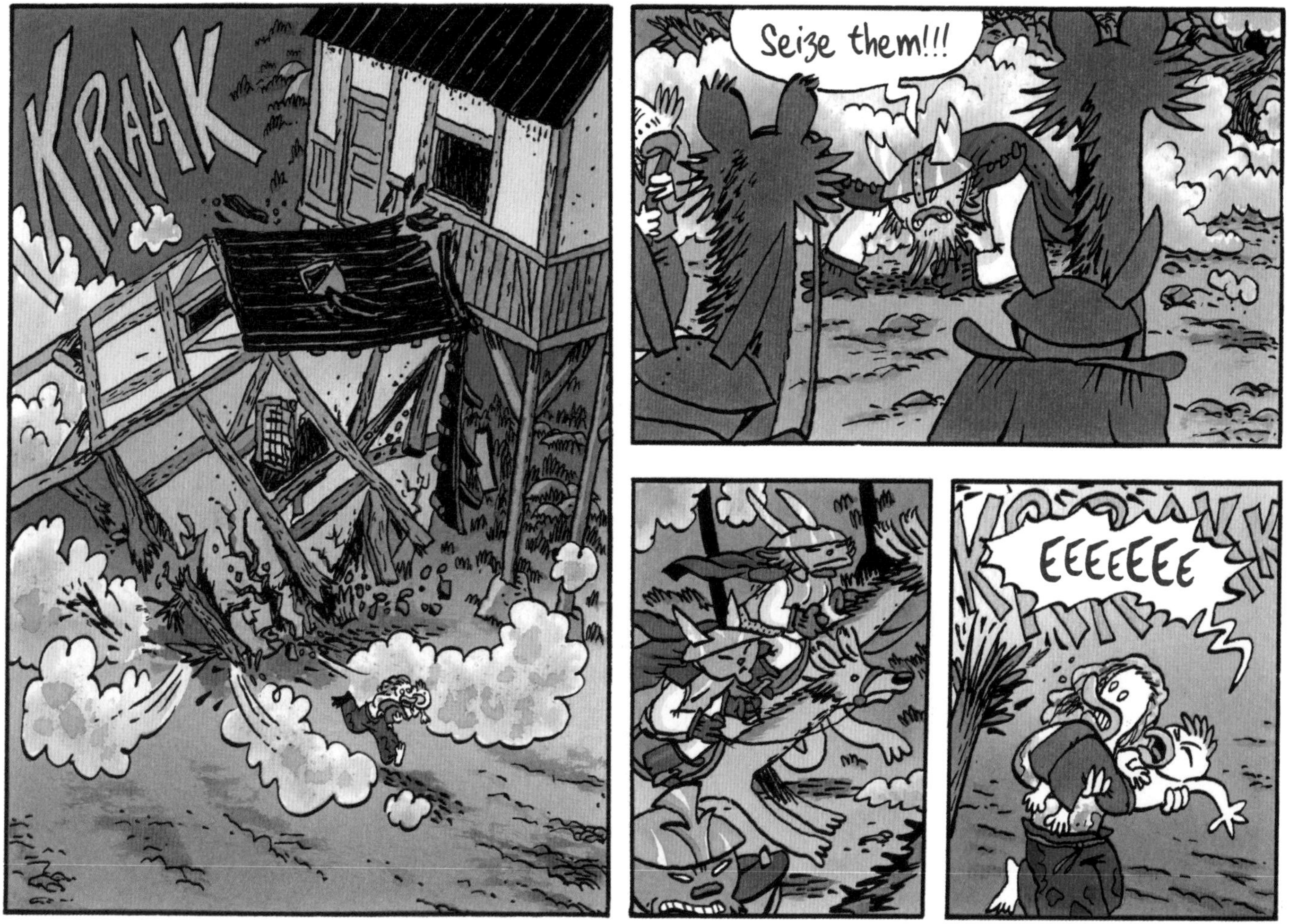
KRAAK
Seize them!!!
EEEEEEE

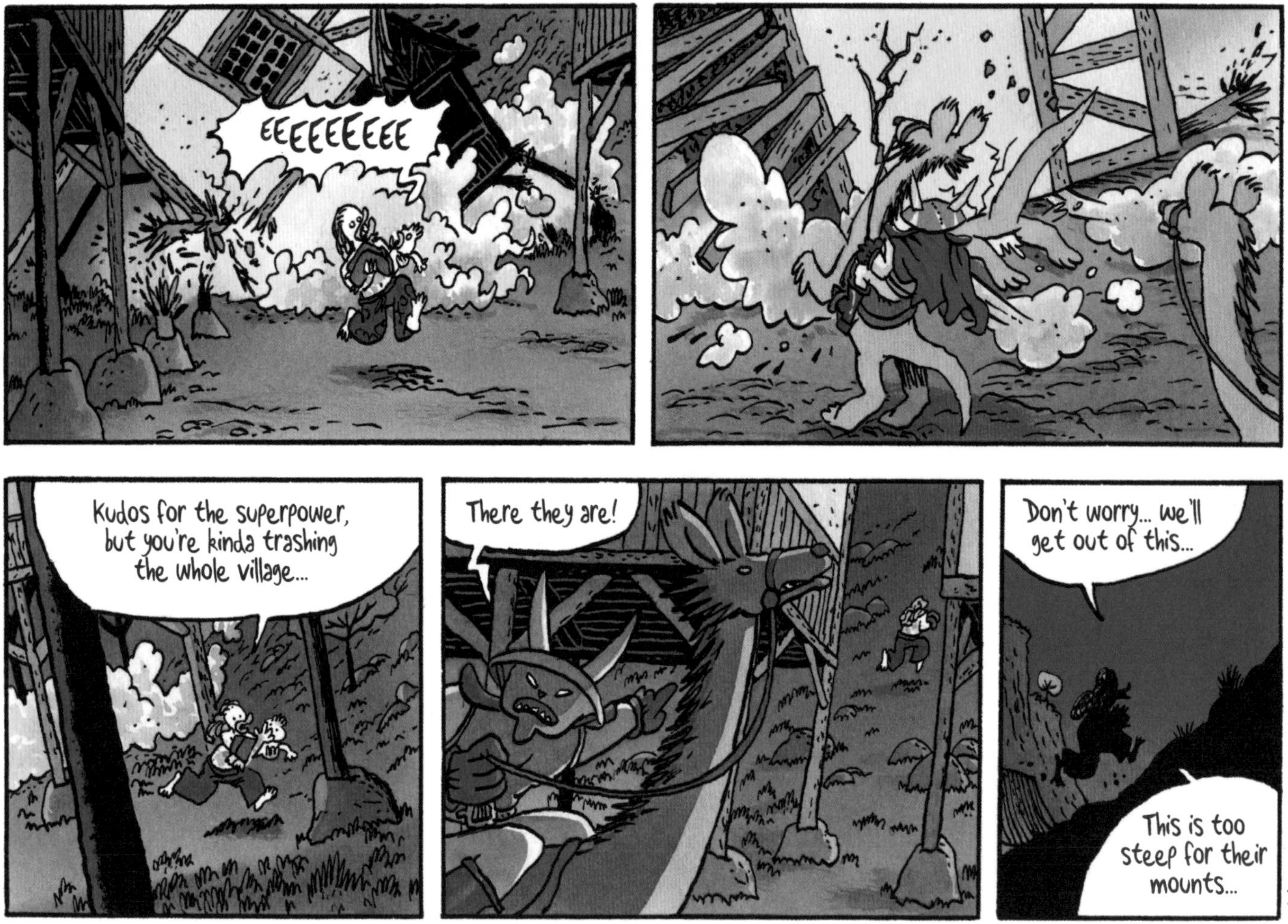
EEEEEEEEE
Kudos for the superpower, but you're kinda trashing the whole village...
There they are!
Don't worry... we'll get out of this...
This is too steep for their mounts...

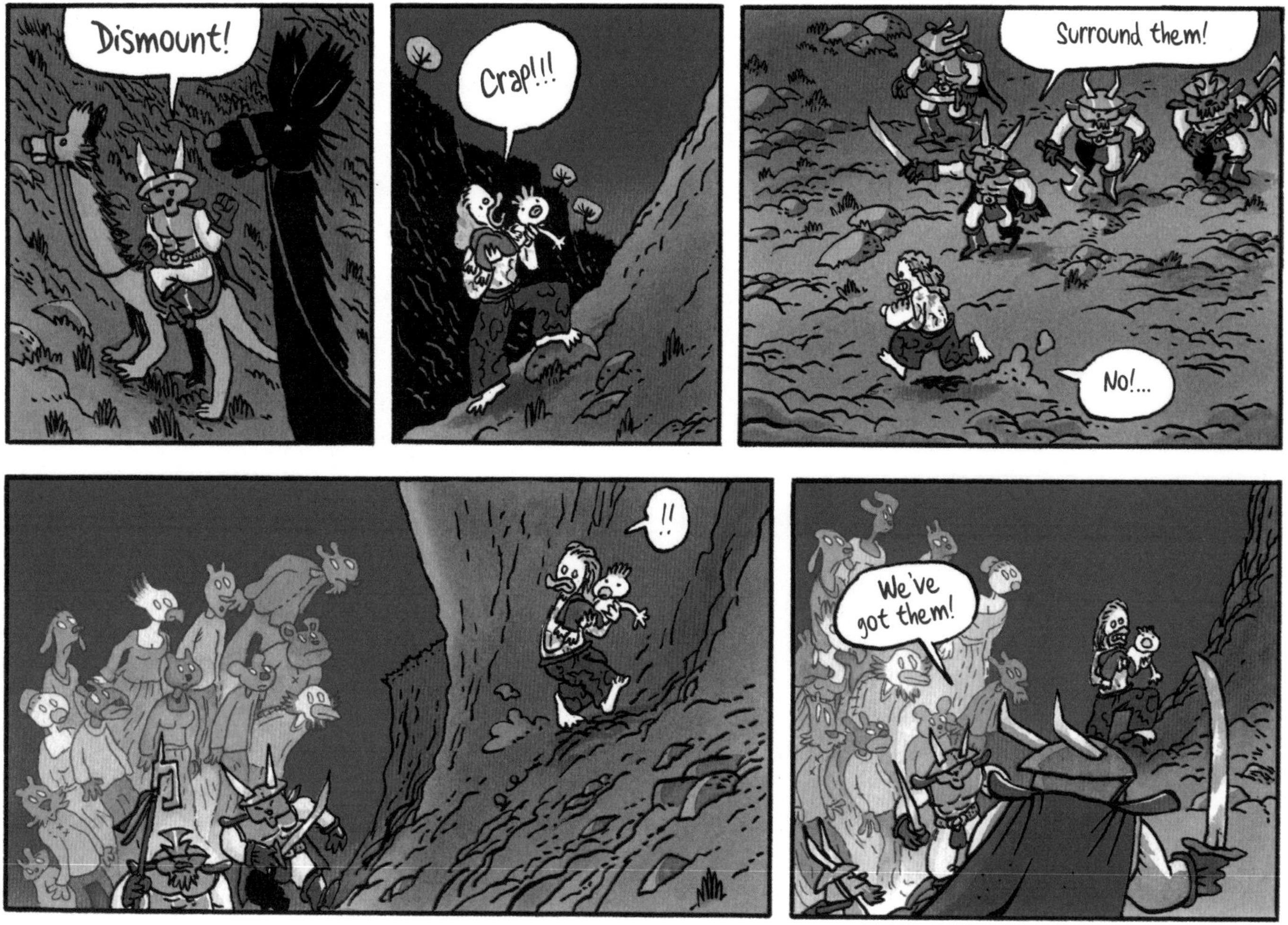
Dismount!
Crap!!!
Surround them!
No!...
!!
We've got them!

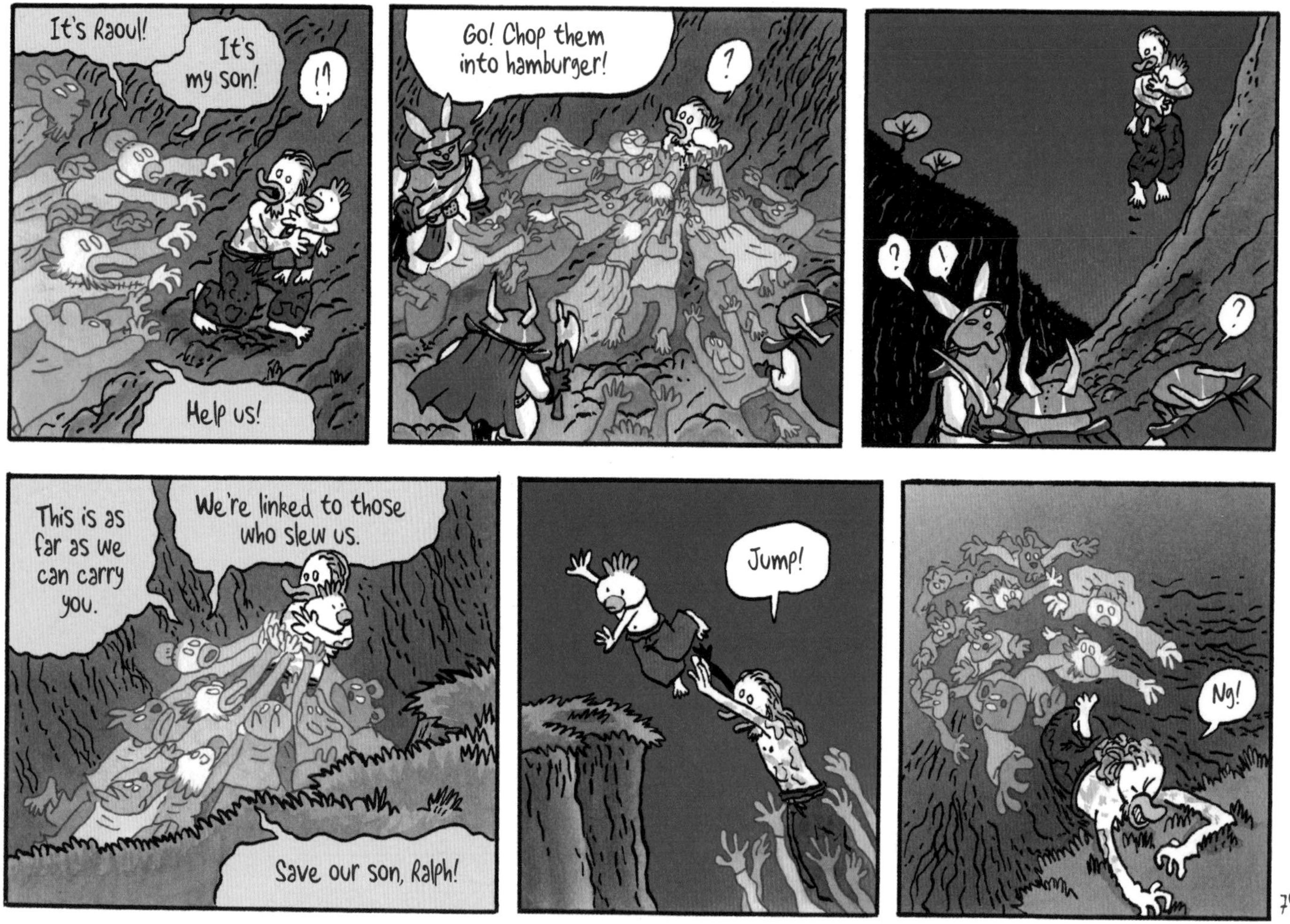
It's Raoul!
It's my son!
!?
Help us!
Go! Chop them into hamburger!
?
? !
?
This is as far as we can carry you.
We're linked to those who slew us.
Save our son, Ralph!
Jump!
Ng!

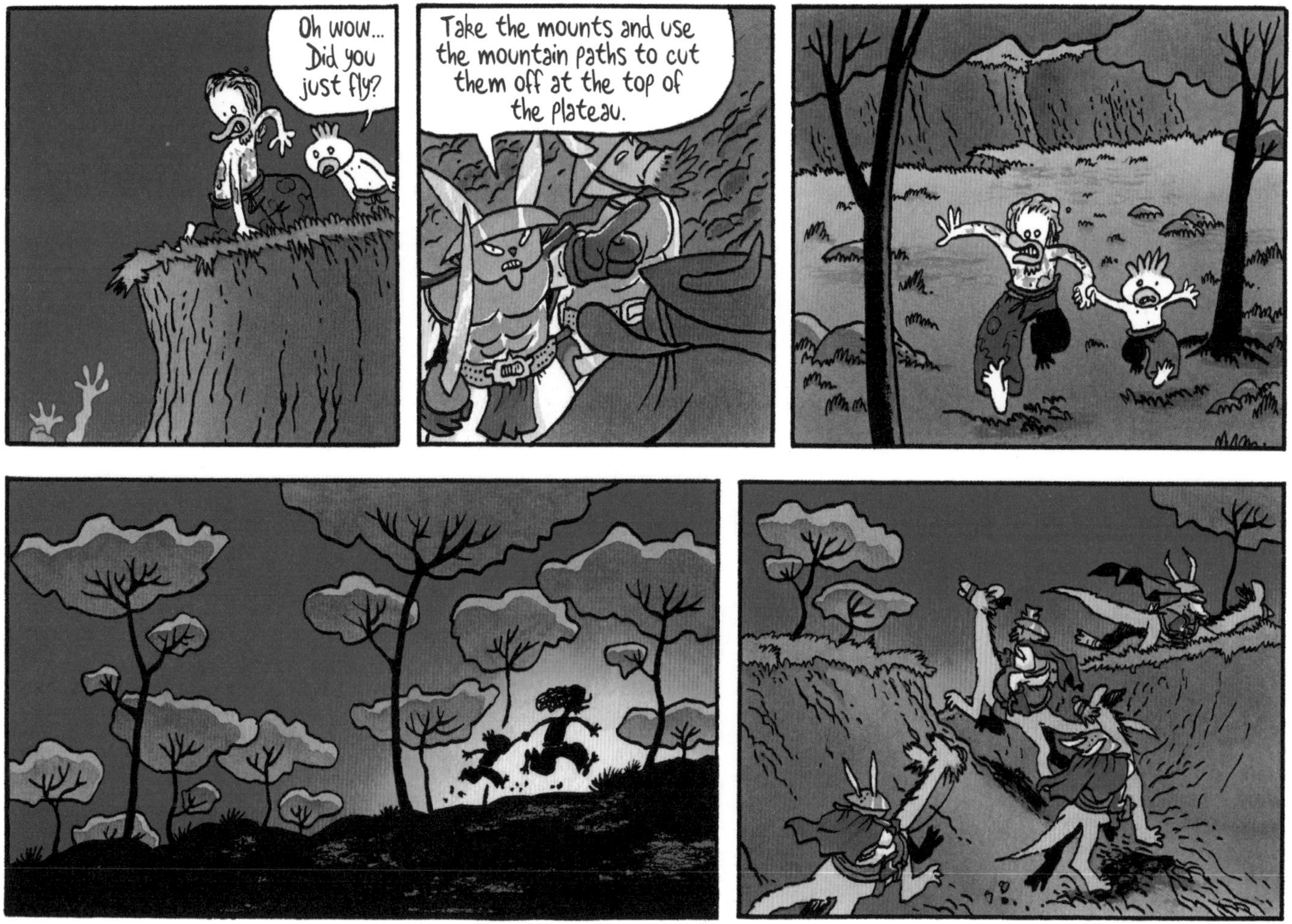
Oh wow... Did you just fly?
Take the mounts and use the mountain paths to cut them off at the top of the plateau.

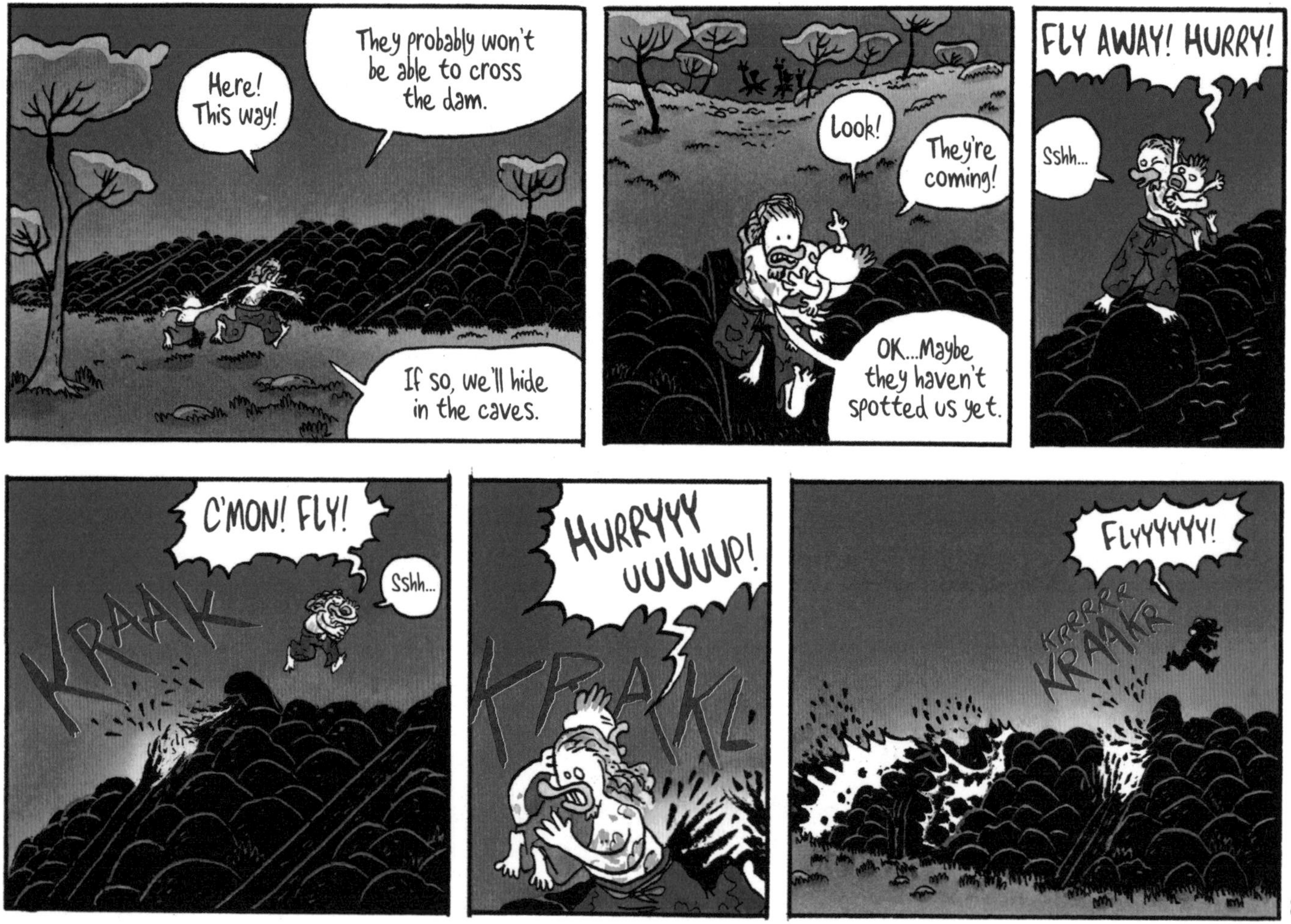

Here! This way!
They probably won't be able to cross the dam.
If so, we'll hide in the caves.
Look!
They're coming!
OK...Maybe they haven't spotted us yet.
FLY AWAY! HURRY!
Sshh...
C'MON! FLY!
Sshh...
KRAAK
HURRYY UUUUUP!
FLYYYYYY!

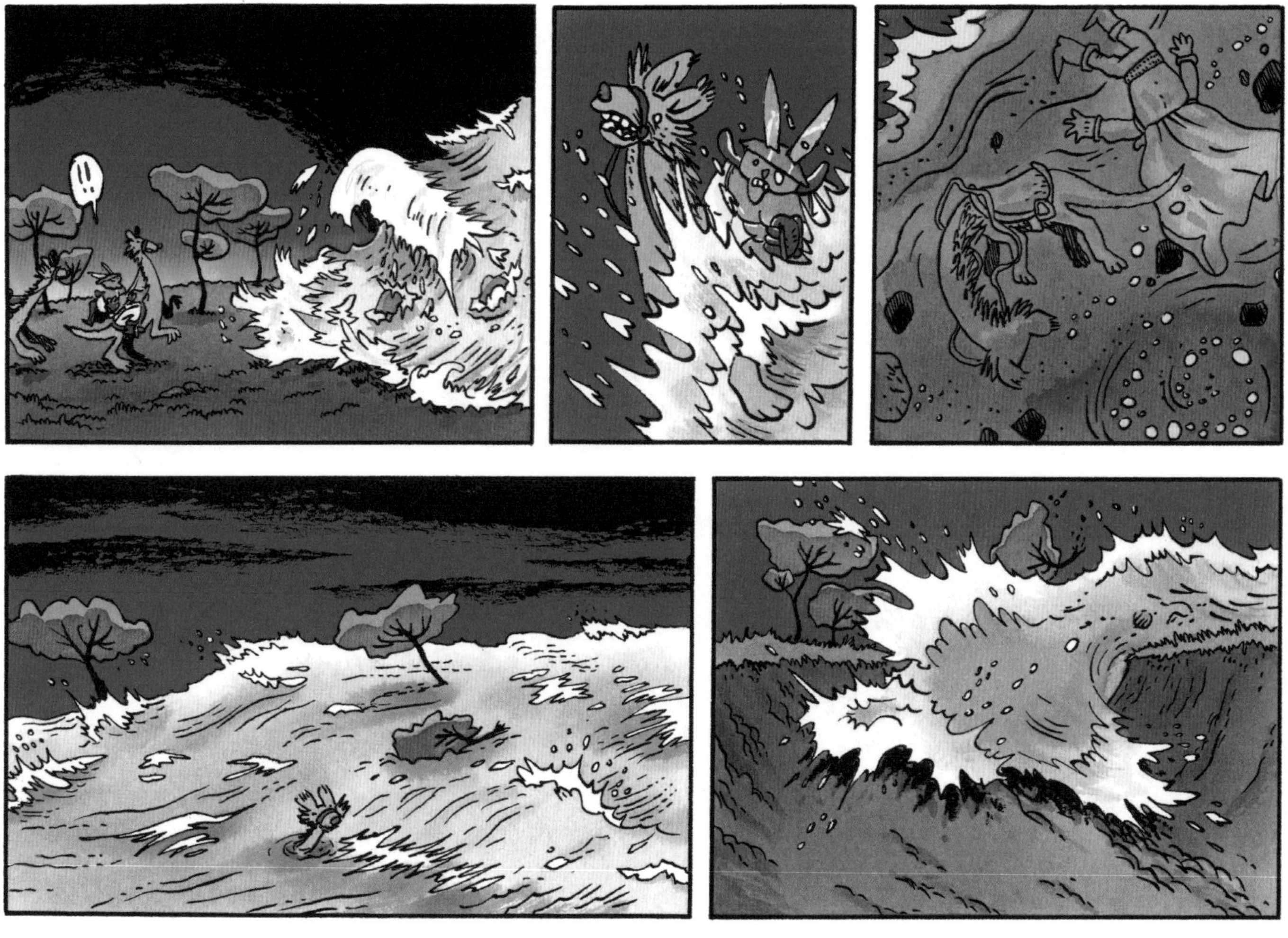
!!

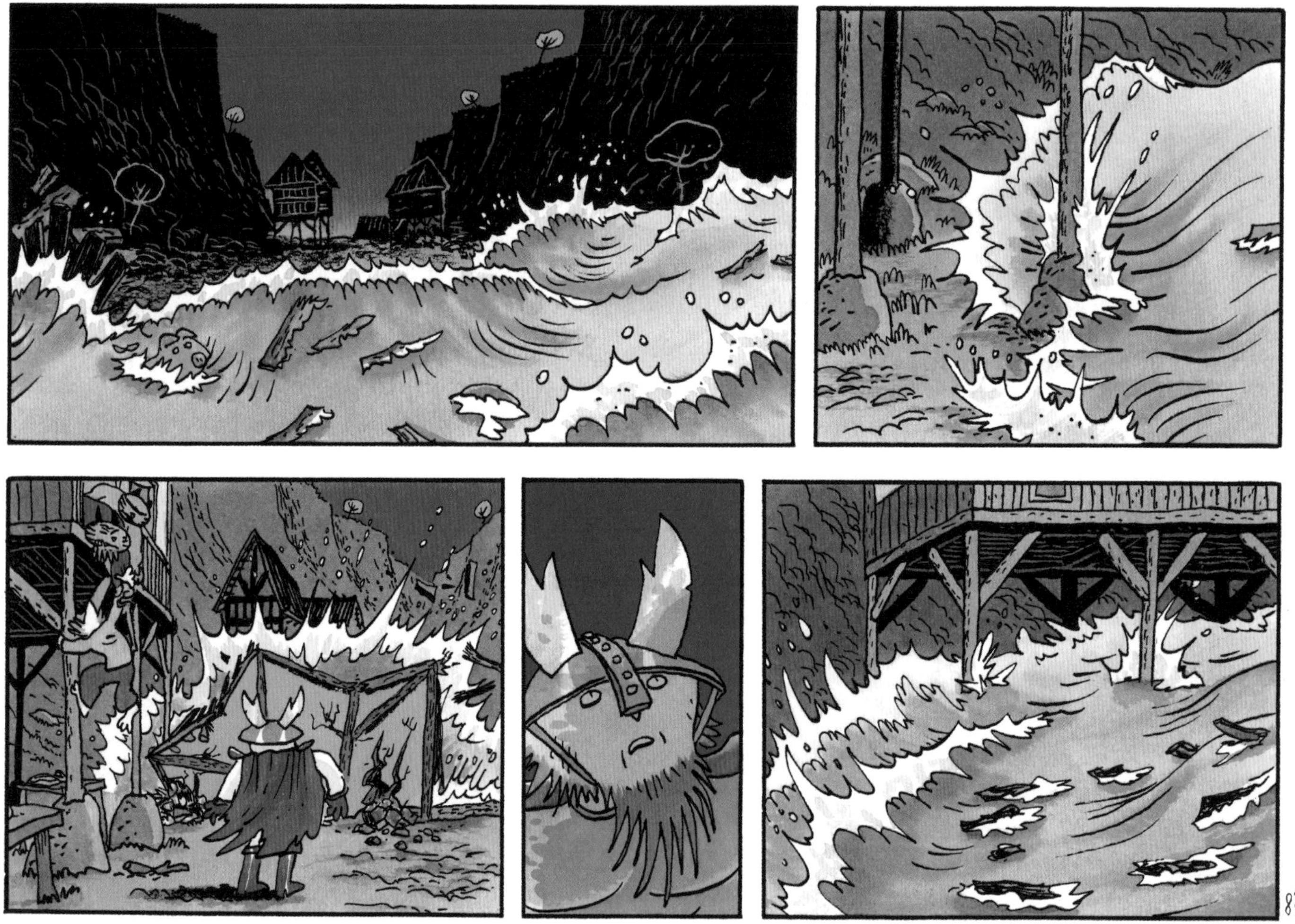

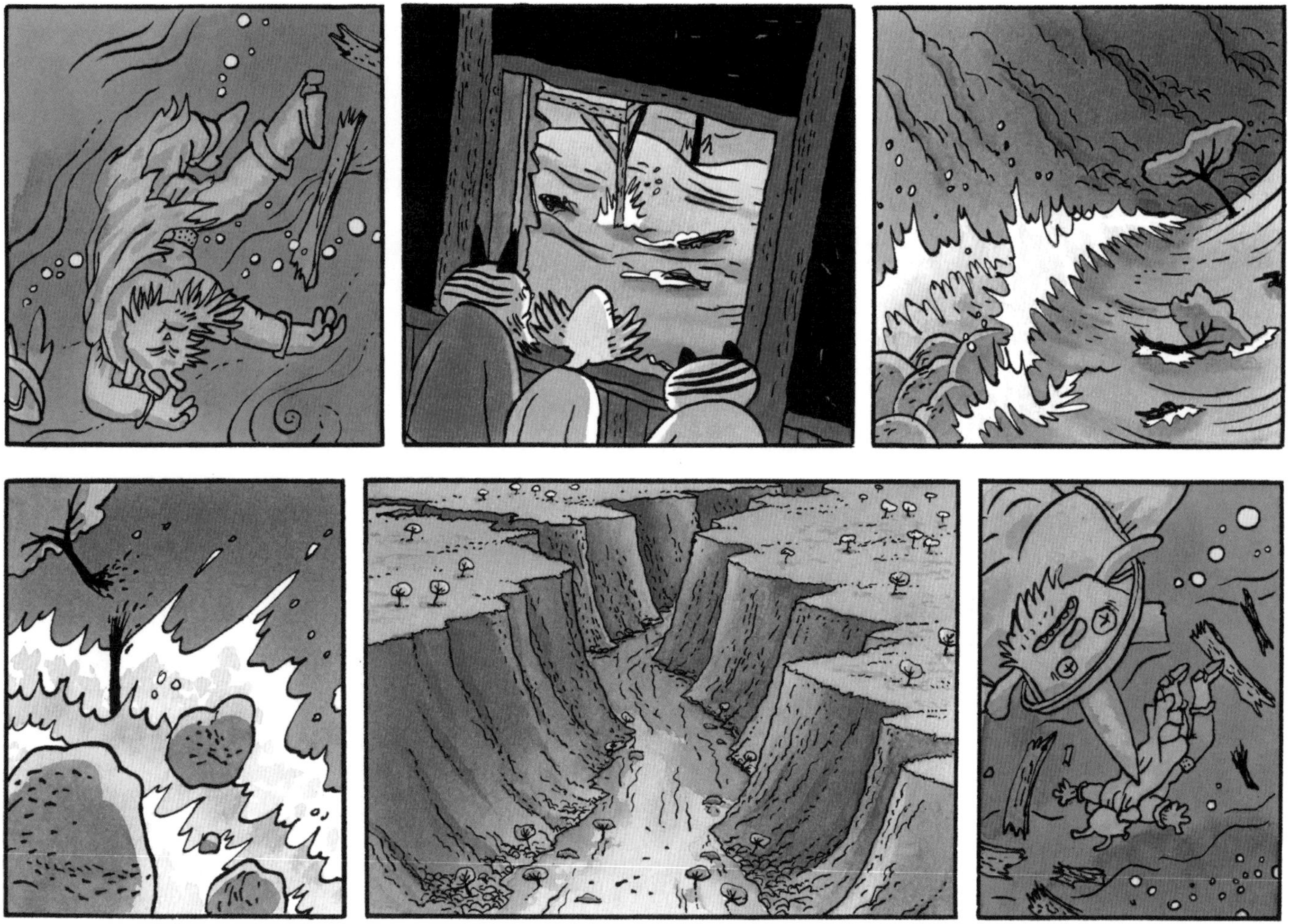

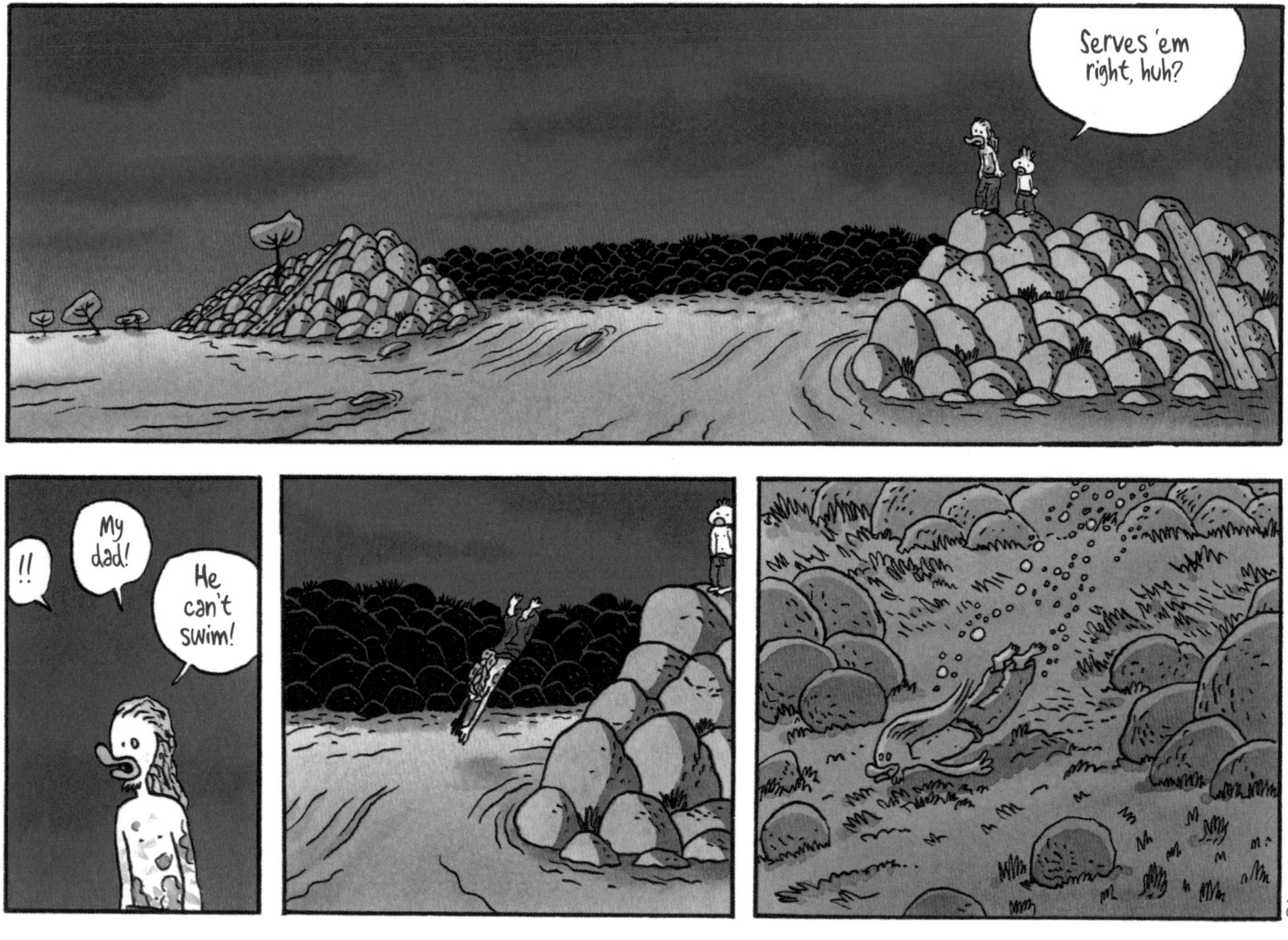
Serves 'em right, huh?
!!
My dad!
He can't swim!

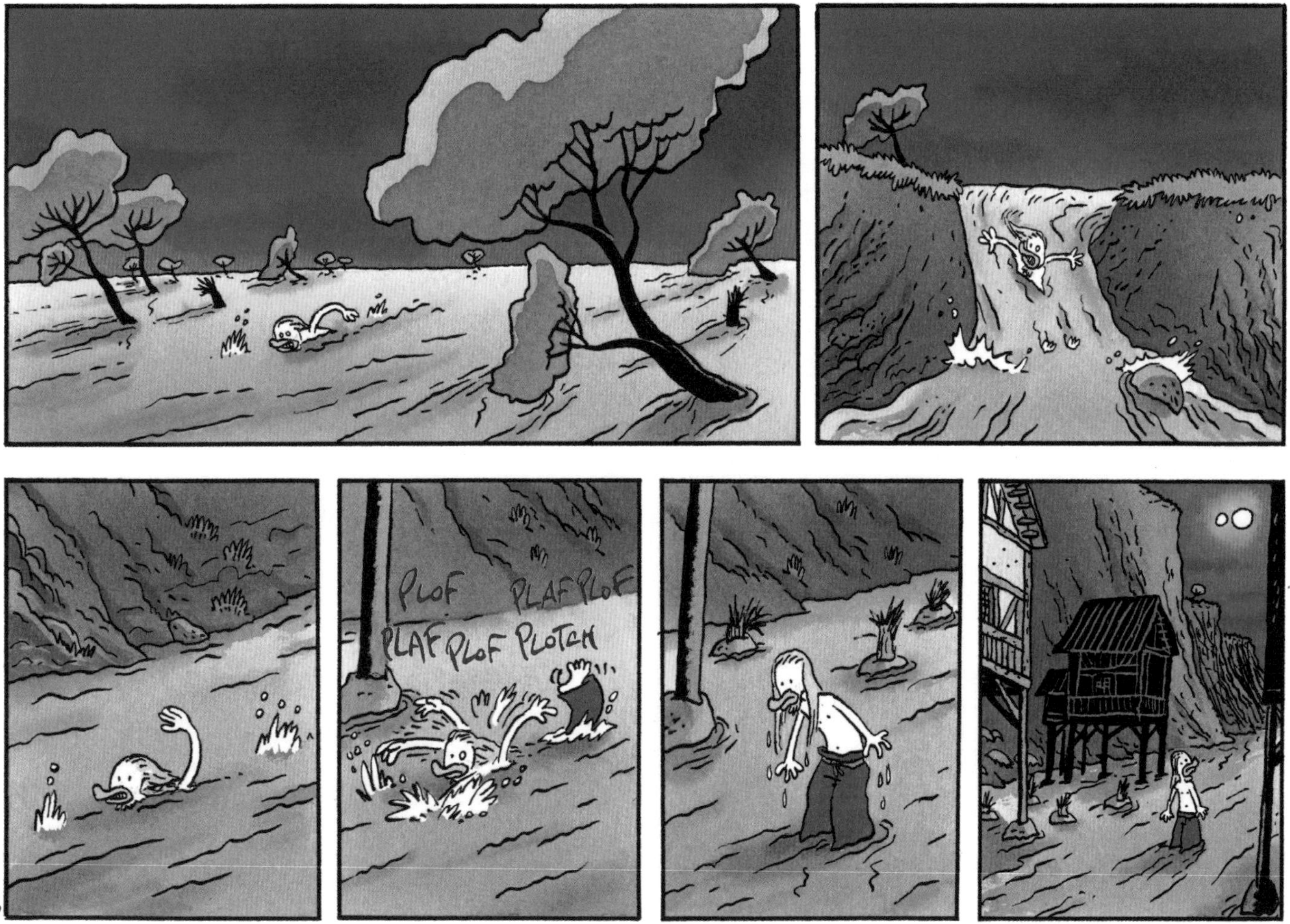
PLOF
PLAF PLOF
PLAF PLOF PLOTCH

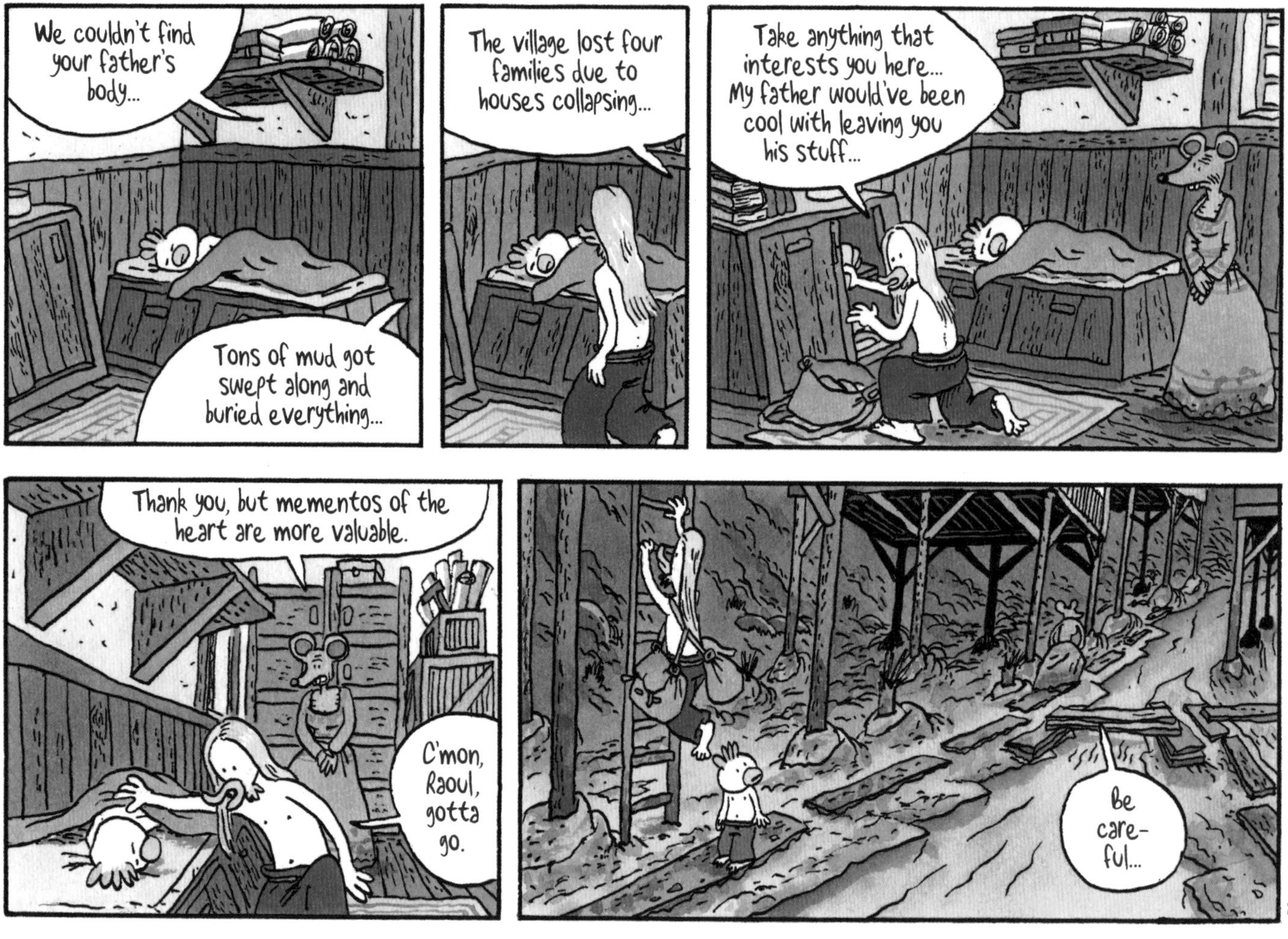
We couldn't find your father's body...
Tons of mud got swept along and buried everything...
The village lost four families due to houses collapsing...
Take anything that interests you here... My father would've been cool with leaving you his stuff...
Thank you, but mementos of the heart are more valuable.
C'mon, Raoul, gotta go.
Be care-ful...

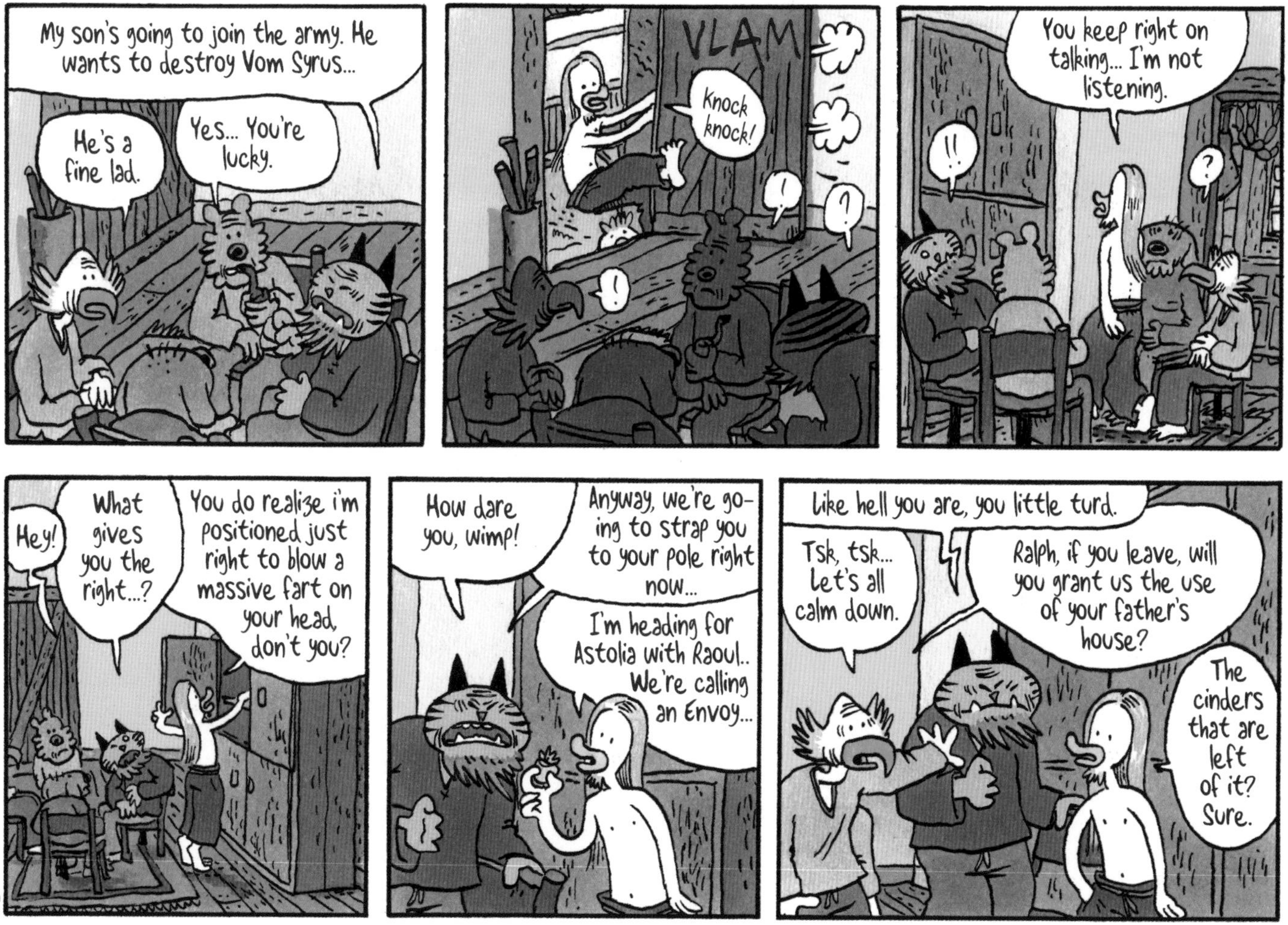
My son's going to join the army. He wants to destroy Vom Syrus...
He's a fine lad.
Yes... You're lucky.
VLAM
Knock knock!
!
?
!
You keep right on talking... I'm not listening.
!!
?
Hey!
What gives you the right...?
You do realize i'm positioned just right to blow a massive fart on your head, don't you?
How dare you, wimp!
Anyway, we're going to strap you to your pole right now...
I'm heading for Astolia with Raoul.. We're calling an Envoy...
Like hell you are, you little turd.
Tsk, tsk... Let's all calm down.
Ralph, if you leave, will you grant us the use of your father's house?
The cinders that are left of it? Sure.

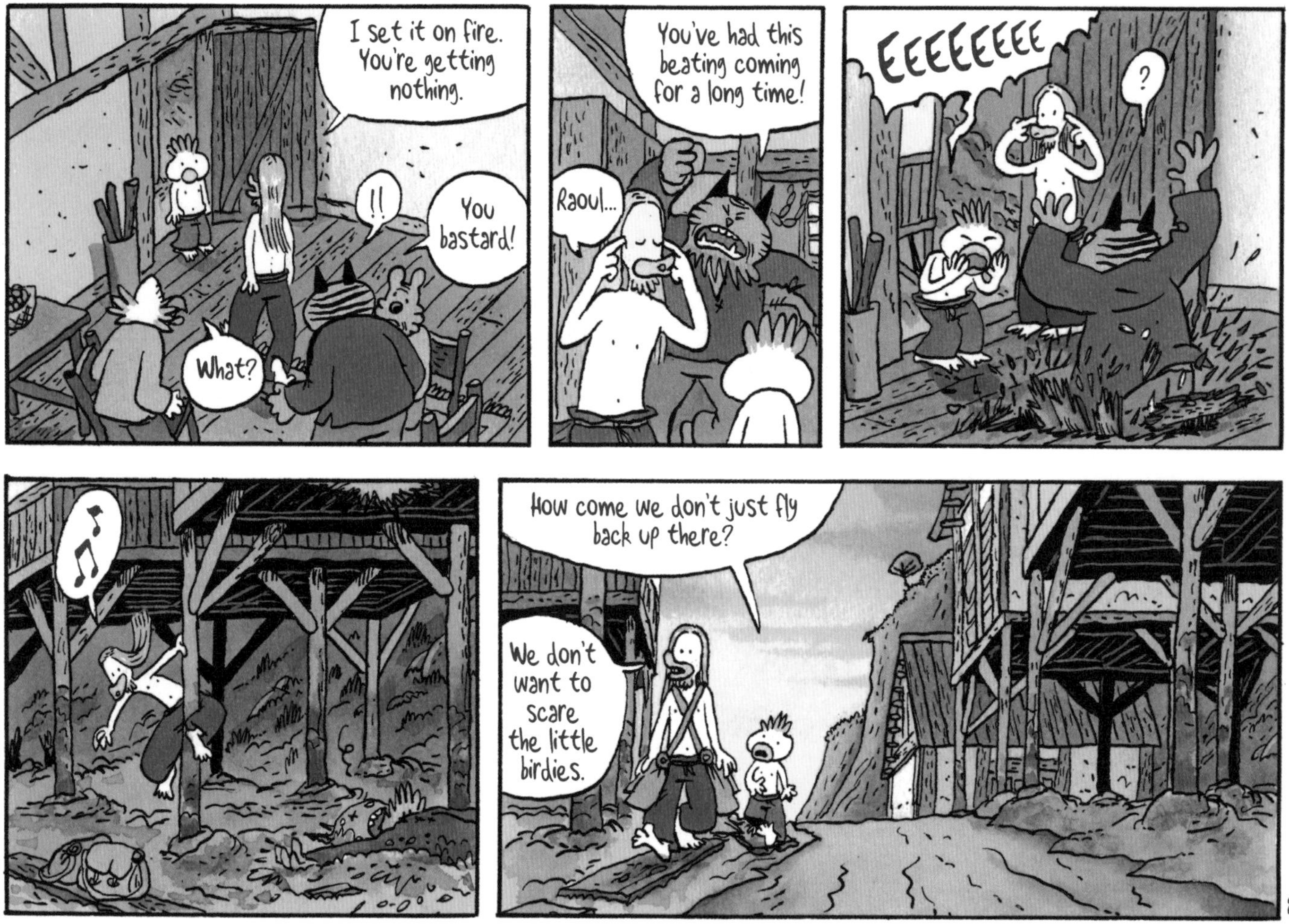

I set it on fire. You're getting nothing.
!!
You bastard!
What?
You've had this beating coming for a long time!
Raoul...
EEEEEEEE
?
How come we don't just fly back up there?
We don't want to scare the little birdies.

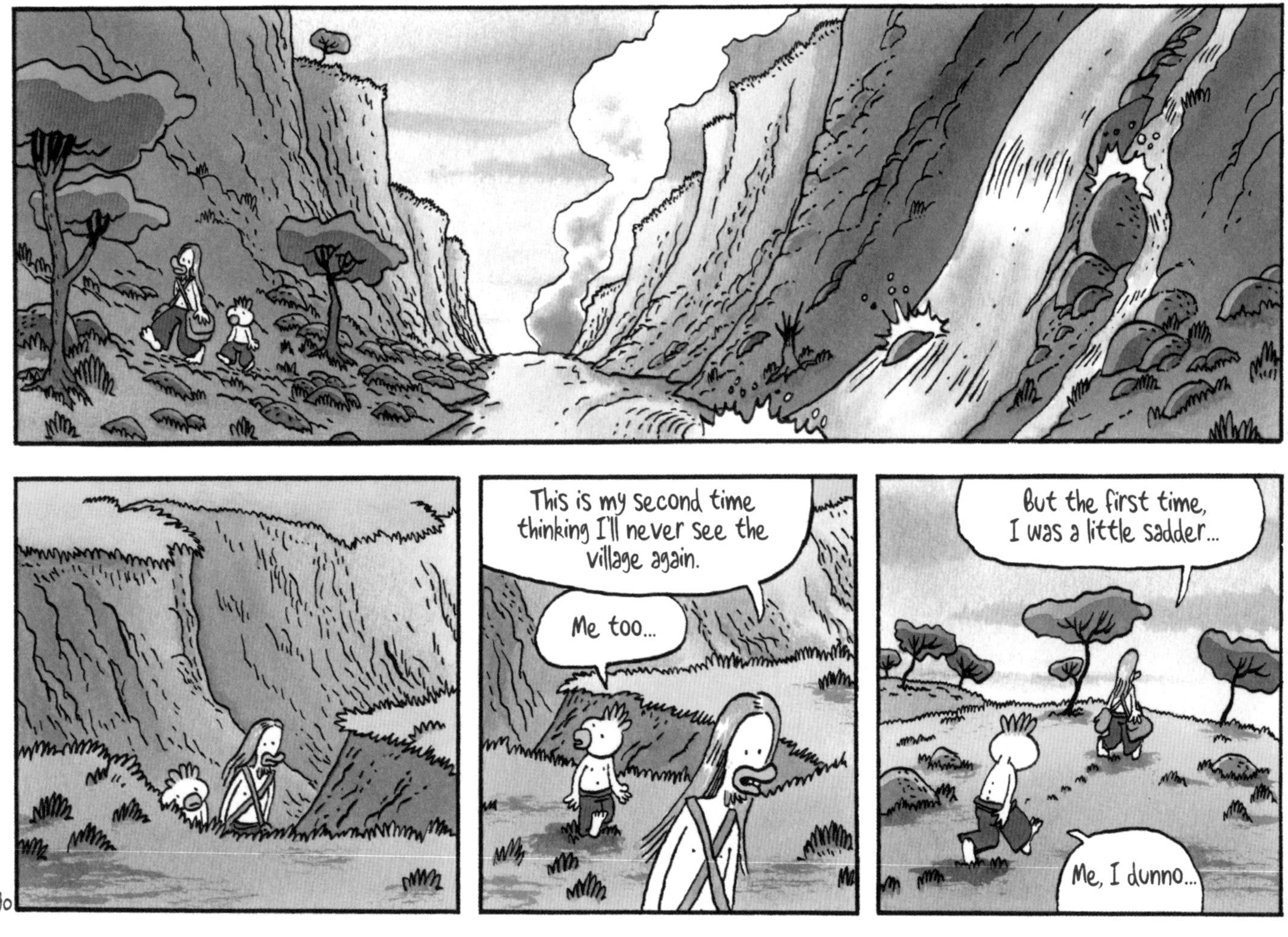
This is my second time thinking I'll never see the village again.
Me too...
But the first time, I was a little sadder...
Me, I dunno...

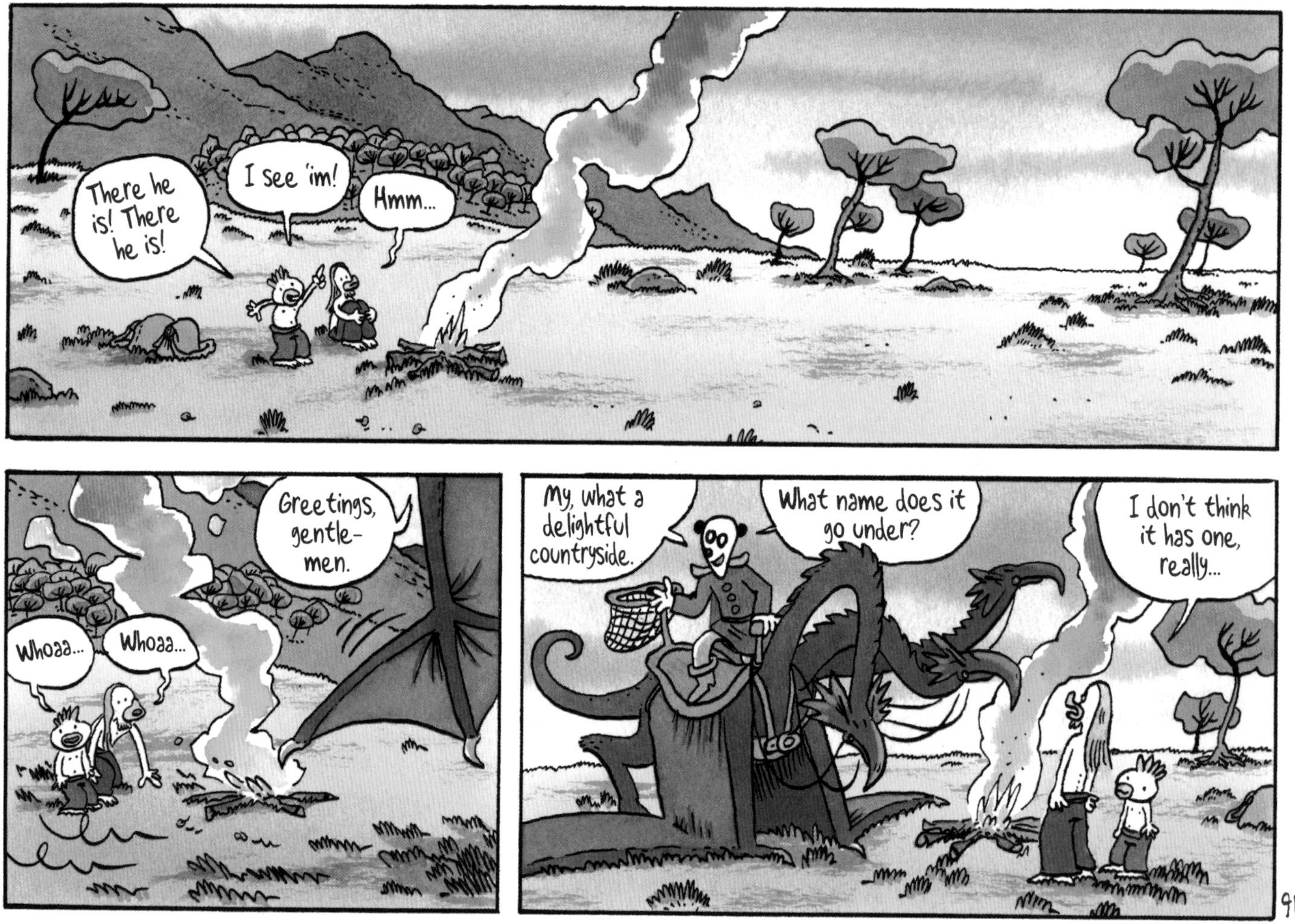
There he is! There he is!
I see 'im!
Hmm...
Greetings, gentlemen.
Whoaa...
Whoaa...
My, what a delightful countryside.
What name does it go under?
I don't think it has one, really...

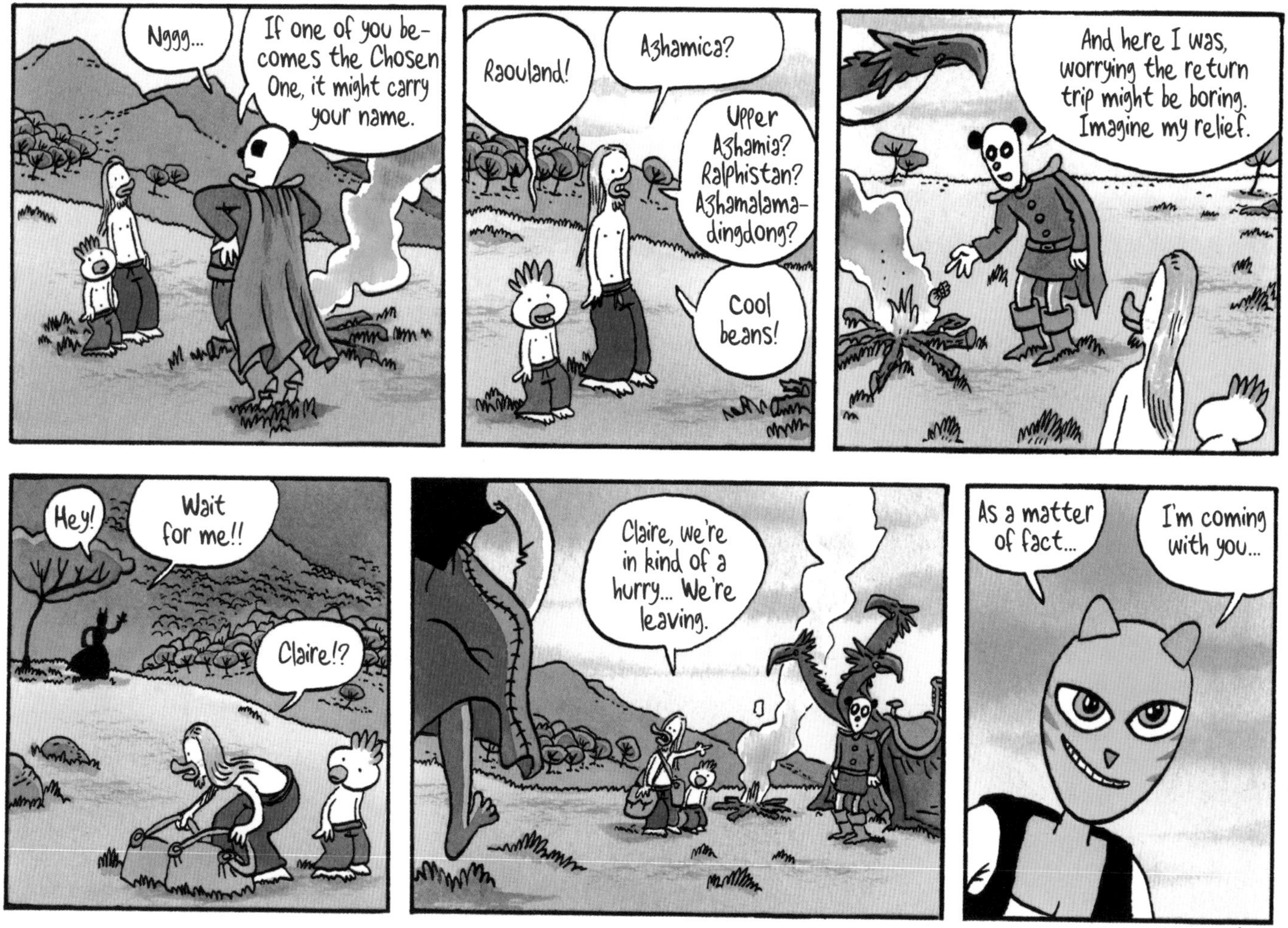
Nggg...
If one of you becomes the Chosen One, it might carry your name.
Raouland!
Azhamica?
Upper Azhamia? Ralphistan? Azhamalama-dingdong?
Cool beans!
And here I was, worrying the return trip might be boring. Imagine my relief.
Hey!
Wait for me!!
Claire!?
Claire, we're in kind of a hurry... We're leaving.
As a matter of fact...
I'm coming with you...

RALPH AZHAM BOOK ONE:
"Why Would You Lie to Someone You Love?"
Originally published in Belgium by Éditions Dupuis under the title *RALPH AZHAM 1— Est-ce qu'on ment aux gens qu'on aime?*

Edited by Kim Thompson.
Designed by Lewis Trondheim.
Lettering and production by Emory Liu.
Associate Publisher: Eric Reynolds.
Published by Gary Groth and Kim Thompson.

Fantagraphics Books,
7563 Lake City Way NE,
Seattle, WA 98115.

Distributed in the U.S. by W.W. Norton and Company, Inc. (800-233-4830). Distributed in Canada by Canadian Manda Group (410-560-7100 x843). Distributed in the U.K. by Turnaround Distribution (44 020 8829-3002). Distributed to comic book specialty stores by Diamond Comics Distributors (800-452-6642 x215).

First Fantagraphics Books edition: September, 2012.
ISBN: 978-1-60699-593-8. Visit the Fantagraphics Books website at www.fantagraphics.com; visit the Fantagraphics bookstore in scenic Georgetown, WA. Printed in Malaysia.

Next...

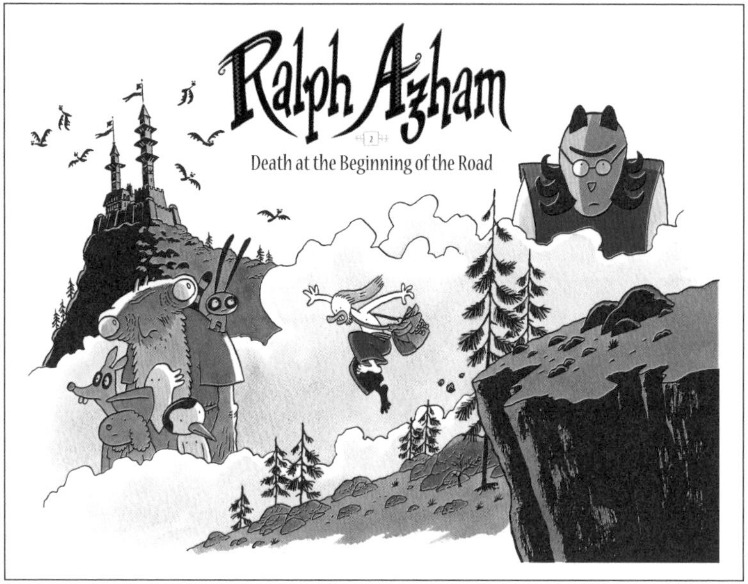
Ralph Azham
2
Death at the Beginning of the Road

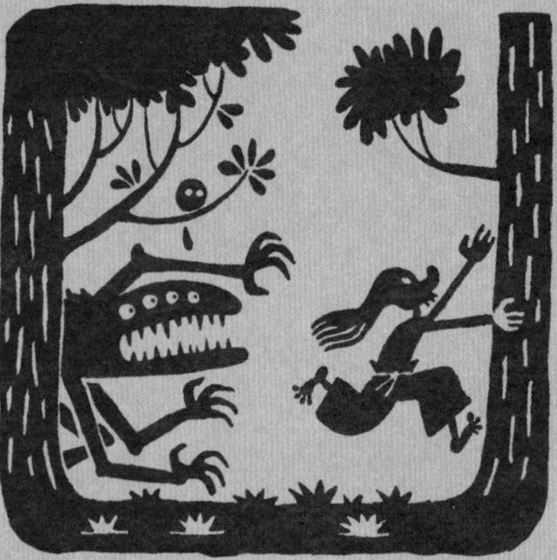
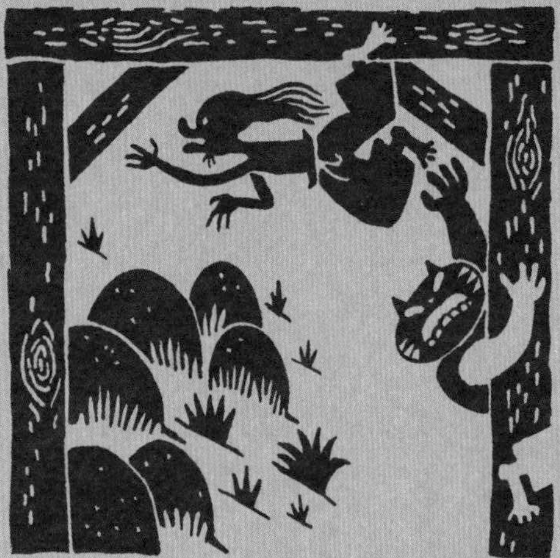
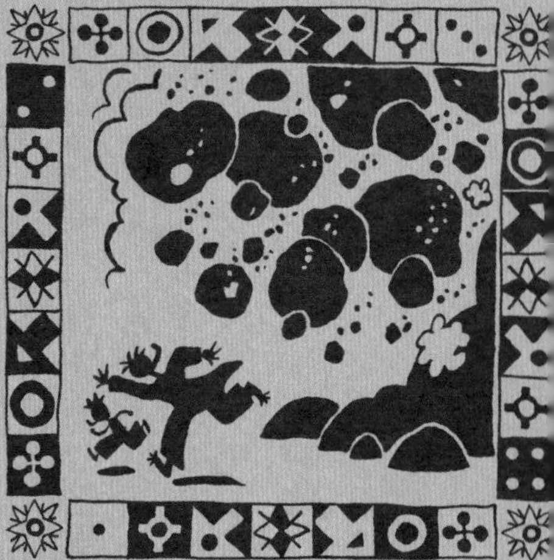
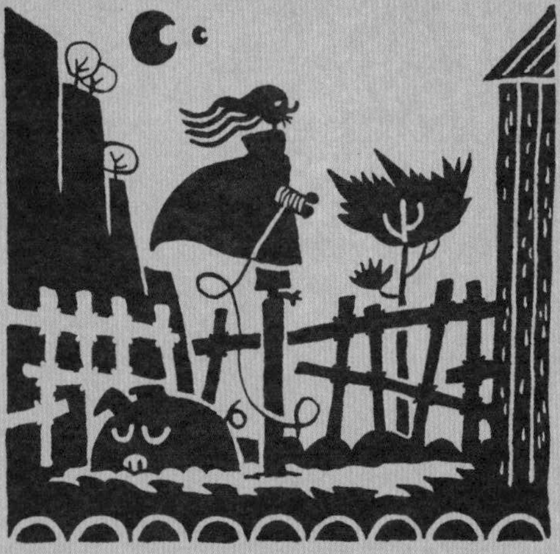
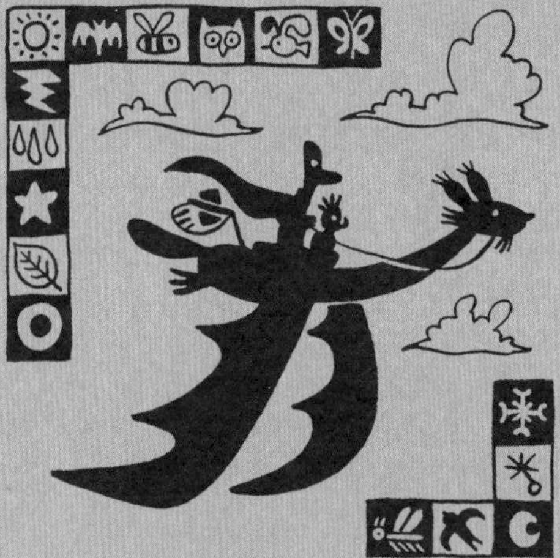
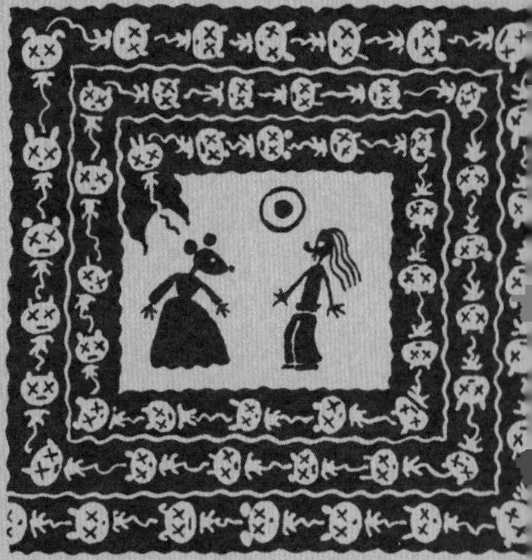